Unfit

Unfit

*The Tale of One Pregnant Teen in the
Bible Belt Before Women Had Choice*

Lani Jo Leigh

Copyright © 2019 by Lani Jo Leigh

Cover and interior design by Roger Leigh

american lifeograph

Published by American Lifeograph
americanlifeograph.com
Inquiries: info@americanlifeograph.com

First American Lifeograph trade paperback edition December, 2019

All rights reserved. No part of this book may be reproduced in any form or by any electronic or mechanical means, including information storage-and-retrieval systems, without prior permission in writing from the Publisher, except for brief quotations embodied in critical articles and reviews.

Library of Congress Cataloging-in-Publication Data
Names: Leigh, Lani Jo, 1954-, author
Title: Unfit: The Tale of One Pregnant Teen in the Bible Belt Before Women Had Choice / Lani Jo Leigh

ISBN: 978-1-7342659-0-3 Paperback
ISBN: 978-1-7342659-2-7 Hardback
ISBN: 978-1-7342659-1-0 EPUB

For Keith
&
In loving memory of Mary Ann and John Lassiter

Audre Lorde called the stories she shared about herself "biomythography." My writing mentor, Ariel Gore, says that all memoir should be labeled fiction because we depend on our own flawed and unreliable memories. I could give you only the facts that are certifiable—my own birthdate from my birth certificate, my son's birthdate from his. But that kind of telling is rather dry, and facts alone cannot recount the story of who I was and who I have become. Think of this then as a story—created from a lifetime of stories that I've told myself and stories that others have told me. As a writer, I've changed some names, altered the timeline, and used other literary devices to create a narrative that speaks my truth.

*There is a pain so utter that it swallows substance up
Then covers the abyss with trance—
So memory can step around—across—upon it
As one within a swoon goes safely where an open-eye
would drop him—
—Bone by bone*

~Emily Dickinson

Part One: The South Canadian 1

    Clean Catch 3

    Unwelcome News.. 18

    Chicken Fried Steak 23

    Roleplaying... 28

    Ugly Shoes.. 37

    The Johnstown Flood 47

    Unhappy Birthday 56

    A Steak Made for Two 62

    The Wrong Movie 65

Part Two: The Mississippi... 69

    Sunday Driving 71

    Babylon.. 80

    Stuck-up.. 87

    The Powers-that-Be 98

    Forget-Me-Nots 107

    Audubon Park 115

    Margaret Haughery.. 119

    A. Wilson, Stalker 126

    Toothpicks 129

    Were You There?.. 132

    Peggy Lee Was Right 138

    Cardboard Breastplates 145

    Wiggling... 153

    Lake Champlain 160

    Christy Makes a Different Choice................................... 164

    Voodoo Queen Marie 166

    On the Banks of Lake Pontchartrain 175

Cotton Candy 182

Glenda Sends Cookies 186

Gin Rummy 194

A Month of Sundays Summer 198

Baby Booties 216

Past Due 221

Out to Lunch 228

One-Mississippi, Two-Mississippi 237

Tiny Blue Bundle 242

It's So Hard 245

Don't Look Back 247

Part Three: Roll On, Columbia 253

Adjusting...255

Finding a Keeper 261

Chanel No. 5...269

Welcome to the Circle 281

The Pathos of Things 291

$400 and 24 Hours 294

Acknowledgements 305

About the Author..307

Part One:
The South Canadian

Uncertainty is the worst of all evils until the moment when reality makes us regret uncertainty.

~Alphonse Karr

Clean Catch

Oklahoma is the body of an old woman, with saggy tits and a thick belly. Her skin is dry and paper-thin and her lips crack from the wind. Winter always comes hard. Icy wind whistles down grass-stained prairies all the way from Canada, through the Dakotas, Nebraska, Kansas, and Oklahoma, until it ruffles the Gulf waters south of Texas.

My junior year in high school was no different. It was January 1971, and on a brutal and cold Monday morning, I waited for my mother on the steps of our concrete porch. The wind stung like my father's belt across my backside. My lips were chapped, my cheeks chafed, but the tears that filled my eyes came from a deep well of dread.

I should have been out the door and on my way to French class, but I had an early morning appointment with Dr. Dycus. For almost two weeks, I had been queasy every day, all through the day, throwing up everything I ate or drank—even water.

As if on cue, the second assault of the morning gathered in the back of my throat, and I was sure I was going to lose my Cocoa Puffs in the denuded branches of my mother's cherished rose bush. To keep myself distracted, I took a deep breath, and focused attention on my reflection in the bumper of the family's '69 Rambler. Two bony knees poked above black and white argyle socks. In Oklahoma, the buckle of the Bible belt, girls weren't allowed to wear pants to school—not even if a blizzard hit and we shivered in temperatures that hovered below freezing.

The screen door creaked. My mother, ever the Sunday School teacher, came up behind me humming "This Little Light of Mine" under her breath.

"Get in the car, Lani. I don't want you to catch your death of cold on top of whatever else you've got."

I slid behind the wheel and started the engine while my mother settled her ample weight on the passenger side of the Rambler's brown vinyl bench seat. "Are you sure you're OK to drive?" she asked. "Want me to take you?"

I shook my head. "No, Ma, I don't want you to take off work. I'll drop you off, and then go see Dr. Dycus. I'll be fine. I feel better already."

When I'm done, I can probably head on over to school. I'm sure it's just a stomach bug."

Keep telling yourself that, I thought, *it's only a stomach bug.*

From where we lived it was only a hop, skip and a jump to Buchanan's Grocery Store on Broadway. In less than five minutes I pulled into the parking lot, and my mom struggled to get out of the car, wrestling with the wind to keep the door open.

"Call me later and let me know how you're feeling. I get off work at six, so if Kathy doesn't have band practice, she can pick me up." She raised her voice, fighting to be heard above the wind's howl. "I've got a pot of beans on for dinner. All you need to do is make some cornbread."

My mom could have stepped right out of the pages of Proverbs 31. Every description of the virtuous woman fit her to a T—she was a hard worker, early riser, kind and generous, a great cook. My mom did whatever it took to keep her five children fed and clothed. My dad was a staff sergeant in the Air Force, and his paycheck didn't stretch far. When we were little, my mom took in laundry with my grandmother, and then a few years later, she wrapped cinnamon lollipops at the only factory in town. Landing the job at Buchanan's was a step up. It meant decent pay and regular hours, and she liked the ribbing she took from the butchers. Spending her days in a freezer did have one drawback, however. Her hands were as chafed and bloody as a raw chuck roast put into the oven before church on a Sunday morning.

I drove back down Broadway past Moore Junior High and Moore Central Elementary and made a sharp right turn onto NW 2nd. As I passed Chestnut Street, I glanced over to where my family had lived when I was a first and second grader, just thigh-high to a June bug.

There was nothing but an empty lot on the corner, but once upon a time, my Memaw's tumbledown house, with its wide, open porch and hiding-place crawl space, filled my world with laughter, tears, and other people's dirty laundry. It was where I first changed my baby brother's diapers. I chased our sweet collie, Patton, around the yard, and when Patton died, it was where we found the black puppy under our Christmas tree, a black puppy that didn't survive more than three months. When Uncle Billy died two days before my brother was born, the whole family—aunts, uncles, third cousins twice removed—came back to the house after the funeral, crowding into the tiny living room like whales in a tackle box.

We moved out of the house when I was in third grade. My dad was stationed in Illinois, and although he traveled alone for most of his assignments while the remainder of the family stayed in Oklahoma, this time we moved with him. With more of her family living in California than Oklahoma, my Memaw headed west to live with Aunt Toni in West Covina. Since my mother's side of the family still lived in Moore, we came back after the six-month stint, but by that time the house had been torn down. All that remained were memories and a crumbling concrete foundation surrounded by a thick jumble of juniper bushes. In the back yard, a rusted clothesline lay bent and twisted on its side. My mind always played tricks with me on this spot, because even in winter, I could smell the sweetness of the honeysuckle that covered the fence.

My hometown, situated between Norman, home to Oklahoma University, and Oklahoma City, the state capital, had only a few thousand residents when my family lived on Chestnut Street. But once the interstate cut through the town's center, Moore grew fast. New housing developments swallowed up the farms that once stretched as far east as Draper Lake. Instead of wheat fields and cow pastures, cookie-cutter houses and strip malls spread north to Oklahoma City and south to Norman.

In the parking lot of the Dycus-Camp Clinic I stayed in the car with the engine idling, staring into the rear-view mirror. As my Memaw would say, I looked all the world like something a dog had been keeping under the porch.

I had bags under my eyes and a big worry line across my forehead. I started feeling sick over Christmas break. No way to enjoy New Year's Eve, even though my boyfriend Randall and I had planned a big date to ring in 1971. Chateaubriand and garlic cheese bread at Steak and Ale, a party with smuggled Coors and friends at Kip's house, but I was home before eleven. New Year's Day we saw *Love Story* at the Bijou. I sobbed so hard; I couldn't tell if it was the greasy popcorn or Jenny's dying that made my stomach do cartwheels.

I had been back at school a week and hadn't taken a single day off from work despite the nausea. I crawled through the days with dry toast and crackers and quick trips to the bathroom between classes. The fear I had about the real reason for my nausea stayed stuck in my throat. I pushed it down and kept repeating in my head, "this too shall pass," like George Harrison's chanting on "My Sweet Lord."

Everything's going to be all right. Hare Krishna, Krishna, Krishna, Hare Rama, Rama, Rama, Hare, Hare.

My appointment couldn't be avoided forever, so I finally dragged myself out of the car and headed into the clinic waiting room. Two thickset older women sat on padded folding chairs; one of them cradled a skein of red yarn in her lap, staring into the abyss while her hands moved the knitting needles. Click, click, click, over and over again. *Click, click, click.*

For as long as I could remember, Dr. Dycus had been our family physician. He took care of my grandma's arthritic hands and heart condition. When I was in second grade, right after Uncle Billy was killed in a car crash and my brother was born, my sisters and I all came down with the measles AND chickenpox. Before we were shuffled off to Aunt Mabel's house, Dr. Dycus was there to prescribe calamine lotion for the blisters and baby aspirin for the fever.

Against the back wall, a milk crate held plastic toys, and a boy who looked about eight, my brother's age, knelt on the floor. "Vrrm, vrrm," he called out scooting a matchbox Camaro across the vinyl floor. A gaunt woman fidgeted with a copy of *Newsweek*.

The room smelled of age and soiled diapers. I picked up a copy of *Babytalk*, scanned a few pages, and quickly put the magazine down.

Before I had time to bolt out of the room and back to my car, Shirley, Dr. Dycus's nurse, led me into an examining room. I smelled alcohol and disinfectant, a welcome relief from the odors of the waiting room. When I climbed up on the table, the paper covering it crackled like Rice Krispies in a bowl of milk.

Shirley pulled up the sleeve of my turtleneck sweater and wrapped the blood pressure cuff around my upper arm. Telling her about my symptoms made my stomach spasm like a cheerleader at a football game doing a back flip. I fought the impulse to throw up while she took my pulse, my temperature.

"I need a urine specimen. Do you know how to get a clean catch?"

I shook my head.

Shirley sighed. "Take this container to the bathroom. Sit on the toilet and spread your legs as wide as possible. Use one hand to spread apart your vagina, and with the other, use this wipe to clean it. Wipe from the front to the back. Then pee a little bit in the toilet before you start peeing in the cup. You only need to fill it halfway up."

"I'll leave you a gown to change into. When you get back, take off everything from the waist up."

Shirley pointed to the restroom down the hall, and I galloped to the toilet just seconds before the Cocoa Puffs. It was a relief to vomit, and for a short minute, I felt better.

Back in the exam room, I undressed and unhooked my bra using only one hand. Randall thought it was a day to celebrate when he learned that move. His arm around my shoulders at the drive-in, then his hand moving down only to snake its way back up under my shirt, a small tug, breasts free, nipples hard and at attention.

Whoosh—a familiar rush of blood went from my head to my vagina and back again, and I blushed thinking about Randall's hands and mouth.

Randall was the most adorable guy in school, and without a doubt, the smartest. He had a rebel's look about him with long hair that brushed his collar, and his dark hazel eyes made me feel grounded and whole whenever I looked into them. I was lucky to be his one and only. We had known each other since seventh grade, and started going steady when we were sophomores, right after my sixteenth birthday. I wore his "drop," and it glistened on my chest just a few inches away from my heart. When my mom went to Moore High School, girls got pinned; but in 1971 the "going-steady" custom was the gifting of a "drop," the boys' three initials dangling from a long, gold chain. Whenever I fingered the R-E-W, I imagined Randall was with me.

In order to shake off the fantasy of playing doctor right there on the table, I stared at the cotton gown, which looked like it was made from old flour sacks, the swirl of colors faded from too many washings. When we were little, my mom used to make all of our dresses out of flour sacks, and I could easily have had a dress in that same floral pattern. My mom was an excellent seamstress—in high school, she annually took home ribbons from the State Fair for her creations. Though my parents had known each other as children, they hadn't seen each other in years until my dad was home on furlough from an overseas assignment with the Air Force. Their courtship was short and sweet, and although my mother had always dreamt of making her own wedding dress, with only a week to plan the wedding, she was resplendent in a borrowed one.

I fingered my drop and glanced up at two body charts that covered the wall, one of bones and another of muscles. *Pectoralis major, Rectus abdom-*

inus, Gluteus medius, sternum, sacrum...up and down the body, each name became part of a new chant to keep me distracted.

Moments later Dr. Dycus stepped into the room holding my chart. Over six feet tall with wispy, sandy-colored hair, his eyes were dark like Hershey's Kisses, and when he smiled, which was frequently, the corners of his mouth crinkled. Besides being our family doctor, he was also David's father, and David was one of my best friends. If I counted up all the hours and minutes and seconds and nanoseconds that Randall and I spent hanging out at the Dycus house, I think we would have found another time-space continuum, since it couldn't have been possible to spend so much time there, and yet still work twenty hours a week, go to school and church, and find time to sneak off with Randall for sex. I liked Dr. Dycus immensely; he and Mrs. Dycus were "cool" parents who drank and smoked and never seemed to give a hoot about what we were doing in their basement rec room. On any other day I would have been happy to see him. If I had a compound fracture from falling off an eleven-story building, brain damage from a head-on collision, or a shot to the heart from my dad's Springfield, there is no one else I would have wanted to take care of me. But on this day, I had trouble looking into his eyes.

"Well, Lani, so you think you've got a bug." Dr. Dycus pulled out a tongue depressor. "Open up and say 'Ah.' How long does the nausea last?"

The tongue depressor triggered my gag reflex, which in turn triggered more stomach gymnastics. I choked back bile.

"Oh, I don't know. Sometimes it can last all day." I paused, forcing myself to form the words. "Usually it's worse in the mornings."

I took off my glasses and held them in my lap. They were my first pair of wire frames, just like John Lennon's. Dr. Dycus tilted my chin and peered up my nose and into my eyes. "And this started a few weeks ago?"

I fought the urge to vomit on his clean white coat. "Yes, sir. A couple of weeks ago. Right after Christmas."

He pulled the gown apart and placed his stethoscope on my bare back. "Now, Lani, take a deep breath. When was your last period?"

The steel was cold, and I shivered while the reason for his question hung between us unacknowledged.

I struggled to breathe slowly—in and out, in and out—like everything was fine. "I think I had one in December. But maybe not. Maybe it was November. I'm not sure."

Without looking at me, Dr. Dycus wrote in my chart. "Well, we need to do some tests. You give me a call first thing in the morning. We should know something by then. You going to school today?"

I nodded.

"Well, take it easy, and drink plenty of water." As he left the room, Dr. Dycus' kind eyes looked kinda worried.

Shirley came back in. She pulled up the sleeve of the gown, tightened an elastic band around my upper arm, swiped the inside of my elbow with alcohol, and then with a pinch and a jab, drew two vials of blood.

Outside the clinic, a new world greeted me. Typical Oklahoma weather, in the space of an hour, the sky had grown dark, the wind had died down, and it looked like it could snow.

It was ten o'clock so there was no point in trying to make my morning classes. I sat in the clinic parking lot a few more minutes before driving the two blocks over to where we used to live on Chestnut Street. My father had told us my grandpa had built the house we used to live in—in fact, he had built all the houses on the block.

I never knew him, my grandfather. He died when I was two. As a kid, hiding in corners, standing in doorways, I listened in on late night grown-up conversations and sometimes the way they talked about him didn't sound pretty. My dad ran away from home when he was fourteen and joined the Navy. Memaw had a hissy fit and wrote President Roosevelt personally to get my dad back. He was already in California, but they caught him right before he was supposed to ship out to the fighting in the Pacific. He wasn't at all happy about being sent home. By the time he turned sixteen, World War II was just months from being over. It didn't matter though; he ran away again, this time to join the Air Force, and there was nothing my Memaw could do about it.

I adored my Memaw. She was a lamb—wouldn't harm a fly, though I saw her swat plenty. Was her husband, my father's father, mean? What we think as children, especially teenagers, can be a far cry from the truth. But if my dad thought fighting and starving and sweating and possibly dying was better than living at home, no telling what kind of man his father was. It's hard to know what makes a man turn mean.

As I sat parked on Chestnut Street, my brain kept skipping around like stones on the river. Small, flat stones. My family. My history. All the people I loved. My best friend, Dayna. Randall.

I never thought of myself as a "bad" girl. In fact, if there had been a contest for Junior class "Miss Goody Two-shoes," I would have been a contender. I was as prim and proper as they came. At least on the outside.

But on the inside? That was a different story. Inside my head, inside my heart, I felt almost the same way about two things that couldn't have been more different—sex and God. And the inside self? It stayed hidden. I never shared it with anyone.

As for the God part, when it came to religion, I was a Christian. But more importantly than being Christian, I was a Baptist. Southern Baptist. My family's life revolved around our church—services on Sunday morning, Sunday night, Wednesday night, all week long if a revival was going on. I went to Sunday school, Bible study, Girls' Auxiliary, Youth Group. We had a zillion rules to follow. Don't drink, don't smoke, don't do drugs. We weren't allowed to dance. At church camp, boys and girls swam at separate times, because the elders believed that being in the company of partially clad bodies might incite us to do who-knows-what. We weren't like the Pentecostals who spoke in tongues or wrestled with snakes; no, Baptists knew how to behave. We sang with passion and lifted up the occasional "amen," but we never got carried away.

I knew the rules. I knew how I was supposed to act. I read the Bible through at least twice. I memorized Bible verses.

His word was in mine heart as a burning fire shut up in
my bones.

I understood the don'ts. On Friday nights when I went to the community center where Randall played rock & roll with his band, I sat on my hands true to my prim and proper outside self, even though my body wanted to take off and fly with the music. But on the inside? As Randall wailed away on the guitar, the high notes ripped through my chest, and I could feel the beat in my arms and feet. All I wanted to do was spin around the room like a ballerina, and then fumble in Randall's Impala and make out to the strains of "Born Under a Bad Sign."

And in church? A few "amens" didn't come anywhere near the crazy love I felt for Jesus. I wanted to be a poet with a mouthful of perfect words to describe my passion.

When love beckons to you, follow him.
I love thee to the level of every day's most quiet need.
I carry your heart with me (I carry it in my heart.)

The depth of my love for God didn't astonish or surprise me as much as the belief that God loved me first. My love for God was in response to God's amazing, unfailing love of me. My soul was thirsty for God like a deer panting for a brook. God prepared a table for me. My cup was full to the brim and running over.

The first song I learned was "Jesus Loves Me." I believed its few simple words deep down in my heart. Jesus loved me, really and truly loved me, and when I sang hymns or prayed, it was almost as if I went into a trance. On those days when I felt sad and alone like an out-of-place ugly duckling, and there were many of those, I knew eventually that I would be okay. With Jesus beside me to love me and guide me, I could believe that I was the daughter of the King, growing into a woman whose price was beyond jewels.

But growing up a Christian was a bit of a mind bender. With Three in One and One in Three, our faith had a split personality like the Joanne Woodward character in *The Three Faces of Eve*. Even though Jesus loved me, God the father was big and old and scary, much like the first pastor I could remember, Pastor Hart at Shields Boulevard Baptist Church in Oklahoma City—gray-haired, red-faced, screaming from the pulpit. This God took vengeance on his enemies.

Your nakedness shall be uncovered, yes, your shame will be seen. For the day of vengeance is in my heart.

It was hard for me to know where I stood with this God. He was a lot like my dad. Loving one minute, angry the next. Or absent.

Even though I knew sex before marriage was wrong—the biggest "don't" of all—after Randall and I had been going out for a few months, we had sex for the first time. I knew I needed to keep it a secret; I couldn't tell anyone, not even Dayna. Surprisingly, I didn't feel guilty; making love with Randall seemed natural, like it was something I was supposed to do. Randall was my soul mate, and God had given us his blessing.

But had we received God's blessing? It didn't seem possible, especially since I was sitting on Chestnut Street in my parents' car ruminating while my urine sample was being sent to a lab. Like the Clairol commercial "Does she... or doesn't she?" I kept wondering "is she...or isn't she?" Was it possible that I could be pregnant?

My eyes were drying out from the hot air and sweat pooled at the back of my neck. I turned off the heater and unbuttoned the top of my coat. I invoked more mantras: *everything's going to be all right. Krishna, Krishna, Hare, Hare, Amen, Hallelujah.*

When it came to sex, Randall and I had been super-careful in a responsible teenage sort of way. He pulled out his cock almost every time before he came. For at least a week before my period, we avoided vaginal sex—heavy petting and hand jobs only. The rhythm method was supposed to work, damn it!

Fortunately, our relationship wasn't only about sex. Randall and I were in love. We made love, even though Randall called it "balling." When we did "it," for a little bit of time I no longer had a hungry, achy, needy feeling.

I clutched the steering wheel as if it were a tree branch in a flash flood. I glanced at my wristwatch. Memaw gave it to me when I was in fifth grade, the Christmas my dad came home from Vietnam and we drove from Moore to Los Angeles for a family reunion. With a huge crowd to herd around—the seven in my family, three aunts, two uncles, five cousins, and my Memaw—we went to Disneyland. She bought the watch there. Snow White with two dwarfs. Dopey and Grumpy.

A large snowflake drifted down, melting the instant it hit the windshield. I looked up into the sky. The flake must have fallen all on its lonesome. Only menacing gray clouds hung above my head. I wanted it to snow. I welcomed snow. I wanted snow to come down hard, cold and white, covering the frozen ground, my apprehensions, my fears.

I said a little prayer. *Jesus, please help me. I'm drowning here.*

It was almost eleven. I put the car in drive and headed east to the high school. I got to thinking about my friend Desiree, and I desperately wished I knew where she was living. We had been friends since fourth grade, ever since we met in Girls' Auxiliary back in the Emmanuel Baptist Church days. But by the time Desiree got into Jr. High, she started getting a little wild—hanging out with the wrong crowd, smoking cigarettes, drinking. The summer after ninth grade, she drove off in a VW van to a rock festival at the raceway in Atlanta. She said that she lost her virginity on top of a mattress in the back of the van under a canopy of bright neon flowers. Fourteen or fifteen people sprawled naked across a filthy twin mattress—everyone fucking everyone else. I was sure she was making it up. How could they all fit?

The festival was more of the same, she said. Thousands of people balling, Janis Joplin and Paul Butterfield blaring through the speakers, pot smoke giving the air a bluish haze.

After the festival, Desiree made her way back home and started tenth grade with the rest of us. But after a few months, her parents said they couldn't do anything with her, like she was some kind of bad hairdo. They sent her to live in a foster home in Norman. She phoned a few times, but kept running away, and then she was gone. She was the only girl I knew who was having sex, or at least the only one who was willing to admit it.

The cafeteria was crowded. Outside in the courtyard, snow began to fall in earnest. I wondered if it would stick. It hardly ever snows in Oklahoma. Winter is the driest time of the year, unlike summer when the heat and humidity are suffocating, and it rains almost every afternoon.

I grabbed some fries and waited for Dayna to get out of class. Dayna and I had been inseparable since seventh grade, our first year of Junior High when we had every single class together, all the way from an 8am English class through Phys Ed after lunch until we found ourselves at 3pm in band practice surrounded by oh-so-cute boys with trumpets and tubas and big bass drums.

Dayna was unlike the other girls I knew. She never made fun of my homemade clothes, my working mom, my too often absent father. Dayna even defended me. In Mrs. Mallet's 7th Grade English class, we read *A Christmas Carol*, and when Scrooge sees Marley's face in his doorknocker, he described it as a bad lobster in a dark cellar. I had never seen a good lobster let alone a bad one, so I asked Mrs. Mallet what that looked like. Mrs. Mallet said the question was the height of impudence and gave me detention. Dayna piped up that she didn't know what a bad lobster looked like either, so she got detention, too.

Dayna had a ¼ inch gap between her front top teeth. I used to have one, too—a gap the size of Texas—until a dentist forced my front teeth together with a rubber band. It seemed like torture at the time, but I didn't mind; I wanted to look as normal as possible. I was always a bit embarrassed about my looks since I had a Mount Williams-sized mole right between my eyes, and there was no fixing that with a rubber band. But Dayna acted like having a front tooth gap was the most natural thing in the world, so natural it was never a topic of discussion, and neither was my mole.

Dayna's father died unexpectedly when we were in 8th grade. I went straight over to her house as soon as I found out. I brought her a potted orchid—just a little purple flower in a little brown pot, but it seemed to mean the world to her. I think that's the one and only time we ever sat together without talking. Usually we rattled on a mile a minute—our thoughts tearing along and tumbling out into the telephone receiver and into our laps, a river of words rushing to the sea—but that one afternoon in her darkened living room we sat, not saying a word, while shadowy figures came and went. We could hear indecipherable adult voices in the kitchen, and every now and then tears would roll down Dayna's face. I held her hand and cried, too. I had never spent any time with her father, and I didn't really know him, but I couldn't bear to see Dayna in such pain.

All through 9th and 10th grade, before I began dating Randall, I spent almost every Saturday night at Dayna's house. My own house was too full of sisters, so in the bedroom Dayna never had to share, one that was all hers and only hers, we read aloud *A Good Man Is Hard to Find* and poems by Emily Dickinson.

I've always loved the way words can sink in deep and take over, and Dayna loved words as much as I did. We ate words—chewing on them in our mouths, delighting in the way they looked on a page.

Cochineal blaze. Sordid excellence. The realm of You.

In the dark of night, we spent hours with our heads in a dictionary, and in ninth grade we decided that once we were out of college, we would move to New York City and write for *The New Yorker*. Dayna said it was the best magazine in the world, full of short stories and poems and interviews and articles written by real journalists.

But I couldn't talk to Dayna about seeing Dr. Dycus. She didn't have a boyfriend, never had sex. She wouldn't understand. And what would this mean for all of our plans? I might not be able to go to college right away, and I could forget about moving to New York with a husband and a baby.

I reasoned as only a teenager can. I knew I could figure everything out. My predicament wasn't a daydream. Seventeen in less than a month, it made sense for me and Randall to get married. Dayna would be the maid of honor. A small wedding, no need to make a big show of it. Randall's mom attended First Methodist, and we would have the wedding there since it had a smaller sanctuary than First Baptist. Even with fewer people, it wouldn't feel empty.

Both families would come without question. Of course, the Bishops would be there—my parents' best friends, and so close that we never used "Mr. and Mrs." with them. All my life they had been nothing other than

Uncle Carl and Aunt Ann. We would invite a few friends from school—Lori, David, Kip, Greg, Patricia. David, definitely, as Randall's best man. Or maybe Randall's brother, Arnold, but he was only in sixth grade. And besides, Dayna would look pretty funny walking down the aisle with him since he was at least a foot shorter. But it wasn't my call; Randall could ask whoever he wanted to be his best man. Just as long as they made it to the church on time.

I would invite Mr. Stevens from work and the Bagleys and the Creigs, maybe even the Friars. I was sure Jean and Warren and Annette would come. Aunt Erma might make the cake. Even Veda Jo and Paul would drive up from Sulpher. Come to think of it, we could fill most of the pews.

We wouldn't need to tell anyone I was pregnant. Yes, yes, people might talk, suspect something was amiss since we didn't wait to get married until after high school, but lots of kids married young. Maybe I could even get away with wearing a white dress. Walk down the aisle on my dad's arm, holding a bouquet of yellow roses. And there would be Randall, standing at the front of the church waiting for me, wanting me. Gazing at me with all the love the world could hold.

The fries were making unhappy noises in my stomach by the time Dayna arrived at my table with a tray overflowing with Sloppy Joes and orange Jell-O.

"Here you are. Where have you been? Mr. Mathis was in fine form this morning. Do you want the homework? Are you all right? You look a little green around the gills." Dayna plopped down and reached across the table to grab a few fries.

"I was at the doctors. I'm fine, just a silly little bug, you know. It's nothing to worry about." I wiped my hands on a paper napkin. "Do you want the rest of these? I'm not very hungry."

Dayna nodded, and dumped the remaining fries on her tray. "Whatever you've got—is it contagious? Cause if it is, please breathe on my Jell-O. I wouldn't mind a good excuse to skip school tomorrow."

"I'm almost over it, I think. I'm not contagious. But I'll breathe on your Jell-O if you want me to."

Dayna lowered her voice like we were co-conspirators in the Weather Underground. "Did you hear? Jimmy Henderson asked Terri Bodine to go out with him. Like Little Miss Everything needed to start dating the sexiest guy in our class."

Terri was our Pastor's daughter. The epitome of a kiss-ass if ever there was one. I felt a small pang of jealousy, and my cheeks flushed. I would never have admitted it in a thousand years, but I lusted after Jimmy and felt woozy every time he walked by my locker. Of course, Randall was my one and only, and I would never act on those feelings. But it was strange to me how I could love someone with all my heart, and still get crazy flashes of desire for someone else.

I drummed my fingers on the table as a distraction. "No, I didn't hear that. Lucky her. Pastor Bodine can't be too happy about it though. Jimmy's sure not the missionary type."

A wave of nausea threatened to steal my shored-up resolve to keep a happy face. "Sorry, Dayna. I'm not feeling so good; I came back a day too soon. I'll call you tonight."

No more snow. The wind scattered what little fell. At home the wind rattled the windows and my nerves. I managed to get through the rest of the day by staying busy. No idle mind or hands for the devil's workshop. Not from me. No siree. I did some laundry, helped my brother Billy and my youngest sister Janet with their spelling and arithmetic, baked the cornbread, set the table, washed the dishes, read a few chapters of *Wuthering Heights*, watched *Gunsmoke*.

Randall called around nine when he got off work at the library. "Missed you today. Everything all right?"

"Yeah, fine, just a bit of a bug."

"Good. Wanna go see *Little Big Man* this weekend? It's still playing at the Plaza."

"Sure. Lori saw it last week and says it's great. Kinda sad, but Dustin Hoffman is amazing."

"I wish we were out at the lake."

"It's kind of cold for that now."

"Not the way we heat up the car."

"Randall, my mom is going to wonder why I'm blushing. I'll see you tomorrow. Goodnight. I love you."

"Love you, too."

As we hung up the phone, I reverted to more sing-song pablum to calm my fears.

Everything's gonna be all right.
Amen. Hallelujah. Hare Krishna.

I would talk to Dr. Dycus in the morning. He would prescribe some antibiotics. I would be fine by the weekend. We would go see a movie, everything back to normal. I was glad I didn't say anything to anyone. And Randall didn't need to know my silly suspicions. As my Memaw always said, "No reason to raise an alarm until there's an alarm to be raised."

Unwelcome News

The next morning my mom left for work at seven with my brother and two youngest sisters in tow. Lucky them, some mornings they got doughnuts at the store for breakfast. I could almost smell the dough rising in the vat of hot oil, and I had a hankering for the sweet, sticky glaze before it was quickly squelched by nausea.

I turned back to my bowl of Cheerios. Since my dad had already left for work at Tinker Air Force Base in Midwest City, I was responsible for making sure my sister Kathy ate something, and that she was wearing a jacket and a skirt that wasn't too short. Kathy was a year behind me in school, and perfectly capable of taking care of herself, but while I might have been "bad," Kathy was wild.

In between trips to the bathroom, I called the clinic. Shirley's cheery voice was on the other end of the line. "Dr. Dycus is with a patient, can he call you right back?"

I paced up and down the short hallway between the bathroom and the living room and walked blindly into Janet's piano. I closed the lid with a bang. In the dining room Kathy finished up some homework in and amongst the clutter of her breakfast. As I carried her dishes to the sink, resentment surfaced. I started to complain, but let it drop, too jittery to fight.

I was rinsing Kathy's cereal bowl when the phone rang. I screamed before she had the chance to grab the phone that hung on the kitchen wall. "I'll get it, I'll get it in mom's room." I darted down the hall into my parent's bedroom where I hoped for a little more privacy. My hand shook as I picked up the pink Princess phone on the bedside table. "This is Lani."

Dr. Dycus cleared his throat. "Lani, I've got some difficult news for you. The test came back positive. You're pregnant."

I didn't respond. I pushed my glasses up to the bridge of my nose. A short span of silence hung between us. I sat down, for the first time in my life unconcerned about mussing the tight hospital corners my mother insisted were the only proper way to make a bed. I couldn't feel the bedspread under my butt or the carpet under my feet.

Dr. Dycus cleared his throat again. "Lani, I know this must be difficult for you. These tests are new, and sometimes there can be a false positive. I can't be definite until I do an internal exam. And I won't do that without your parent's permission."

Another longer span of silence. I wrapped the telephone cord around my ring finger. I couldn't tell my parents. For sure it would break my mother's heart when my father killed me. I started to crumple, the floor spinning out from under me.

"Get back to me on this. Either way, you need to start taking care of yourself."

"Yes, Dr. Dycus," I mumbled. "I'll get back to you."

I bit my lower lip and hung up the phone, fighting back tears.

"Lani?" I heard my sister's voice coming from miles away, high and strident. "The bus will be here any minute. What are you doing? Who was on the phone?"

The last thing I needed was Kathy's prying.

I got up from the bed and stumbled on my way back to the living room. Kathy stood near the front door holding a book bag and the hard case holding her flute. The long denim strap of her shoulder bag looked out of place under her wool muffler. Kathy's long brown hair came nearly to the small of her back and it was so straight it coulda been rolled out like pie crust. She was wearing her winter coat unbuttoned, and beneath it the waist of her skirt was rolled up exposing three-quarters of her thigh.

"Good Lord, Kathy, you can see from here until Christmas. You pull that skirt down right now or I'm telling Ma."

Just then the school bus stopped across the street from our house, and Kathy stuck out her tongue and rushed outside. Sometimes I really hated being the oldest. Siblings can be such pains even in the best of times, and Kathy, the second in our band of five, was so ornery she could make a preacher cuss. "Hold the bus," I yelled, grabbing my coat and bag.

On the bus I gripped the seat backs and found an empty space near the rear. The outside temperature hovered below freezing, and the little bit of warmth generated by the bus's heater didn't penetrate past the fifth row. We crossed the railroad tracks and drove past the O'Neil farm. The verdant fields shimmered with blankets of winter wheat that seemed to defy the gray and cloudy January skies.

A spit wad came flying by my head, barely missing me by inches. A couple of junior varsity guys in first year letter jackets looked back sheepishly. I gave them the evil eye, and they turned around and ignored me.

Pregnant girls weren't allowed in school, so I wondered if I might have to drop out, at least for a while. Maybe I could get an extra job. My mom already worked too hard, and our family couldn't afford another mouth to feed. We needed a baby like I needed water in my lungs.

I forced my gloom and doom thoughts into the belief that Randall would do right by me. We would get married. My folks would be there to help out. We could fix up his parents' garage as a little apartment until we graduated. Randall would make an excellent father. I would be the best mother ever. Yes, everything was gonna be all right. Amen. Hallelujah.

The diesel fumes triggered another wave of nausea. I pulled a piece of dry toast from my coat pocket and nibbled a little to keep my stomach in check. My little bug had a big name—morning sickness.

Through crowded halls, I walked with head bent, eyes fixed on the scuffed floors. Conversations were hushed, and it seemed like folks stopped talking mid-sentence whenever I walked past. Like most self-centered teenagers, I believed all the conversations were focused on me. How could they know already? I only found out myself minutes ago.

My first class of the morning was French, upstairs in Room 219. This was my second year of French, and one of my favorite subjects. The previous year our teacher, Mrs. Tourney, took us to Oklahoma City on a field trip to see *The Umbrellas of Cherbourg* with dinner at La Citrouille afterwards. Stiff white tablecloths and napkins, more than one fork in the place setting—the fanciest restaurant I had ever seen. They served escargot as an appetizer, all slathered in butter and garlic, and the mere thought of it made me gag.

The previous December, right before Christmas break, I was in French class when I heard the news about Sean's death. Sean and I had been friends since seventh grade. In tenth grade, our Honors English class held an end-of-year party next to the Duck Pond on the campus of Oklahoma University in Norman. We had a potluck picnic, read poetry, acted out scenes from Shakespeare, and pretended we were as grown-up and sophisticated as college students. To celebrate, Sean brought along a bottle of Chianti. Being Irish Catholic, Sean was an oddity at our school, and his parents kept wine in the house. They even let him drink it, because Catholics, unlike Baptists, don't believe that drinking alcohol is the biggest sin in the world.

At the picnic, our teacher, Mrs. Sanders, smiled and looked the other way. I guess she figured "what the fuck" since she had already been called on the carpet earlier in the year for letting us read *The Catcher in the Rye*.

Besides, she and her husband were moving to Newfoundland that summer. At the time, I was a little worried about taking my first drink. A good Baptist doesn't drink. But good Baptists don't have sex before marriage either, and by that time, Randall and I had been fucking for more than a month. The wine was warm; it made my throat and belly burn, and I liked the free and easy way it made me feel.

I wished Mrs. Sanders still lived in Moore. I knew I could talk to her about Sean. I knew I could talk with her about my pregnancy. Sean's death was incomprehensible. He stumbled down the stairs to his basement, got tangled in a rope and choked to death. It was a freak accident. It had to be a freak accident, no matter what the newspaper reported. Sean was quirky, irreverent, funny, generous. He had a chipped front tooth, and a big cowlick on the right side of his forehead that forced his long hair over electric blue eyes to stick out at strange angles. He had everything to live for, and I refused to believe the dark rumors that spread around town.

I bawled for hours after Sean's funeral. Randall held me, and when my wails reduced to whimpers, we made love. And that night, I really needed him to come inside me.

In Honors English, my second class of the morning, I caught Randall's eye and smiled. In that moment I noticed how long his hair was getting; it almost reached below the collar of his shirt. Funny thing about being a teenager—I could fly emotionally from deep to shallow without blinking an eye. I wanted to take him out in the hall and kiss him senseless. Even in the midst of all my sadness over Sean's death and my worry over being pregnant I was still getting turned on. "We need to talk," I mouthed silently, "after class."

I glanced away as Mrs. Massenger began speaking. "I've typed up parts of *In Memoriam A.H.H.* by Alfred, Lord Tennyson," she said. "This poem, hundreds of lines in length, expresses Tennyson's struggle with the unexpected death of his close friend, Arthur Henry Hallman. Tennyson took more than seventeen years to write it, and it's considered one of the greatest poems of the nineteenth century."

"So, get in groups of three or four, read the poem, and discuss what it brings up for you."

I picked up the mimeographed sheet and formed a circle with David, Lori and Greg. Lori offered to begin:

> *Oh yet we trust that somehow good*
> *Will be the final goal of ill,*

I couldn't make sense of the words. The cadence rocked me into a trance, and I felt like I had left my body. I was a spirit hovering above the room, and I examined the faces of people who were my whole world. Sean's death had struck a huge crack in it. What would this pregnancy do?

A wave of nausea pulled me back into my seat. Lori was still reading,

> *So runs my dream: but what am I?*
> *An infant crying in the night:*
> *An infant crying for the light:*
> *And with no language but a cry.*

After lunch, our weirdo group of irregulars gathered outside the cafeteria in the smoking area. The wind was vicious as it whipped down from the northern plains, and the breezeway lived up to its name. David had trouble lighting a cigarette. Randall opened up his arms for a hug, and I sank into them. Tears held off and on in check all day now descended like the tumbling waters of Falls Creek in early spring.

"What's going on with you?" he asked perplexed. "Oh, nothing, just got a lot on my mind. I love you," I nuzzled in his ear. "Yeah, me too," he whispered. His hand cradled the small of my back before his fingers migrated to the curve of my hips.

I broke out of his grasp and drew my coat closer to my body. I was worried I would tell all, and this was neither the time nor the place for a confession. I laughed at something Dayna was saying. Randall could think I was "on the rag" and hormonally moody. Hormones were raging, all right, but for a different reason.

Chicken Fried Steak

Friday after school, I asked Randall if we could take a drive to visit Sean's grave. Lilac Hill Cemetery, Sean's final resting place, was about five miles south of Moore, just before the turn off for Indian Hills Road.

Maybe there I could give Randall the news about the baby. Maybe there we could gain some perspective on the fragility of life and our place in the world. Maybe there we could find acceptance for our predicament and make plans for the future.

On the bench seat of Randall's '67 Impala, I scooted over until I pressed against his side. His arm brushed my breast as he reached to turn on the radio, and a wonderful shiver of desire raced through my body. *Hare Krishna, Krishna, Krishna.* It was no time to start thinking about sex. I placed my hand over his. "Babe, if it's all right with you, can we stay quiet for a while?"

I needed the comfort of silence. I had too much to think about. I had to tell Randall about the baby. The secrecy was eating me up, but my mind drew a complete blank when it came to the right words for sharing what might be unwelcome news. My tongue felt like it was swollen to twice its normal size. Saliva pooled in the back of my throat, but I couldn't swallow. I started to panic, afraid that I might choke.

"Randall?"

"What is it, Lani?"

"Nothing really." I held my peace. The time wasn't right. Randall seemed to have a lot on his mind, too.

"I just wanted to see how you're doing. We haven't talked much this week."

Since getting the news on Tuesday, I had spent most of my time buried in school and work. I kept telling myself that I needed to be comfortable with the pregnancy, and sure of the direction we needed to take before I explained it all to him.

We drove the rest of the way to the cemetery in silence. Randall kept both hands on the steering wheel, in the 10 and 2 position, and stared ahead. He was always such a careful driver. Everything would be fine. He was going to make a wonderful father.

It was almost dusk when we arrived at the cemetery. The moon, although not full, hung huge and bright in the dimming light. The sky was clear, and a million stars were beginning to peek out over our heads illuminating the circular drive.

Randall parked the car and headed toward the gravesite, completely forgetting to open my car door. I pushed it open. The temperature had dropped. I wrapped my arms around my body, shivering in the harsh wind. My face felt raw, my eyes were scratchy. The frozen ground matched the frozen skies, and I slipped on icy grass.

"Fudge," I said under my breath.

I walked toward Randall where a mound of dirt rose above the ground.

Sean's burial service had been short. The priest sprinkled holy water on the empty grave and Sean's coffin. "Grant him eternal rest, may light perpetual shine on him, may he rest in peace," he intoned before Sean's body was lowered into darkness.

The little light that was left quickly drained away, and neither Randall nor the mound gave off any shadows. We stood together in silence, and I choked back tears. "It's still hard to believe he's gone."

I stood there a moment brooding over Sean's death and my pregnancy, when a song popped into my head. "What do you think, Randall? Are we all just part of one big circle of life? One life ends and another begins? You know—like in that Blood, Sweat & Tears song 'And When I Die'."

"That's ridiculous, Lani, people die, and people are born and neither has anything to do with the other," Randall sneered. "The only thing real in that song is that heaven doesn't exist, and the ground we're buried in is as cold as the moon."

I felt hit by another icy blast, and this time it wasn't the wind.

Randall and I trudged back to his car. Once again, he forgot to open my car door, and I slipped on the slope of the drainage ditch. I felt a run starting in my stocking. "Double-fudge."

I got in the car. Instead of scooting over to my customary spot under Randall's arm, I stayed on the passenger side—sad, worried and pissed. Randall turned the key in the ignition and put the car in drive.

The time to tell him had come—it was now or never.

"I don't know how to tell you this, so I'm just gonna blurt it out. Randall, I'm pregnant."

He looked over at me, his face ashen. He put the car in park and turned on the radio. The sound of "The Long and Winding Road" filled the distance between us. It was our song; we played it all the time. It came out the previous spring right after we had started making love, and everything in the song was about us. The road leading us home and to each other.

I wanted to believe that Randall was my home. I wanted to believe that I was his. I wanted to believe that we would happily welcome the baby into our home and that none of us would ever be alone anymore.

"*Before you, I was alone,*" I sang with the radio in the background.

Randall was silent.

"*Alone, I cried and cried,*" I whispered.

Randall hit the steering wheel with a clenched fist.

"*And you will never know,*" I blubbered. "*How hard I've tried to bring you home.*"

The dark night was ready to engulf us. We sat a moment without speaking, and then slowly drove away.

A few moments later, I wiped away tears and realized I was starving.

"Can we go get something to eat? Please?"

Randall shrugged, and we headed to Del Rancho on Main Street for chicken fried steak sandwiches. Like most Okies, I believed that no one can stay upset when eating chicken fried steak.

We pulled up to a speakerphone and placed our order. Once we knew sandwiches, onion rings, and cherry vanilla cokes were on their way, Randall turned to look at me.

"I can't believe this is happening. This is so fucked up. We've been careful. Are you sure?"

I looked out the window, avoiding Randall's piercing eyes. "I saw Dr. Dycus on Monday. I've been sick since Christmas. They did blood tests, urine tests—I talked to him on Tuesday and he said I was pregnant." I turned back to face Randall and attempted my best Elmer J. Fudd impersonation with exaggerated downturned lips. "Guess I killed da wabbit."

Randall shook his head. "This isn't funny. Why didn't you say something earlier? Have you told Dayna?"

I was hurt by his question. "No, I wouldn't tell anyone before I told you." I reached out and placed my hand on his thigh. "And I didn't tell you earlier because I wanted to figure things out."

I moved to scoot closer, but Randall kept his hand on the seat between us. His voice was stern.

"I don't want you saying anything to anyone until we've had a chance to sort this out. And you should've told me right away. Sometimes these things are better handled early."

Something in his voice didn't sit right. Randall and I never had a "how many kids do you want" conversation. I always figured we'd have at least three. There were three kids in his family, and five in mine. I couldn't wrap my mind around what he seemed to be implying.

"What things? What are you talking about? An abortion? Are you talking about an abortion?"

Randall nodded.

I was stunned—who was this stranger sitting next to me? Randall was supposed to stand by me. He was my road home, my bridge over troubled waters. My throat tightened. I felt hot, nauseous. Something was seriously wrong here. Randall wasn't behaving like the same boy I knew and loved.

"I can't get an abortion, they're illegal. And even if they weren't...." I stopped mid-sentence.

Randall patted my shoulder like I was an unreasonable three-year-old. "It's an embryo. Tissue. But we don't need to have this conversation now."

"Well, when can we talk about it? We've got to talk about it!" My voice was thin and sharp, and grated on my own nerves.

The carhop knocked on the window. As Randall rolled it down, the smell of toasted bread, grease and cooked meat wafted into the car along with a sharp blast of cold wind. He passed over the cardboard tray holding our drinks, and I wanted nothing more than to puke—all over his vinyl seat, all over his chicken fried steak, all over him. I rolled down my window, and stuck my face out, tears stinging my eyes.

"I thought we'd get married."

"Lani, roll up your window. It's freezing in here." Randall took two straws out of the bag and pulled off the protective paper wrapper. "Of course, we'll get married. We just can't get married right now."

"Why not?" I grumbled.

I rolled up the window and stabbed the straws through the holes in the plastic lids and handed Randall one of the cokes. He set a red-checked paper food tray filled with a large order of onion rings on the seat between us.

"Because we're sixteen. Because I work at the library for $1.25 an hour. Because we don't have any place to live. Because we still have to finish high school. Enough reasons for you?" By the third "because," his voice sounded like it was being cranked out of the speakers at a Led Zeppelin concert. His face turned red, and then in an oh, so familiar gesture, he reached up, brushed his hand across his long bangs, and pushed his eyeglasses against the bridge of his nose.

"You don't have to shout," I complained. "Besides, I'm almost seventeen, and our parents would help us out."

"Don't be so sure about that," he muttered.

I ignored his remark. "But what about the baby?" I took a long sip of coke. "We're going to have a baby."

Randall reached back into the bag and pulled out a steak sandwich. "Here, eat your food. I'm almost late for work. Let's drop this for now. We'll go out tomorrow the same as usual. Later we'll tell my folks, and then we'll all go over to talk with your parents. Doesn't the Bible say there's strength in numbers?"

"I guess so. A man may prevail against the one, but two will withstand him; and a threefold cord is not quickly broken. Ecclesiastes, I think. And now there's three of us—you, me, and the baby."

"I don't…" Randall's voice trailed off.

I bit into my sandwich. I loved Del Rancho chicken fried steak, but that afternoon, I might as well have been eating cardboard. Our conversation hadn't turned out the way I expected. If my Memaw had been there she would have said I'd been rode hard and put away wet.

I forced myself to chew and swallow. Randall made a rubbing motion around the corner of his mouth.

I scrounged around for a napkin and wiped mayonnaise off my chin. I was taught that all things work for good to them who love the Lord. I was also taught that God's ways are not our ways. Sometimes when God answers prayers, the answer is "no." I decided to give prayer a chance anyway.

> *God, you know I love you. And Randall and I love each other. He's just feeling confused right now. The best thing is for us to get married and have this baby. Work some good here.*

Roleplaying

Randall rang the doorbell around six on Saturday. We both had worked eight hours—Randall at the public library and me at Steven's Pharmacy—and we were hungry, tired, and cranky. "Wanna get some pizza at Orin's?"

Underneath his leather trench coat, he was still wearing the clothes he wore to work—a blue button-down long-sleeved shirt, gray wool herringbone pants and Dexter shoes. Randall was quite the dresser and rarely wore jeans and t-shirts. Even when he played with his band, he dressed up. His sound may have been psychedelic rock, but his look was all British Invasion.

I wore the clothes my mother made me—dresses for school and some polyester pantsuits for work—but they were more her taste than mine, and certainly would never have graced the pages of *Seventeen*. I never cared about how clothing looked; I dressed for comfort.

"Sure, Orin's sounds great." I grabbed the heavyweight pea coat I had picked up in the fall from the Army Navy Surplus Store in Norman. The wind had died down, but the temperature hovered in the low thirties.

I peeked into the kitchen. My mother stood at the stove with her back to me, both hands busy chopping lettuce and tomatoes. A metal bowl the size of a cantaloupe overflowed with grated cheddar cheese. The big cast iron skillet sizzled with browning ground beef and onions. In a moment she would fill the smaller skillet with Crisco and fry up tortillas until they were hot but not crispy.

Feeling guilty I turned back to Randall. "Wanna eat here?"

He shook his head. "No, thanks. Besides, we need to talk."

"Ma," I yelled. "Randall and I are going to get some pizza down in Norman. I'll be back by ten."

"Don't be late," my mother hollered back. "Church tomorrow."

We headed to Norman on the old Highway. It used to be the only way we could get there before they put in Interstate 35. It was a far prettier trip for sure. They built the interstate smack dab in the middle of a big expanse of nothingness. The old highway passed the country store at the intersection of Seven Corners, and at night the lights of farmhouses in the distance looked like God winking. The highway had a fair share of dips in the road that we could take flying, our stomachs doing flip-flops like we were on the Big Dipper at Springlake.

Lilac Hill Cemetery was off of the old Highway, too, and when we passed it, I thought about Sean's final resting place. A deep sadness settled in. At Sean's funeral we prayed for him to be surrounded by perpetual light, but I was terrified by the thought that he would never again see the light of day.

Randall and I didn't talk on the way. For a couple of people who needed to talk, and who used to have an ever flowing artesian well of words in each other's company, it was strange to have the poetry dry up and catch in our throats.

I tried to start up a conversation. "How was work? Were you busy?"

"Listen, Lani, I've got a lot on my mind. Just let me focus on the road."

Orin's was our go-to place for pizza—much, much better than Pizza Hut. Besides, it was right on Campus Corner near the college bookstore and a head shop. Randall went there to pick up nickel bags when he couldn't find any pot on Paseo Street. And the previous year, just a week before we had sex for the first time, we played hooky from school with Lori and Buzz, caught the bus to Norman and walked to campus. All sorts of anti-war protests were taking place on the South Oval, but on that warm and bright May Day we were still innocents. I brought a copy of *The Prophet*; Randall brought Walt Whitman and e.e. cummings. We hung out at on the Oval, listened to speeches, smoked pot, read poetry, and Randall and I kissed until I thought my tongue would fall off.

Later that week cops arrested twelve thousand people in Washington D.C. for protesting. But that wasn't the worst of it. On May 4th at Kent State things got really ugly. The Ohio National Guard shot and killed four kids—two who just happened to be in the wrong place at the wrong time. Suddenly, the world grew dark, and it seemed as if all we'd been doing up to that point was nothing more than game-playing. I had a hard time finding my Pollyanna self, and I became less hopeful. I had serious doubts we could change the world and stop the senseless unending war.

Once at Orin's, I found a booth in the back corner while Randall ordered mushroom and pepperoni pizza. He carried two large red plastic glasses to the table.

"Coke, OK?" he asked.

"Sure, fine." I tore the top off the paper wrapper and stuck a straw into the glass. "Want to tell me about your day now?"

Randall was still wearing his trench coat. He stood up, took it off and hung it on a peg attached to the side of our wooden booth. "Want me to take your coat?"

I shook my head. "No, not yet, I'm still a little cold. It's really frigid out tonight."

Randall sat back down in the booth. "What do you think? It's January."

I took another sip of coke. "So, are we going to talk, or what?"

Randall hesitated before speaking. "Listen, I, I talked to my parent's last night after I got home."

A huge sense of betrayal washed through my body. "I thought we were going to tell them together. Remember? Strength in numbers?"

Randall sighed. "I know them better than you do. I knew they'd want to hear it from me without any outside influence."

"Outside influence!" Tears welled up along with my anger. "I'm pregnant with their grandchild. I'm not some stranger with no stake in this." On top of the table, I clenched my right hand into a fist.

Randall reached across and closed my hand in his own. "Calm down, Lani. We need to be logical about this. My parents want to help us, they want to help you, but we have to think beyond today. What we decide will affect us for the rest of our lives."

"I *am* trying to be logical. But I can't put the genie back in the bottle." I pulled my hand away and started picking at a torn cuticle. "I'm pregnant."

"Well, what if we could make you not pregnant?" Randall paused and took a sip of coke. "My parents can help."

"Weren't you listening to me yesterday? How can you even suggest that?" I pounded my fist on the table. "And even if I felt differently, it's illegal. Your parents know some guy in a back alley?"

Randall shook his head. "No, it's legal in Colorado, and they would help you get there and pay for the procedure."

"I don't care where it's legal. It's out of the question."

A deep voice came across the intercom. "Pizza for Randall."

Randall left the booth, and I held my head in my hands.

I knew there was no way I could have an abortion. My church taught that the Bible was the Word of God. Everything in the Bible was true and infallible. In the book of Jeremiah God said, *"Before I formed thee in the belly I knew thee; and before thou camest forth out of the womb I sanctified thee…"* That meant that God already knew and loved my baby. God had plans for my baby. I started to sob.

Randall came back to our booth with the greasy pizza.

"Lani, stop crying. I don't think you understand." His voice was stern. "What's out of the question is getting married and having this baby. My parents won't stand for that."

I fought the nausea, trying to make sense of what Randall was saying. "What do you mean, they won't stand for it. If you want to get married, then we get married."

Randall lifted a slice of pizza from the pan and placed it on a paper plate. Cheese dripped from the tip. "No, Lani, we don't get married." His voice turned pleading. "I'm only sixteen. I can't get married in this state without my parent's permission and they're not going to give it."

"Then we'll go to another state." I sounded like a beggar. "If we can cross state lines for an abortion, we can cross state lines to get married." I picked up the pizza slice and brought it to my mouth. We had been at Orin's the previous fall when we heard the news that Janis Joplin died of a drug overdose, and the sharp smell of pepperoni took me back to the despair of that night. I looked down at the table, not sure of what I was seeing.

Internally I told myself, "This is a saltshaker. This is grated Parmesan cheese. Hot pepper flakes. Garlic powder." But all of these familiar, unfamiliar things seemed covered in loss. Loss of hope, loss of light, loss of life. I put the pizza back down on the plate with tears streaming down my face. "But what about the baby, Randall? What about the baby?"

Randall was insistent. "Lani, I agree with my parents. I'm too young to get married. And I'm certainly too young to have a baby." He took a bite of pizza. A string of melted cheese hung from his mouth down onto the plate. "I've got college, I want to travel. Listen, you don't want to get tied down, do you?"

Randall washed down his last bite of pizza with a sip of coke. "My first choice is no baby, period. But if you don't like that idea, then you've got to consider adoption if you want to stay with me."

"You don't want to marry me?" A deep, pain welled up in my chest. I had never felt that kind of anguish before, like a knife slicing me apart. "You don't want to have our baby?" I pushed my plate away.

"Lani, someday we can get married." Randall took another bite of pizza, and his words were garbled and clear. "But no, I don't want to have a baby. Not now, maybe not ever."

On the way home Randall made a familiar right turn off state highway 77 and onto SE 119th Street, heading east towards Kitchen Lake. My mom used to play half-court basketball with the Kitchen girls, perky twins with bouncy names something like Billy or Dottie. She showed me some pictures of their team in the Moore High class of '49 yearbook, and the twins had more than just bouncy names going for them. Twenty years later, their farmhouse sat abandoned, and the dirt road meandering to the deserted barn made a perfect spot for "parking." At least it was perfect before it got so cold. Randall had the heat blasting in the Impala, and I could feel sweat dripping down the back of my neck.

I was pregnant and craving Randall—the very thing that got me in this mess. For a minute he sang along with the radio, oblivious. KATT, the only radio station in Oklahoma playing something on the air besides oldies or country, was blaring "White Room," album version. Randall loved Cream, and he leaned over and turned the music up louder. "This is a Pete Brown lyric."

"The guy who wrote 'Tales of Brave Ulysses'?" I asked, feigning interest.

"No, but he did write 'Sunshine of Your Love' with Clapton." Randall made a left onto the unnamed dirt road. The car bounced up and down. The shocks were on their last legs.

I could only remember a few of the lyrics, but they seemed appropriate for the pickle I found myself in—something about waiting for an eternity to get to the place I needed to be. I scooted closer on the bench seat, "Oh, God, Randall, I don't think I can get through this."

We came to a full stop in front of the barn. Randall shut off the headlights and the black night seemed to absorb the car and everything in it, including me and Randall. I felt small. The sky had cleared, and a million stars were visible in the heavens.

Randall reached over and began to unbutton my wool coat. "Let's just take this a day at a time, OK?"

"What do you think you're doing?" I asked, pushing his hand away.

"You know what I'm doing, Lani." He pushed the glasses up on his nose and leaned in for a kiss. "Or do you want to be Betty tonight?"

I don't remember how it started, but at some point in our short-lived courtship, we began some silly role-playing games. I would be Betty, the good girl cheerleader, and he'd be Bubba, first-string quarterback. We had a couple of different scenarios, but basically, Betty and Bubba would go parking, Bubba would make his move, Betty would resist, but only up to a point. Then we would start in on some heavy petting, which always culminated in full-on, pants around the ankles, heaving-breathing, heart-pounding sex. We hadn't played this game in a while, because it only worked in the car. Popular kids never had sex in their bedrooms with sixth-grade brothers listening outside the door.

"I don't know if I'm supposed to, well, you know, do it while I'm pregnant," I protested. "Won't it hurt the baby?"

"It's not going to hurt the baby, I." Randall looked exasperated. "Don't you know anything about procreation?"

"I guess I don't have to know much." I held my arms tight across my chest. "I got pregnant just fine being an ignoramus."

"Listen, I'm sorry." Randall placed his hands on my forearms. "I was just thinking, you know, once your parents find out they might not let us spend any time alone."

"I'm not really in the mood, Randall," I lied as I leaned over and kissed his cheek, "but I guess you're right." I uncrossed my arms and unbuttoned my jacket. "Do you want to get in back?"

"Betty, why don't you give me a real kiss?" Randall pressed his mouth against mine, and his tongue started exploring the back of my throat. Instantly, I felt some of the tension leave my body. After a minute, Randall came up for air. "I made that last touchdown just for you."

"I saw you looking over at me." I tossed my head, imagining a long, blonde ponytail instead of my thin dishwater blonde hair blunt cut just above my shoulders.

Randall placed his hand under my T-shirt. "Yeah, it was hard to keep my head in the game." His fingers inched their way up my stomach. "You look so cute in that short skirt."

"I'm getting awfully hot. Let me take my coat off." I pulled my arms out of the sleeves and laid it across the back of the seat. But without the wool's comforting warmth, I trembled, partly in anticipation and partly from the temperature. "Could you see my panties when I jumped up and down?"

Randall's fingers found their way beneath my bra, and he caressed my erect nipples. "Yeah, and when you bent over, man, it was almost impossible to keep from getting a hard on."

I giggled. "I guess it's pretty hard to play football with a hard on."

"I've got one now, Betty." Randall guided my hand to the crotch of his grey wool slacks. "Go on. Touch it."

"I don't think I'm supposed to do that, Bubba." I pretended to pull my hand back, and Randall tightened his grip. I weakly protested, "Good girls don't touch their boyfriend's thingies."

Randall took his hand out from under my shirt and unbuckled his belt. "Come on, Betty, please touch it." He quickly unzipped his pants and reached into his underwear and pulled out his penis. "I promise it won't bite."

At the sound of the zipper and the sight of his cock I felt myself flushing, straining against my jeans. I kept playing our little game. "Oh, it's so hard, Bubba, and so big, just like a tire iron. It scares me." My breath came in short, sharp pants.

"Betty, it won't hurt you. You gotta trust me. Pull down your pants." Randall reached out and fumbled with the snap on my jeans.

I unzipped my pants and lifted my butt up so I could pull them down along with my panties. When they were below my knees, I sat back down. The leather upholstery was cool on my skin. I leaned over to take off my tennis shoes.

Randall watched me and kept stroking his penis. "Don't worry about your shoes, Betty. Just turn over."

"Randall, what are you doing?" I straightened up to look at him. His face was in shadow, the only light coming from his bright teeth. "You want to do it doggy style?"

Up to that point we had never done it that way before.

"Use Bubba. It's OK, Betty. Get up on your knees and lean against the door. It's going to feel good; I promise."

I rested my elbows on the armrest. My face was pressed up against the glass. The cold reminded me of Sean's dark tomb, and I shook in my thin T-shirt. I was exposed and vulnerable. Randall's belt buckle and zipper grazed my ass as he positioned himself behind me. He was having trouble finding my opening. I reached back to help, but Randall grabbed my arm and pushed it towards the window.

"Why don't you finger me a little?" I asked, but Randall didn't answer. There was a hard thrust until he was in. Usually I melted when I had him inside me, but that night it felt different. Randall seemed angry. He pushed harder and harder, faster and faster. His slacks were scratchy. Without meaning to, I started to cry.

"Ah, Betty, cut the crap. You know you want it." Randall's jaw sounded clenched.

I looked for movement in the brambles near the barn, but I couldn't see anything except my breath as it fogged up the window.

Within seconds Randall shuddered, then emptied himself into me. He pulled out and sat back on his side of the bench seat. I uncurled my legs, stretched them out, and leaned to one side. I worried his cum might stain the upholstery. I looked over at the side of his face. Randall stared straight ahead while he zipped and buckled his pants. I grabbed my jeans and panties, and then lifted my butt once more to slide them up to my waist. I picked up my coat from where it had fallen on the floor, slipped my arms into the sleeves and drew it close to my chest.

Randall put the key into the ignition and started the car. Usually after our late-night trysts, I would scooch under his arm and rest my head on his shoulder. But on that night, I stayed on the passenger side. Randall didn't speak a word during the rest of the ride home.

When we arrived at my house, I was anxious to get out of the car. I hated the stickiness between my legs. I turned to face Randall. "So, what now?" I asked.

"Tomorrow my parents and I'll come over and we'll explain to your parents what's what." Randall didn't look at me.

"You mean about adoption." My throat closed around my words, and without breath they were almost inaudible.

"Yes, about adoption if you refuse to consider the other." Randall spit his words at me.

"OK, I'll see you tomorrow." I leaned in for a kiss, but instead of reaching for my lips, Randall pecked my cheek.

Usually we would goodbye for hours—kissing, nuzzling, and whispering endearments. But that night I got out of the car, and Randall backed out of the driveway, speeding away without a backward glance.

I stood on the porch for a few minutes trying to compose myself. I felt like I could cry for hours; pain was bottled up inside me like the Southfork Dam holding back Lake Conemaugh. My chest hurt. My head hurt. My eyes hurt.

My mom sat on the couch waiting up for me with some sewing. She was wearing her oldest housecoat, the one covered in blue forget-me-nots, as frayed on the edges as the furry pink mules she had slipped off. She stretched her legs out in front of her, resting bare feet on the coffee table. My dad had made it out of wood from a Monkey Pod tree when he was stationed in Hawaii right before I was born. The wicker sewing-basket we gave her for Christmas two years ago was below her legs, nestled on the shag carpet. She threaded a needle, and then looked up to examine my face with the same intensity. "You OK, Lani? You look like you've been crying. You two have a fight?"

"No, Ma. It's been a hard week. We passed the cemetery on our way to Norman, and I got to thinking about Sean." I took off my coat, walked the half dozen steps across the room and hung it in the closet on an empty metal hanger.

Our living room was tiny. In four steps, I crossed the width of the room and stood at her side. "I'm beat. I'm going to go to bed. Goodnight." I leaned over and kissed her cheek. She smelled like talcum powder, and for the first time I noticed a few gray hairs in her short-cropped auburn hair. "See you in the morning."

She refocused her attention on the needle and thread, and the skirt of the dress she was hemming. "Sleep tight. Don't let the…."

"…bedbugs bite." I finished her sentence and walked down the hall to my room, weary and beat. In her bottom bunk, Kathy's breathing was deep and regular. I climbed up into my bunk, crawled under the covers completely clothed. I stared at a wall poster of John Lennon, listened to the long, low whistle of a train in the distance, and willed myself to fall asleep.

Ugly Shoes

Sunday morning came early. I glanced out my bedroom window. The cloudless sky—savage, cerulean—offered no place to hide. The psalmist wrote, "thou art my hiding place; thou shalt compass me about with songs of deliverance." Could God really be a hiding place? Because that's all I wanted to do—hide from my parents, hide from the world. I especially wanted to hide from Randall.

After breakfast, Kathy and I laid out our clothes for church. She fiddled with the radio, but it was against house rules to listen to music or watch TV before church on Sunday. We were supposed to have our mind on the Lord. I heard the bathroom door open and started to head in there, but Kathy beat me to it. With four girls, it was a dog eat dog world when it came to the bathroom.

I turned the volume down. There was absolutely no reason for me to get in trouble for Kathy's crappy music. She listened to pop not rock—the Monkees, Partridge Family, The Jackson Five. She wouldn't have known Cream if they came and sat in her lap.

The station played oldies, too, and within minutes Johnny Mathis's velvet voice filled the room.

"Until the Twelfth of Never" was one of my favorite songs. I loved Johnny Mathis, but I only admitted it to a few people, since liking him was about as cool as the heavy stockings my grandmother wore for her varicose veins. Randall knew—Randall knew everything about me, and in early fall he had taken me to see Johnny Mathis at the Civic Center—our first truly grown-up date. I wore Kathy's maxi dress, a dark green polyester knit with a princess waist and halter-top. It was low cut in the back, and I couldn't wear a bra. Lucky for me, it didn't matter since I still had a teenager's perky tits. Randall kept running his hand up and down my spine all through the concert. Talk about goosebumps. The following week we saw The Moody Blues, and Randall dared me not to wear anything at all underneath my peasant skirt, but I didn't take him up on it. One of my mother's maxims was to always wear clean underwear in case we were ever in an accident, so I kept my panties on until after the concert.

I always believed that Randall would love me that long—until bluebells forgot to bloom, until poets ran out of rhymes. And just like in the song I wanted him to hold me and never let me go. But he seemed so angry with me.

Why couldn't he understand? I didn't get pregnant on purpose. I wasn't trying to trick him into marrying me. I truly believed that we loved each other. Getting married was what people in love do, especially when they were going to have a baby together.

Kathy came back wrapped in a bath towel, her long hair dripping wet.

"Don't you know how to dry off?" I asked her. "You're getting the floor all wet."

"What's your problem? You're not the boss of me." She threw the towel on the footboard of my bunk. "Are you crying? You've been acting weird lately."

"Leave me alone. It's been a rough week."

She shrugged and scrounged in her drawer for some clean underwear.

On the radio The Turtles sang "Happy Together." I turned it off with an open-handed bang.

As soon as church let out, everyone piled into the family station wagon to rush home for lunch. Mom put a pot roast in the oven when she got up that morning, so it would be ready to eat by the time we got back. Sometimes Pastor Bodine spit hellfire and raised damnation with an altar call that lasted an eternity, and the roast would burn to a crisp. But on this day, we were lucky. Super Bowl V was on in the afternoon, so Pastor Bodine's sermon didn't drag on endlessly. The men were itching to get home to watch football, and so at our house, the meat was juicy and tender from its long, slow cooking, and no one could ever tell it was a cheap cut.

Normally, I luxuriated in the smells of the kitchen, but when we entered the house, I took one whiff of the potatoes, onions, and carrots surrounding the meat and I was hit with a wave of nausea.

I was so tired. All I wanted to do as go to my room and lie down, but my mom had other plans. "Lani, start setting the table."

She rummaged in a drawer for an apron, found the orange one she usually wore in the fall for canning, and put it on to keep the grease off her Sunday dress. I looked down. The floor could use a good mopping.

Potatoes peeled and dropped into boiling water, my mom started on the gravy, stirring flour in the meat drippings. She was still wearing her dress pumps. "Let me do that," I said. "You go change your shoes." I heard the TV blaring in the other room. We were never allowed to eat in front of the television set, but for something like the Super Bowl my dad might make an exception. "Ma, just this once, let's eat buffet style. Whatcha think?"

Randall called later that afternoon. The dishes were done; the kitchen was empty. "My folks and I are ready to head over," he said.
"Are you kidding? The Super Bowl's on. My dad's still watching the game." I stopped short at the chorus of "No!!!" coming from the adjoining room.
"Then tomorrow after dinner? Would that work?" Randall sounded exasperated.
I cradled the handset against my left ear and twisted the phone cord in my right hand. After years of pulling by childish hands, it no longer resembled a corkscrew or a pig's tail. I took a deep breath.
"No, not tomorrow. It's my mother's birthday. She's gonna be forty. I can't tell her on her birthday. We'll have to wait until Tuesday."
Randall was silent for a moment, and then I heard a deep sigh. "OK, Tuesday it is. I guess I'll see you in school tomorrow."
I started crying. "Randall, I love you." I waited expectantly for the usual response, but he simply added, "Yeah, me too" before he hung up.
In the den I sat on the floor next to the couch and watched the end of the game. With only five seconds left in the fourth quarter the Colts kicked a 32-yard field goal. Final score–Baltimore Colts 16, Dallas Cowboys 13. My dad, a big Cowboy fan, was disgusted and we scattered to our separate rooms. It was a good thing he was a deacon, or a few choice four-letter words would have flown around.

Tuesday afternoon I called my mom from work. She was at Buchanan's in the meat department and several minutes passed before she came to the phone. "This is Mary Ann."
"Ma, I'm having dinner with Randall tonight. OK?"
"Sure, I guess so. I was just gonna pick up some footlongs from Dairy Queen. I don't feel much like cooking."
My mom sounded as weary as a coonhound out chasing rabbits. Hearing the tiredness in her voice, I felt sad. "Too much of a big party last night, huh?"
She seemed to perk up. "It was a nice party, Lani. Your grandma did herself proud. And you girls were a big help, too. I'm just tuckered out."

"So, pick up footlongs. It's the Tuesday night special, isn't it? Five for a dollar?"

"Well, you know your brother can eat five all by himself." She laughed.

I heard the front doorbell, and a customer entered the store.

"He could probably eat ten. Is Daddy home?"

From behind the pharmacy counter Mr. Stevens in his brown Mr. Rogers' sweater gave me the stink eye.

"No, he's got a Deacon meeting at church. The Ladies Auxiliary is gonna feed them." Mom sighed.

"But he'll be home later, right?" I knew I couldn't put off telling them for another day.

"Oh, sure, hon, he'll be home by six-thirty."

Mr. Stevens glared at me. I needed to get out on the floor.

"OK, so I'll see you later."

I paused and added almost offhandedly, "Love you, ma."

My mom sounded surprised. "Why, I love you, too, Lani. See you at home."

Randall picked me up after work and we drove back to his house. Usually, we headed to his bedroom to do some homework and make out. It had gotten so cold in the previous few months, we had even been having sex in Randall's bedroom. No one bothered us, and after some pretty heavy petting with most of our clothes on, we could get right down to business and get it done in less than three minutes. Arnold, Randall's kid brother, sometimes tried to sneak peeks, but it was easy to shoo away a sixth grader with the promise of a dollar. We turned the music up loud to cover any sounds we might make, although neither Randall nor I made much noise.

This time, however, we didn't head back to Randall's room. Mrs. Wallace greeted us at the door without a smile. I looked around for Mindy, Randall's sister, but she and Arnold were nowhere to be seen.

Randall's parents were older when they married—both in their forties. Now Mr. Wallace was more than sixty with hair the color of meringue on lemon pie. Mrs. Wallace was in her late fifties and she dyed her thinning hair the color of a Halloween jack-o-lantern.

Mr. Wallace was super-smart and worked as a scientist for the government, out at Tinker where my dad was stationed. But he was civilian, not military like my dad. Mrs. Wallace didn't have to work. With all that time on her hands, I thought she might have been involved in clubs and volunteer activities, but she spent most of her time reading, and the floor of the living room was covered with stacks and stacks of books. Randall's parents were considered eccentric, especially for a small town in Oklahoma, but I always thought they were part of what made Randall so wonderful.

A few generations earlier, the Wallace family emigrated from Wales. On a carved wooden stand in the living room they displayed a big family Bible that was written in Welsh. Randall said it was more than a hundred years old. I didn't know why they displayed a Bible in their living room. Randall and I never discussed it, but the tittle-tattle around town was that his father was an atheist. In Moore being an atheist was about the same as being a Communist, which was another rumor about Mr. Wallace.

Mrs. Wallace kept the family presentable by going to the Methodist church. Like Baptists, Methodists were Christian and upon death would be glory bound for heaven. But every good Baptist could testify that Methodists were still pretty suspect when it came to religion because they were sprinklers, not dunkers. They baptized infants and kept whiskey in flasks for fortitude. They also allowed dancing, which made me forever jealous of my fourth-grade friend, Pam, who strutted around in the sweetest pink tutu before, during, and after her ballet recital.

I sat on the edge of the couch in the Wallace living room like I had been invited over for a cup of English tea. Back straight, skirt pulled down over my knees, I could have been wearing white gloves with my pinkie stuck out, sipping from Wedgwood bone china. Randall sat to the right of me. I wanted him to reach out and touch my leg or put his arm around me, but he kept his arms at his side.

It was hot in the room, and I didn't know whether or not I should take off my coat. Mrs. Wallace didn't offer to take it. She sat on the chair across from me and glared at the painting behind my head. She didn't look at me, acknowledge me, or offer me a piece of pie. I wanted to scream or beat my fists on Randall's chest, but I smiled instead. Not my typical smile—broad, open-mouthed, showing all my teeth—this was a thin, tight smile that could easily have passed as a grimace.

I didn't see Mr. Wallace, but I heard him in the kitchen. I hadn't eaten, and I had hoped they might feed me, but it looked like they were done with dinner. Mr. Wallace was finishing up with the dishes like he did every night.

In my family, my dad did absolutely no housework. He came home from work and he expected to be fed. Then he sat in front of the TV, and one of us girls had the odious task of rubbing his feet. His toenails were yellow and ragged, and the bottoms of his feet were hard and calloused. Still, every night he got a foot rub. My mom worked a full day, too, but when she came home from work, she cooked our meals, sewed our clothes, did our laundry. At least five times a week she ironed my dad's uniform. Unlike Mrs. Wallace, my mom was involved in all sorts of clubs—the PTA, the Moore Historical Society, Ladies Auxiliary. She was even in charge of the nursery at church—infants through kindergarten—probably more than thirty kids to care for every Sunday. And nobody rubbed her feet ever.

Mrs. Wallace definitely wore the pants in Randall's family, and she was the one who did the talking. I never heard Randall's dad speak more than a word or two. Now she barked, "Mr. W., your presence is required."

Mr. Wallace ambled into the living room drying his hands on a dishtowel. He hadn't had a chance to sit down before Mrs. Wallace declared, "Lani, I take it Randall has shared our position."

I stared at her shoes. They were the ugliest shoes I had ever seen in my life. They looked like a boy's Hush Puppies; footwear fit for a nun.

"Yes, ma'am."

I decided she must have some kind of foot problem. No one in their right mind would wear shoes that ugly without a reason.

"So, there's really nothing to talk about, now is there?"

I kept my eyes glued to her shoes wondering if my baby might inherit her feet.

"No, ma'am." The baby would most certainly inherit my feet.

Mrs. Wallace stood up. The conversation was over before it began. "Then let's get over to your house and explain it to your parents."

I was hungry. Lunch had been seven hours ago, and I puked most of it up. I had hoped Randall and I could drive over to my house in his Impala and stop for a burger on the way. As we left the house, however, Mrs. Wallace gave me a hostile stare, and steered us over to the family station wagon. On the ride across town, Randall and I were careful not to sit too close together.

Since it was after seven, I knew my dad would be home from his deacons' meeting. But I had totally forgotten that Tuesday was family Bible study night. At church they stressed "the family that prays together, stays together," and "train up a child in the way he should go," so my father decided we would read scripture together at least once a week. I got a pass because I was usually working, and if she had band practice, Kathy got out of it, too. Unfortunately, the three youngest in the family were stuck.

At least family Bible study was better than "spare the rod, spoil the child," a proverb my dad adhered to for most of my young life even though that saying isn't in the Bible, not in those words exactly. Dad threw it out whenever he pulled off his belt or grabbed a wooden spoon from the kitchen or cut a switch from any tree that was handy. By the time I was 13 I was too big to paddle, and my Dad pretty much stopped spanking all of us. Except Kathy. She got whupped for sucking her teeth or rolling her eyes. She always seemed to know how to get on my dad's dark side.

As soon as I opened the door my parents could sense that something was wrong. Randall and his parents were at my back, so that was one huge clue. Even though Randall and I were nearing our one-year anniversary of going steady, this was the first time my parents actually met Mr. and Mrs. Wallace.

My dad was parked on the piano bench with Mom on the divan to his right. My younger brother and sisters sat in a semi-circle on the floor at their feet. Kathy was absent, so she must have gone to a friend's house after band practice. As soon as we walked through the door, my dad closed his Bible and set his eyes hard against me.

"Go get ready for bed now," he yelled at my three youngest siblings.

Carla immediately started whining. "It's not even eight. I want to watch the end of 'Mod Squad'."

Dad turned on her. His voice wasn't raised, but if the inside of a freezer had a sound, this would have been it. "Keep it up and you're gonna get a switchin'. Like I told you, get ready for bed, and stay in your room."

It was the voice that made us sit up straight, and respond with an immediate, "Yes, sir."

Carla, Janet and Billy scrambled to their feet and dispersed in various directions. Carla and Janet shared the room at the end of the hall across from my parents' bedroom. Billy had a small area that had been partitioned out of the den, created from one-half of our garage.

My mom's hands were shaking along with her voice. "Go on ahead, Billy, I'll be there in a minute to tuck you in."

With the kids out of the way, my mom motioned for Mr. and Mrs. Wallace to sit in the two side chairs, across from where she was sitting. "Can I take your coats? Would you like some coffee?"

Mrs. Wallace shook her head. "We're not staying long."

I could feel my mom's eyes on me. I wanted to look at her, but I knew if I did, I would burst into tears, so I struggled to avoid eye contact.

Randall and I had no place to sit. We could either scrunch up next to my mom on the couch or get down on the floor like my sisters and brother, so instead we stood next to the front window in the spot reserved for our Christmas tree.

Everyone was looking down at the brown, green and orange shag carpet. I never realized how ugly it was until that moment. Strange the things I took for granted and never seemed to notice—ugly shag carpet, ugly brown shoes, nice feet.

My dad was the first to speak and he didn't mince his words. "So, what's all this about? Is Lani in some kind of trouble?"

Like me, Mrs. Wallace was staring intently at the living room carpet. She looked up briefly and addressed my dad. "Mr. Lassiter, we're all in a bit of trouble here, I should say."

I broke down crying, "Mama, I'm sorry, I'm so sorry. I'm going to have a baby."

My mom covered her face with her hands. Sobs quickly racked her body. My dad had a quick sharp intake of breath, and his words come out labored as if there was not enough air to carry them forward and across the room.

"So, what do you plan to do about this, young man?"

Randall remained silent.

Mrs. Wallace continued. "Randall, along with his father and I, will help with any financial concerns you might have. We've talked it over and Lani is going to give this baby up for adoption. Given their ages, it's best for all concerned."

My mom lifted her head up and looked at me, "Lani, is this true? Is this what you want?"

Of course it wasn't what I wanted. Up until that moment I thought of nothing but getting married to Randall and having our baby. I had planned the wedding, making a home in his parent's garage, finishing school, putting off college, whatever it took to make a life together. But Randall wanted none of that, and I couldn't imagine a world without Randall.

I nodded. "Ma, Randall's got lots of plans for his life. We're really young. A baby would mess that all up."

Like many of the women of my mother and grandmother's generations, my mom always kept a freshly laundered and perfumed handkerchief in her shirtsleeve. She pulled it out and blew her nose. "But surely…"

I don't know why, but I felt protective of Randall. I reached out and grabbed his hand. "Randall says he loves me, and we'll get married someday, but right now we're too young to take care of a baby."

I was being rent right down the middle. I wanted to believe Randall, and defend this decision, but I hated myself with every word. Did I have a choice? Should I drop out of school and stay home and hope that Randall changed his mind? Did I believe that once the baby came, he would marry me, and we could live happily ever after?

Instead I followed my script. "He's got too much to think about, he's got college, and maybe I'll go to college, too. How can we do that with a baby?"

Mrs. Wallace took charge of the conversation again. "There are places designed to take care of girls in need. When and where is up to you, and Randall will pay his fair share, be sure of that."

She got up out of her chair. Mr. Wallace got up, too. Randall opened the door for his parents, and a sharp blast of January wind burst into the room. "We'll be in touch," Mrs. Wallace said as they left the house. Randall's face looked carved in stone.

"Lani, go to your room." My dad sounded like he could put a hole in a wall just by looking at it. "We'll talk about this tomorrow."

My mom stayed on the couch crying. Her whole body shook like she had a bad case of the flu with fever and chills. Her family didn't have the best of genes, in fact her father died on her eighteenth birthday, when she was just a year older than I was. Poof. Dropped dead of a heart attack, just like that. Nobody ever saw it coming. Even though my mom and I had typical mother-daughter arguments, I dearly loved my mother, and I prayed that my news wasn't killing her.

In my bedroom, I undressed in the dark and climbed up into bed. I never got any dinner, and I was still hungry.

Kathy came home around nine. She flipped on the light switch. The glare hit me in the face, and I blinked swollen eyes.

"What's going on? Where's mom and dad?" Kathy threw her jacket on the floor. "It's early. When'd you start going to bed with the chickens?"

"Kathy, God gave you two ears and one mouth for a reason, so just shut up."

Kathy shrugged. "You shut up. What'd I do?"

She was right. She wasn't my enemy. All I had to do was look in the mirror to see my own worst enemy. There was no reason to take this out on her. And I needed a confidant, a friend; I needed my sister.

"Listen, if you go fix me a sandwich, I'll tell you all about it."

The Johnstown Flood

My mom called and made an appointment with Pastor Bodine for late Thursday afternoon. I overheard her whispering on the phone with Mrs. Alden, the church secretary. "Just a little bit of Pastor's time, we've got a family emergency."

I asked my boss, Mr. Stevens, for the afternoon off; Mom and Dad took off work early. When they picked me up from school, my dad looked as happy as a wet hen.

Pastor Bodine's office was in the administrative wing of the church underneath the Youth and Adult Sunday School classrooms. To get to his office you had to check-in with the gatekeeper, Mrs. Alden. Her job was keeping all the church gears greased. She also was a total busy body, and I knew as soon as my parents and I headed down the hall to Pastor's office, she would be on the phone to Mrs. Grayson, First Baptist's biggest gossip.

I wondered if my getting pregnant would affect my dad's position as a church deacon. Would they think he was unfit to serve because of me? Would it be a case of the sins of the children being visited on the father? I knew it would never be "if you are without sin, cast the first stone."

We passed offices for the rest of the paid staff. Youth Minister, Christian Education Minister, Music Minister, and several Associate Ministers.

We were short an Associate Minister since Pastor Allen was fired the previous summer. Someone saw guys drinking beer on his front lawn. A construction crew had been putting on a new roof, and then throwing back a few cold ones at the end of a long workday. A well-meaning Baptist busybody tattled to the church elders, and the next thing we knew, Pastor Allen was history.

Mrs. Young, the Christian Education Minister was responsible for all Sunday School classes, Training Union, Girls' and Boys' Auxiliary, and Vacation Bible School. But she wasn't allowed to preach. In the Baptist churches I attended, women weren't allowed to preach, and they couldn't vote in all-church meetings. In fact, women weren't even allowed to speak up in a church meeting. If a woman wanted to make a point or bring something up, she had to first tell the pastor or her husband. If, and only if, he felt it was worthy of discussion, he could bring it to the attention of the congregation. If a woman didn't have a husband, then she probably didn't have anything worth saying. This system seemed to work out all right for men.

But it was the faith and hard work of women that got anything done. They taught Sunday school, cooked and served the meal before Wednesday night Bible Study, filled the choir, raised money for missions with the Rummage Sale, and took food to shut-ins. As the nursery school coordinator, my mom spent an untold number of hours every week planning lessons, training teachers, even cleaning out the diaper pails. Basically, women were the legs, hands and heart of the church. Men? Mouth, teeth, tongue, and fists. They yelled at the world and all of us in it through a bullhorn.

Pastor Bodine seemed younger than my dad, but then, no matter the age, my dad always looked older than his years because he was bald. His hair started falling out before he turned twenty-one, so he had been bald my entire life. Pastor Bodine had a thick head of coal black hair, with eyebrows stretching halfway to the crown of his head.

My mom said I should trust him. "He's here to help you, Lani. Pastor's the shepherd and we're his flock." But I wondered whose side he was on. Was he with God the judge or Jesus the lover?

When we got to his office, Pastor Bodine shook Daddy's hand, patted Mom on the shoulder and handed her a box of Kleenex. If you were coming to see Pastor, you had a reason to cry about something. They probably had a secret closet filled with nothing but boxes of Kleenex.

Pastor Bodine motioned for my parents to sit in the two leather-upholstered chairs facing the desk. I stood, waiting. There was no place for me to sit, and Pastor motioned to the open doorway. "Lani, why don't you go get a chair from the meeting room?"

Some subterfuge. It was obvious he had set it up this way so they could talk about me. I left them alone and went down the hall for a chair. When I returned, we sat in a small semi-circle facing the Pastor's desk. The shiny black surface was neat—nothing on it but a few framed photographs and a Bible. Behind his chair, shelves stretched floor to ceiling, filled with thick, heavy books and more family photographs. *Strong's Concordance*, a book about Jeremiah, Matthew Henry's *Complete Bible Commentary*. Photographs of his twins Sheri and Teri, also juniors at my high school, were cradled in gold frames much like the school pictures that sat on top of the piano in our living room.

Pastor Bodine cleared his throat. "Let us pray."

My mother reached for another tissue. My dad didn't look like he had moved a muscle. We bowed our heads, closed our eyes, and I took a deep breath.

"Heavenly Father, we know that the devil surrounds us, leading us into temptation. But you are stronger, O Lord, and you can bring us back to the path of righteousness."

I peeked out through half-lidded eyes. *The devil didn't have nothin' to do with this.*

Pastor continued in a deep and resonant voice. "Good can come from evil, Father. Give us wisdom to know thy will, and the strength to do it."

We lifted our heads. Pastor Bodine fixed his gaze on me. His eyes were kind. "Lani, your parents shared your predicament. I'm sorry we have to meet under these circumstances. But I'm here to help you make the best decision for everyone concerned."

I tuned him out. Voices circled the room around me. I heard sketches of "all things work together for good of them that love God, to them who are the called according to his purpose." I felt numb inside. A heavy weight descended on my shoulders, and I wanted to crawl into a hole and never come out.

Pastor Bodine rifled through some folders in his lower right-hand desk drawer, and then handed my parents a pamphlet. It was from Sellers Baptist Home and Adoption Center in New Orleans, Louisiana. The picture on the front was a drawing of a woman's face, half in shadow. Her eyes were downcast, and she held her face in her hand.

My parents poured over the pamphlet's short list of questions and answers. *What is Sellers? When was it established? What is its purpose?*

I knew all about Sellers. The previous summer, on a Girls' Auxiliary trip to Knoxville for the National Convention, we made a stop in New Orleans for the sole purpose of visiting the home even though it was out of the way. The Youth leaders wanted to remind us that sex was a sin. *Look what can happen if you're not good. You'll pay mightily if you engage in IT.*

I remembered the Home as a big red brick building in the Garden District. White columns in front. Lots of flowering bushes with a smell wet and sweet. We were told that whenever visitors came to the Home the girls stayed in their rooms. We didn't see anyone except a secretary and the social worker giving us the tour. She told us they hid the girls to protect their identities. She tried to make their lives seem full and interesting.

Sellers was more than just a home for unwed mothers—after the babies were born, they stayed in a large upstairs nursery until they were placed for adoption. We weren't allowed to see the babies or the nursery. Instead, we went upstairs and peered into two bedrooms. I felt weird looking at the girls' meager possessions on display—a cross between junk set out to be pawed over in a garage sale and priceless artifacts behind glass in a museum. Who were these invisible girls—one with a threadbare white bear on a bed, another with a ceramic ballerina on the nightstand? Who owned the scuffed house slippers peeking out from under the bed covered by a blue chenille bedspread?

As we headed back to the bus, I stopped in the middle of the sidewalk and turned back to glance up at the second story where the bedrooms were located. I saw a girl, who couldn't have been much older than me, peeking through drawn curtains.

I drifted out of my musings at the sound of my mom's voice. "It looks nice, John. The Home Mission Board runs it." Her spirits seemed to pick up. "They have a housemother, three nurses, social workers." My dad barely grunted out a response.

Pastor Bodine piped up. "I can make the necessary arrangements. Of course, there's a substantial charge for the excellent care, but the boy's family should shoulder most of the burden. She can probably go right away, if there's an opening."

He turned to face me. "Lani, I know this must be difficult for you. It must be a frightening time. We'll do everything in our power to help you with this transition. And you will always be in our prayers."

I remained silent. Go right away? I wasn't even showing. It would be months before I got to that stage. My baby and I were being shoved under the carpet. Everyone wanted me gone. Not one person asked me how I felt or what I wanted.

My mom nodded. "Thank you, Pastor, for helping us. As you can imagine, this is something we never dreamed could happen. Lani's always been so…" She started to tear up again. "Any way, we're grateful for your strength in our hour of need." She slipped the Sellers brochure in her purse.

We stood up to leave. Pastor Bodine came around from behind his desk to accompany us out the door. "I'll talk to the Wallaces about the financial arrangements," he told my parents. "I can appreciate that you might not want to deal with them." Then as an afterthought, he turned to me. "Lani, you may not feel this way now, but you're making the best out of a bad situation."

I sighed and looked down. My mind fled to thoughts of an apocalypse. Over Christmas break in ninth grade, I read a Reader's Digest Condensed version of *The Johnstown Flood*. Days and days of heavy rain in Pennsylvania, warnings sent by men trying to save the dam, ignored communications. In the end, the dam burst and Johnstown was hit by a hill of water sixty feet high rushing forty miles an hour. No one could fight that force of nature. More than two thousand people drowned. Right then in that moment, I was drowning in my own great flood. I couldn't fight against nature or the hand of God or my mom and dad or Randall or his parents or Pastor Bodine. I was sixteen, and if Randall wouldn't marry me, what choice did I have but to tread the path that lay out before me? Desiree hit the road for a concert in Atlanta, but I didn't have that option—not in January, and not pregnant.

A new thought pricked my mother's conscience and she started to sob. "But what do we tell...." Pastor Bodine patted her shoulder, hushing a crying child. "There's time for all that later."

Pastor Bodine shook my father's hand, and my parents shuffled down the hallway. I started to follow them when Pastor Bodine grabbed me by the shoulders. This was not the gentle shushing of a child. His grip grew tighter, ever tighter, while he whispered in my ear.

"Remember, when you lie with dogs, you wake up with fleas."

It was a little before five when we got home. Kathy wasn't there. The three youngest were watching television in the room we called a den. I didn't know what to do with myself. I was being sent away, soon by all accounts, and nothing seemed to matter anymore.

I didn't bother to take off my coat. "I'm going to Dayna's house," I yelled to my mother who had just walked into the kitchen. "I've got to borrow the car."

"Now?" she yelled back. She returned to the living room drying her hands on a stained dishtowel. "It's time to start fixin' dinner. I could use your help."

I shook my head. "Ma, she's my best friend. I gotta tell her sometime." I realized I had been holding my breath, and I released a sigh. "She must know something's wrong. We've barely spoken this week. And I want her to hear it from me and not from some nasty gossip Mrs. Alden will spread around."

"Lani, what a thing to say. You know she wouldn't do anything of the sort. But I guess I can't stop you." Now it was my mother's turn to sigh. "But please be back by six. I don't need any more aggravation today."

I nodded and headed out the door.

It took less than ten minutes to get to Dayna's house. She lived on the north side of Moore in a newer housing division with homes twice the size of ours. No one answered the doorbell. I figured Dayna was still at band practice like my sister, and her mom was not yet home from working at the First National Bank of Oklahoma City. Dayna's little sister was most likely at a neighbor's house. It was too cold to wait on the porch, so I went back to the car. Even though night had fallen, and the sky was dark, I had parked a ways down the street in a lame attempt to remain incognito. When Lori's car pulled up in front of Dayna's house, I ducked down behind the steering wheel so they couldn't see me or my shadow in the streetlight. Lori was a friend, just not a great friend, and I didn't feel like chitchat. I heard the sound of an engine idling, a car door opening, laughter, then Dayna's clear and unmistakable voice.

"He's gonna get the nickname 'Bean' with that kind of toot."

More laughter. "See you tomorrow, Lori. Thanks for the ride."

A car door slammed shut. I heard it shift into gear. Then footsteps on a concrete path, and a screen door creaked.

I waited to sit up until Lori's car sped past me. Dayna stood at her front door, fumbling in her purse for the house keys. I slipped out of the car, crossed the street and reached the sidewalk before Dayna even saw me. "Boo!" I yelled. Startled, Dayna dropped her purse, and turned towards me. "Heavens to Betsy, Lani. You almost gave me a heart attack. What do you mean sneakin' up on me like that?"

We both leaned over to pick up the scattered pens, tubes of Chapstick, and pennies, bumping our heads in the process. Her fuzzy blue knit cap pushed back to expose a soft pink ear. "Hey, watch it," Dayna said.

"Sorry. I don't know what I'm doing these days." Pain long held in check careened through my body—up my legs, up my arms, down my head until it all pooled in the center of my chest. My ribs cracked open and a torrent of pain flowed along with my tears until, like Alice in Wonderland, I was sure I was standing in four feet of water.

"Lani, whatever is wrong with you? Get inside before someone sees you."

Dayna ushered me into a living room that was dark and stifling. The heat had been turned up all day even though no one was home. Dayna dropped her purse, book bag and flute case on the floor and reached for a box of tissues. "Here, blow your nose. I can't talk to you with all that snot on your lip." For a moment I felt free of the pain trap and laughed.

Dayna took off her coat and held out a gloved hand for mine. "That's more like it. Come on, let's go back to my room so we can talk." I handed her my coat and leaned over to grab her book bag. My car keys dropped from my hand into the blue shag carpet.

"Where's your purse?" Dayna asked as she leaned over to pick up her flute case. Again, we almost bumped heads like we were stuck in some stupid Three Stooges movie. Her breath was sweet and smelled like oranges and peppermint. I wanted to hug her, kiss her, and have her tell me that everything was going to be okay. "My purse? I left it in the car," I blubbered in a five-year old's whine. I laughed again, then cried again at the gravity of life, the ridiculousness of my predicament.

"What am I ever gonna do with you?"

I followed Dayna down the hallway to her bedroom. We dumped everything on the floor—coats, bags, scarves, gloves—kicked off our shoes and climbed onto the bed.

Dayna's room had the same blue shag carpet as the living room, and all of her furniture was white. Dresser and vanity table with a large oval mirror, a bed designed for a princess. Four tall bedposts that almost touched the ceiling held up a white canopy. Dayna was the only person I knew who had a canopy bed. She had fancy pillows that weren't even used for sleeping and they matched the bedspread with its hot pink paisley pattern with subtle hints of lime green. Dayna was so stylish; her room looked like it had just stepped of the pages of a decorating magazine like *Good Housekeeping*.

Now she fluffed a fancy pillow and leaned back into it with her arms open. Finally, a welcoming embrace from my friend, my dearest friend.

I lay back against the pillow, too, and pressed my face against her chest. My silent tears flowed like a deep, slow river.

"So, what's going on, Lani?" Dayna turned on her side to face me. "You've been acting mighty strange lately. In fact, you haven't seemed yourself for more than a week now. What's this all about? Is it Randall? Did y'all break up?"

My tears fell harder. They rushed down my face, no longer the slow South Canadian, but the fast, raging Colorado. My breathing became shallow and my voice caught in my throat like a boulder in the river.

"No, we didn't break up, but I'm......I'm......"

Dayna's body stiffened. She moved her arm from around my neck and sat straight up. "You're what? You're pregnant?" She almost growled. "You've been having sex with him? With Randall? How long has this been going on? You are so deceitful. Why didn't you tell me?"

I sat up, too, and hung my legs off the side of the bed. "I couldn't tell you. I didn't think you would understand." With her reaction, couldn't she at least understand my reluctance to confess this to her then or now?

Dayna came around and sat in the window seat across from me. "You didn't tell me because you knew I would tell you the truth. You knew I would tell you that this is so wrong. It's wrong and you know it. And now look what's happened. I can't believe you've been lying to me this whole time."

"No, I wasn't lying." I shook my head. "No lying. I just didn't tell you about it."

"You are lower than a snake. You know that, right, Lani? Best friends are supposed to share everything, but when it came to this, you...you...."

My voice was pleading, "Dayna, I'm sorry, I'm so sorry. You're right. I should have talked to you. I never dreamed in a million years that this would happen, that I would get pregnant."

Dayna scoffed. "What? Are you crazy or just duller than dishwater? Girls get pregnant all the time. What do you think happened to Cynthia Logan, huh? So, what are you going to do? Get married?"

"I wish." I started crying harder although I didn't think it even possible. "No, we're not getting married. Everyone says we're too young. Randall's parents, Pastor Bodine. My parents would be okay with us getting married, but his folks won't stand for it. Can you believe it? They even wanted me to get an abortion!"

The briefest smile flickered on Dayna's face. "So, you're not getting married." She stood up and faced the window. "That's a relief. I mean, you're too young to get married, and you and Randall aren't meant for each other anyway."

The dam held and my crying stopped. How could Dayna say such a thing? "No, it's not like that at all. Randall and I still love each other. In fact, we're madly in love and we're going to get married just as soon as we graduate high school. He promised as much. We're going to get married. He just isn't ready for a baby right now."

Dayna bit her lip as she turned to face me. "So, are you gonna go live with your relatives in California?"

"No, I don't think they'll even tell them. This is supposed to stay a secret."

"So, what will you do? You can't hide in your house for nine months."

"They're sending me to Sellers. I'm supposed to give the baby up for adoption once it's born."

"Sellers? That place in New Orleans we visited last summer?"

"Yeah, pretty unbelievable, huh?" The dam was breached again, and sobs racked my body.

Disdain dripped from Dayna's pursed lips. "I still can't believe this is happening. You always have to make everything about you. But now I guess you're just gonna hafta pay the piper."

"Dayna, I need you on my side right now. You're my best friend. I know I screwed up. Randall and I both screwed up, but I don't need a bunch of stupid platitudes." I looked for my coat and keys. "I gotta go help my mom with dinner," I said as I headed toward the door. "You don't need to show me out. I just need you to promise me that you won't say a word of this to anyone."

Dayna's honeyed voice was familiar—comforting and familiar. "Sure, Lani, whatever you say."

Unhappy Birthday

My birthday came while the paddle wheels of a no-good gambler's boat seemed to push me down the Mississippi to New Orleans. I was finally seventeen, and certainly old enough to get married, but the reality of my situation smacked me upside the head when a packet of information arrived from Sellers, my soon-to-be home away from home.

I had no reason to celebrate since we were making plans for me to leave, but I hung onto the belief that Randall and I were soul mates. After school he gave me a bottle of Tigress. He wrote a new poem he titled "Wake Forest" and stuck it inside the box. *Was he having second thoughts?* The words were sweet and sad, something about sitting on the banks of a fast-moving river, holding my tiny soft hand, gazing into pools held captive in my eyes.

I desperately needed Randall to love me, and I held tight to the hope that he might change his mind, and together we could change his parents' minds. Come fall we would be one incredibly happy married couple with a newborn baby.

Randall had to work, and my dad stayed away, too, but my mom tried to make my birthday supper feel special. She made my favorite cake—red velvet with cream cheese icing—and she invited my grandmother to dinner. At that point we hadn't officially told my littlest sisters and brother about the baby, so it would have seemed strange not to celebrate my birthday a little.

Billy couldn't care less about my birthday, which was the same day the Apollo 14 lunar module landed on the moon. He ran around the house with a cardboard box on his head. Every eight-year-old boy wanted to be an astronaut in those days.

I didn't get to buy anything from Wards, our go-to place for new clothes and our usual big birthday treat. Instead, my mom made my birthday outfit—a pink polyester pantsuit. The top had a white Peter Pan collar and large white buttons down the front. Pink has always been my least favorite color, and in that pantsuit, I looked like cotton candy at the State Fair. My mom didn't use a maternity pattern—she bought the material before she found out I was pregnant. She and I both knew that it wouldn't stretch along with my belly, but my mom sewed elastic into the waistband, and she hoped that it would hold out for another month or two. If I were lucky it would last until school let out—if (an even bigger if) girls in New Orleans were allowed to wear pants to school.

After dinner, I opened birthday cards from relatives. Memaw sent two dollars. She didn't know about the baby either. My parents had decided to wait and tell the California relatives until after I was safely ensconced at Sellers. Though I'm not sure they ever told anyone the entire truth. As my Memaw used to say, "You're as happy as a dead pig in the sunshine," which was her way of saying ignorance is bliss.

February 5, 1971

Dear Memaw,

Thank you so much for the birthday card and money. I'm going to use it buy the latest album by Simon and Garfunkel, Bridge Over Troubled Water. Do you know their music? You've probably heard the song "Mrs. Robinson," because they play it all the time on the radio. It's the one with the line about Joe DiMaggio. I love everything they've ever done. You might like it, too, if you get a chance to listen to it. It's mostly folksy with pretty melodies.

Everyone here is doing just fine. We had a cold January, but the weather turned unseasonably warm last week.

Give everyone a big hug from me, and thanks again for the birthday money.

Love always,
Lani

When the dishes were done, and the girls and Billy had gone to bed, my mom sat in her usual spot at the end of the living room couch wearing a pink and blue flowered housedress. Mending, my mom was always mending.

"So, what was in that package from Sellers?" I asked.

"There wasn't much in it." My mom looked cross-eyed at the needle in her hand. "A list of clothes to pack, a bill for the first month. And that director, Mrs. LaPrairie, sent along a letter."

"And?" I raised my eyebrows above my wireframe glasses.

"And she sounds nice." My mom sighed and reached up to scratch the side of her face where the skin was red and blotchy and flaked around scraggly eyebrows. "I don't know what you want me to say, Lani." Her voice started to waver. "She says you'll be well taken care of; she says you're doing the right thing."

She shrugged. In her mind the conversation was over, but I struggled to keep us talking.

"Do I really have to leave so early?"

"What do you mean, hon?"

"Well, I'm not showing, I probably won't be showing that much by the time school lets out. And we've got all these baggy styles now, you know, baby doll tops and empire waists. Half the girls at school look pregnant."

"Lani, what a thing to say."

"But it's true, Ma. I'll just look like I'm getting fat. And I want to finish the year out. I want to try out for Select Chorus, which isn't until May. Next year's editor for the paper won't get picked until April. And what if I can't go to school there? I won't be able to graduate with my class."

"Pastor assures us you can go to school. They've asked for your transcript. The folks at Sellers are very supportive of a girl's education. It says so right in their brochure. As for those other things, I'm sorry. It can't be helped. Besides there's an opening now and this way you can start seeing a doctor right away."

"But I don't want to go now. I want to stay here and finish school."

"You better mind your Ps and Qs, young lady."

My mom looked up from her mending with a face like a James Cagney gangster. Her voice was softer though, and trembled.

"We've already made all the arrangements. Get to bed."

Great. I was leaving home early because everyone believed it was best for me and the baby. I wished everyone would quit telling me I was doing the right thing, because right thing or wrong thing, it didn't seem to matter. As far as they were concerned, leaving for Sellers and leaving now was the only option available.

Some birthday. My mother said they got a bill. Even though Sellers was part of the Home Mission budget, it cost a bundle to stay there—about

$300 a month. Randall and his parents were paying for half, but coming up with $150 a month was a hardship on my folks. As my Memaw always said, we were never ones to walk in high cotton—we weren't rich and there was no chance of it happening, either. Even though having enough money to make ends meet was always a struggle, my mother never let us suffer. This was yet another year where she wouldn't get herself a new Easter dress.

Alone in the bedroom I shared with Kathy, I folded my new pantsuit and placed it in the bottom dresser drawer. I substituted my jeans for a pair of flannel pajama bottoms and left on my bra and "The Man from U.N.C.L.E." t-shirt. I hated sleeping in a bra, but my mother told me I needed to wear one all the time now. "Don't go without a bra for even one minute," she said, "or you'll be sorry."

Dayna ignored my invite to birthday supper, and she didn't call me either. Usually we talked on the phone for hours every night, but ever since I told her about the baby, she had been standoffish. I passed it off as just the shock of everything. I wanted to believe that we were going to stay best friends forever. That was what we had promised each other. Forever.

A week passed and my mother told my youngest sisters the truth about my condition. Sister number two, Carla, eventually stopped speaking to me. Carla was in eighth grade, and unlike the rest of us, she was popular and hung out with the in-crowd of cheerleaders and jocks. When Carla heard the news, she cried, "How could you?" I was selfish, she said, and I'd ruined her life. Her silence was a vast improvement. On the other hand, my sisters Kathy and Janet were sweet and promised to write. My brother Billy didn't know the real reason I was leaving. My folks thought he was too young to understand. He was eight at the time, so they told him the same story they told everyone else. It was the story I told my boss, Mr. Stevens, when I turned in my two-week notice. I was going to New Orleans (true) to help some missionaries (true) with their children (sort of true). Ever the good Christians, my parents didn't want to outright lie, so they had to make up something that was as close to the truth as it could be.

It did make some sense that I might be helping missionaries. My dad met so many when he was stationed overseas. In Vietnam, Ethiopia, or Brazil, he always went to the local Southern Baptist church. And when the missionaries came back to the states on sabbatical, if they made their way to Oklahoma, they stayed at our house and gave a slide show at church. Lots of photos of open-air primary schools and baptisms in a river. My dad took pictures when he was away, too. When he came back from Vietnam, he gave a slide show to my sixth-grade class. He couldn't show the photos from Ethiopia, though, because there were too many bare-chested women.

One evening not long after, my sisters and Billy were watching television and I was on the living room divan reading *One Flew Over the Cuckoo's Nest*. As my Memaw would say, "Little pitchers have big ears," and I overheard my parents in the kitchen arguing about the trip.

"Mary Ann, I can drive there in one day. If we leave at two in the morning, we can be there by four in the afternoon." My dad's voice sounded tight. "It'll save us the cost of a motel and a meal."

I could see my mother from where I was sitting. She wiped up spilled gravy from the oilcloth covering the dining table and glanced in my direction.

"But, John, that's sixteen hours without any stops. You can't put Lani through that."

There was a long pause. My dad's back was to me; he was still wearing his Air Force khakis. He got up to pour another cup of coffee. Whenever we traveled, even if we were crossing the country from Oklahoma to California and back, as long as my dad had a thermos of hot, black coffee, he could keep the pedal to the metal and drive. Every vacation we went for hours and hours without stopping. My dad's bladder must have been made of steel. In the back seat, Billy peed into a jar, but my sisters and I learned how to hold it, no matter how painful it became.

"Mary Ann, you know that dog won't hunt." His voice was tired; I heard weariness in each syllable. "Lani's got precious little to say about any of this. She brought this on herself."

I felt ashamed, mortified, and mad enough to bite nails. I wasn't the only person involved here. It wasn't all my fault. I didn't want to go to Sellers. And I certainly didn't want to go before school let out in May.

In the letter received from Mrs. La Prairie, Sellers' director, she said that I needed to arrive on a weekday when the regular staff was in the office, so my folks finally decided that my father and I would leave early Sunday morning before my sisters and brother got up and ready for church. We would drive as far as Alexandria and stay the night in a motel. By leaving at a decent time the following morning, we could get to New Orleans and Sellers by Monday afternoon.

At times it seemed that I needed to pee every hour on the hour, but I decided not to worry about bathroom breaks. Unless my dad wanted smelly, wet upholstery, he better plan on some stops.

A Steak Made for Two

Valentine's Day fell on a Sunday. Randall and I had an actual date—the first one since telling my parents about the baby. We booked a table at Steak and Ale, the nicest restaurant on the south side of Oklahoma City. It was our special place. We went there in October on our first driving date when Randall turned sixteen and got his license and the use of his dad's yellow '67 Impala. We went there to celebrate the New Year.

Randall wore a suit and tie; the same one he wore to Sean's funeral. I wore Kathy's green maxi-dress, the same one I had worn the previous year to the Johnny Mathis concert. My breasts had gotten bigger. I looked down at Randall's drop trapped in my cleavage. I wondered if Randall noticed the difference.

My mother insisted on scraps of enforced modesty, so she gave me my great-grandmother's red shawl to wear in the restaurant. Green dress. Red shawl. I only needed to add a few twinkling lights and I would have sparkled like a Christmas tree.

The hostess seated us at a small table by the front window. We took a moment to read through the menu but ended up ordering the same thing we'd had on the last two visits. For starters, cheesy garlic bread and French onion soup along with some stilted conversation.

"Apollo 14 made it back to earth safely."

"I know. Glad it wasn't a 'successful failure' like 13."

"The earthquake near LA killed more than fifty people."

"Yeah, I heard they had to evacuate 40,000. They think the earth is splitting open—could be as big as the Grand Canyon."

We ordered Chateaubriand; a steak made for two. I was sure it was another positive sign of our togetherness, but only small talk continued.

"I hear they're predicting snow for later this week."

"You're kidding. It was almost 60 degrees today."

"I finished reading a new collection of H.P. Lovecraft stories."

"I've never read any of his stuff. Seems more like a guy thing. Are they horror or science fiction or both?"

Over a shared plate of New York cheesecake, we exchanged gifts. The previous week in an antique store in Norman I found a hardback copy of *Leaves of Grass*. Whitman was one of Randall's favorite poets, and when we played hooky on the South Oval, Randall read aloud parts of "Song of Myself." The book cost me almost a whole week's wages, fifteen dollars, but it was published in 1921 and had a forward by Carl Sandburg, so it seemed worth it.

Randal gave me a copy of *Jonathan Livingston Seagull*.

I was disappointed. I was leaving home in two weeks to have HIS baby, so I felt I deserved more than an insipid feel good book I could read in twenty minutes. "Gee, thanks, Randall, this is great." I tried to express enthusiasm, but honestly, he might as well have given me *The Little Engine That Could*.

New mantras had replaced "everything's gonna be all right." Now it was buck up, keep your chin up, press on. Persevere, surmount any obstacle, you're doing the right thing, the right thing, the right thing, when all I wanted was to get married and keep my baby.

We left the restaurant and drove back home without talking. Randall lit a joint, and I rolled down the window to keep the smell from lingering on my great-grandmother's shawl or my sister's dress. When we got to I-35, I started to feel sick.

I thought for a moment it might have been the wine sauce on the Chateaubriand. But I knew it was more than that. I wanted to wake up from a nightmare. I wanted someone to ride in on a white horse and make everything okay. I wanted my parents to stop walking me to the gallows.

I worried as we neared Crossroads Mall that Randall would turn off the highway and go parking down Sooner Road, but we stayed on I-35 all the way to Moore. As we pulled up in front of my house, I wondered if we would ever make love again. This night, unlike the last time we pulled into the driveway, Randall put his arm around my shoulders and pulled me in close.

I buried my head in his chest. He lifted my chin and gazed deeply into my eyes.

"I do love you, Lani, you gotta know that." His tongue made its way around my starving lips. He was reading from the old memo. "Everything's going to be all right, you'll see."

I choked back tears, grateful for his tenderness. I stayed a moment longer with my head on his chest. He was wearing the Royal Copenhagen I bought him for Christmas. I don't know what it was about that smell, but the smallest whiff made me ready to take my clothes off and throw care to the wind.

That night, as the sweet, woodsy scent wafted over me, my body ached for Randall in a way I never dreamed possible. A searing pain sliced through my chest.

"I know. I love you, too." I opened the car door and stepped into thin night air. The wind had picked up, blowing hard from the north, and it rattled the metal mailbox hanging from a peg on our front porch until it groaned like Marley with his chains.

I picked up the shawl from where it had fallen on the floor and wrapped it around my shoulders. "Thanks for the book, Randall. I'll take it with me."

Maybe it would inspire me to fly.

The Wrong Movie

February is the shortest month of the year, and in 1971, its close came much too soon. My last two weeks of work flew by, and soon I told lies and goodbyes to teachers and acquaintances and cried over farewells with the few close friends who knew the truth. I called Dayna repeatedly, but I could never catch her in. At least that's what her mother said. Then, on the last Saturday of the month, I packed a familiar green suitcase. Hard and indestructible, my family had used it for every big trip we had ever taken. The previous summer, when I carried it to the Girls' Auxiliary National Convention in Knoxville, I never dreamed I would be packing it for a trip like this.

I didn't take a lot—only two books, *The Prophet* and *Jonathan Livingston Seagull*—though I decided to bring most of my albums. *Crosby, Stills & Nash*; *Tea for the Tillerman*; *Clouds*; *Sounds of Silence*; *Ladies of the Canyon*. I knew that if I left them at home Kathy would have them scratched up by the time I got back.

I owned a few Rod McKuen albums at the time—*Listen to the Warm, The Sea, For Lovers*—and I left them for my sister Janet. She was only in sixth grade, but she was the only one in the family besides me who seemed to appreciate poetry. Several times I caught her listening to them, rocking back and forth like the ward of a nut house. Janet and I were similar emotional beings, and like our mother, we cried at the drop of a hat.

I threw in six pairs of new panties with the stretchy front panel, two bras, some blue cotton pajamas, one of my mother's nightgowns, and my going-away gift from Mr. Stevens—a new box of neon blue and orange stationery.

I packed the maternity outfit we bought at Wards, and the pink polyester pantsuit my mom made for my birthday. She wanted me to wear it my first day at Sellers; she thought it would help me make a good impression—pink was a good color for me, she said. I thought I looked like a dork, but I would wear it to please her. It was little enough to honor her request given all the pain I had put her through.

I crammed a small canvas toiletry bag with my toothbrush, a tube of Crest, a hairbrush, a tube of liquid Prell, a blue jar of Noxema. I stuck the toiletry bag in the top of the suitcase along with the white Bible my grandma had given me when I was baptized, and the marble egg Dayna bought me at the State Fair the previous September—a *Funny Girl* memento.

I decided not to bring Randall's drop. Since the day he had given it to me I had never taken it off. I even wore it in the shower. I loved looking down at it, cradled between my breasts, breasts that Randall stroked and kissed, breasts that were getting bigger by the hour, breasts that my baby would never suckle. My drop meant more to me than anything else I owned, and when I saw it against my clothes or my skin, or when I was anxious and rubbed it between my fingers, I felt as if Randall was right there beside me, loving me forever. But the Sellers' instructions said to bring nothing of value. I pulled the drop up over my head, and for a moment, it became tangled in my hair. With a quick tug I pulled it out. I laid the drop on the red velvet lining of my jewelry box, a small black lacquered one that my father brought back from Vietnam. I closed the lid, determined not to think any more about it.

Randall came over after supper. My mom and dad were polite, but not pleasant. Thankfully they left us alone, but instead of holding hands and discussing our future, it was only more small talk.

The invasion of Laos.

Evel Knievel's plan to jump 19 cars in California.

The recent assignment of *In Cold Blood* for Mrs. Massenger's Honors English Class.

I felt like I was in a movie and I had been plopped down in the wrong scene. My life felt like it was happening to someone else. On the couch, Randall and I sat too far away from each other.

When "Mary Tyler Moore" finished at nine, my mom shooed my sisters out of the den and on to bed. She stopped on her way to the hall bathroom. "You've got a long drive tomorrow, Lani, better call it a night."

"OK, Mama, I'll just walk Randall outside."

I didn't grab my coat, and the cold night air sliced through my joints and stopped my breath. Randall leaned in to kiss me.

I wanted a kiss that would last forever, but this kiss was short, and not particularly sweet—a romantic comedy kiss. We were Cary Grant and Audrey Hepburn. A peck on the cheek. A slight brushing of lips. I wondered what had happened to our passion. Maybe we were afraid to fire it up since we were hurtling headfirst into a long separation. Randall seemed indifferent to what was happening, unmoved by the gravity of our situation. I kept hearing a verse from Proverbs in my head: *Who hath woe? who hath sorrow? who hath redness of eyes?* The answer was me, Me, ME!!

My voice was barely audible. "I'll write as soon as I can."

"I don't know if I'll have time to write. If there's a phone, send me the number, and I'll call you on Thursday night." Randall turned toward his car, parked behind my dad's Mercury.

As he walked away, I imagined it all so differently. This was the movie scene I wanted: Randall would take me in his arms and hide me in the back seat of his yellow Impala. We would run off to the abandoned house near Draper Lake and fuck until the sun came up. I would take him inside me again and again and again, until every pore on my body had memorized every pore on his. Then Randall would realize that he couldn't live without me. We defy his parents and in the bright light of day drive to Texas to get married.

As Randall opened the car door, I called out, "Hey, I couldn't reach Dayna tonight. Will you tell her goodbye for me?"

"Sure thing, Lani. Take care of yourself. I'll call. I promise."

As he backed into the street, I played out a new movie scene. The heroine lifts her hand in a feeble wave and bites her lip. She floats above the ground, emotions in check, and then slowly she turns and walks back to the house dry-eyed.

Cut.

I crawled out of bed the next morning and dressed in the dark. Our departure was set for 4am, hours before my brother and sisters would wake; only my mom was there to see us off.

My dad and I waited near the front door, and I felt like my heart would burst. Other than the two-week trip to the Girls' Auxiliary National Convention in Knoxville and a few one-week stints at summer church camp, I had never been away from home. Now I was staring at almost six months away from everyone I knew and loved. Blood is thicker than water, my father said. Without family, we couldn't survive, my mother said. But I was supposed to say goodbye to my mom's cooking and bickering with my sisters and late-night phone calls with Dayna and sweet loving trysts with Randall. My mother was right; I wouldn't survive. But for everyone's sake, I had to force a happy face. When asked how I was doing, I would simply say "Fine, everything is fine."

My mom came in from the kitchen carrying a thermos of coffee and a brown paper bag. The green suitcase sat on the floor where I had left it the previous night. My dad took the sack lunch and thermos and headed to the car, giving my mom and I a moment alone. She started to say something, then abruptly went back into the kitchen. She returned with a box of saltines. Her chin quivered.

"Ma, it's going to be OK. Really."

She put her arms around me, and for a moment I rested against her chest. I thought of a baby's chubby fist held tight inside its mother's hand.

"I know, I know," she whispered. "It's just I worry so."

I kissed her cheek and pulled out of her grasp. I straightened my shoulder bag, took the saltines, and picked up the suitcase.

"I'll be all right. You'll see. I'll write as soon as I get there."

I walked to the car determined not to turn around. My dad threw the suitcase in the trunk. I settled into the front passenger seat and he handed me the thermos. "You're in charge of pouring the coffee when I need it."

As we backed out of the driveway, I saw my mom's face framed in the doorway. I raised my hand to wave goodbye. She started to wave back, but quickly placed her hands over her face before backing up and closing the door.

Part Two: The Mississippi

Wisdom is learning what to overlook.

~William James

Sunday Driving

We followed the old highway down to Norman, past Lilac Hill Cemetery, where Sean was buried, and then headed down State Highway 9 that ran along the South Canadian. It was one of the routes my family took when we went out Sunday driving, making our way to Holdenville and Aunt Ethel and Uncle Earl's house.

Some of my favorite childhood memories are from these Sunday drives. All seven of us piled into Nellybelle, one of those amazing '57 Plymouths with enormous fins in back, rising up from either side of the trunk like two great white sharks. My dad picked her up in New York after one of his tours of duty, and he drove her all the way across the country in just three days. The color of desert gold with a shiny grill across the front, we named her after Pat Brady's jeep, and we drove her until all the life was out of her.

Aunt Ethel and Uncle Earl lived down the street from Uncle DV and Aunt Marie. Aunt Ethel and Uncle Earl never had any children, but from front porch talk, it seemed it wasn't for lack of trying. Uncle Earl was wounded in the Great War, World War I, the War to End All Wars, and his voice was raspy from the gas he inhaled in the trenches.

DV and Marie were what we called "characters"—DV tuned pianos and invented all kinds of strange instruments. On Sundays, we had a big lunch of country-fried chicken, biscuits and gravy, and fresh-picked poke salad that had been boiled three times and fried up in bacon grease. Then the whole family gathered on the front porch for some visiting. Swapping stories, sharing memories, conversations about nothing in particular. That pretty much summed up "visiting." Sitting in the heat, swatting away flies. The smaller children ran around in the front yard listening to the blink, blank, blink of a homemade banjitar, and the plink, plank, plink of DV and Marie's wads of chewed up tobacco and saliva hitting the spittoon.

I always felt my mom was a bit above the country simplicity, even though she was born and raised in Moore. After she married my dad, they were stationed in Hawaii where I was born. She shared wonderful stories about her job at the private school Kamehameha, and Hawaii seemed like a place filled with fairytale magic—black sand beaches hugging warm teal waters filled with turtles, whales and fearsome barracuda. Then, just after my third birthday, my dad was stationed in England. Within a few months, my mother, my two sisters and I followed him there. We lived on base for the first couple of years, and my youngest sister was born outside of Liverpool. Our last year in England, we moved to a large house in the village of Abbotsley, not too far from Cambridge. An English Lord owned the house and surrounding property, and he rented it cheap to American servicemen, a bit of a "thank the Yank" for America's participation in WWII. This was his simple country home, but to us it was a mansion. We had an Irish housekeeper/nanny, five bedrooms, three fireplaces, a gardener who gave us rides in the wheelbarrow, an abandoned tennis court where we learned to roller skate, a plum orchard, a ten-pound calico cat that liked to steal our fish and chips, and a white picket fence covered in pink tea roses. Since we weren't too far out of London, sometimes my mom and dad drove there for the theater in my dad's two-seater red convertible MG.

I remember thinking that my mother was the most beautiful woman in the world. When my mom and dad went out, she looked just like a movie star in a boatneck dress deeper than the color of midnight and splattered with large, crimson roses. I loved watching her get dressed. The golden tube of ruby red cream that she applied to her lips. The shiny, green fairy dust that seemed to make her hazel eyes dance all the brighter. Her dark auburn hair falling in natural curls just above her soft shoulders. My dad got gussied up too; but not in his Air Force dress blues, in his Sunday-go-to-meeting suit and tie. When my mom was ready and my dad first laid eyes on her, a huge smile would cross his face. "Honey, you look like a million bucks." She smiled back with a glow that could shame a thousand suns.

My mom was the kind of person who could fit in anywhere. She was loved by everyone who met her. Even though I thought she deserved better than her life of continual give and give, she seemed to enjoy our Sunday drives and the visits with my dad's relatives in Holdenville. And she never complained, not even when she got stuck washing the dishes each week.

There was one Sunday drive I should have gone on but didn't. The first time Randall and I "did it," my family was down in Holdenville. Mother's Day, the week after the Kent State killings. At the time it felt like the whole world was coming apart, and we needed to grab what little pleasure we could. That was what my friend Desiree believed. She wasn't embarrassed at all to talk about all the guys she'd balled, or how good they felt inside her. And it wasn't just Desiree and all her big talk. Sex was as rampant as the kudzu I saw growing out of control on the trip to Knoxville. Airline stewardesses offered coffee, tea, or me; Goldie Hawn danced in a skimpy bikini on "Laugh In;" "Light My Fire" played non-stop on the radio. Even in Moore, a Bible-thumping small town, the world throbbed with the message that a sexual revolution was going on all around us, and I had better be a part of it.

My dad interrupted my thoughts, "Lani, I'm 'bout ready for that cup of coffee."

I held the thermos in my lap between my legs, and carefully unscrewed the top. The Coleman thermos was an antique. It had belonged to my grandfather, my mother's father, the one I never met, the one who died on my mother's eighteenth birthday in 1948. I loved the way the steam rose up out of the thermos and filled the car with the scent of black pepper and caramel. My grandfather's thermos—cool green steel on the outside and thick glass inside—kept coffee hot all day. I poured some into the metal top that served double duty as a cup. On those bumpy Oklahoma roads, I had trouble keeping the coffee from sloshing on my thighs. Even through my jeans, my skin smarted from a single spilled drop.

I was thirsty, and would have loved a cup of coffee, but I wasn't allowed to drink it—too young, my mom said—though I had been sneaking around and drinking it behind my parents' backs for more than a year. I didn't smoke cigarettes or pot. I didn't drink alcohol, but I had two secret pleasures—sex and coffee.

When we were past Norman, instead of continuing on Highway 9 east toward Holdenville, we followed the south fork of the Canadian River where it winds its way down to Noble and beyond to Slaughterhouse. I forgot to bring a book to keep me occupied in the car. Being left with only my own thoughts for company was pure torment. I couldn't stop thinking about Randall. I hadn't been gone for more than an hour and already I missed him so much I couldn't stand being alive. I didn't know how I could be away from him for six months. Looking out the car window, I had serious doubts I would survive.

Randall didn't seduce me, coerce me, or bribe me. I wanted to be with him. My body longed for his.

On the Sunday we first made love, my family left for Holdenville after church. I was supposed to be going to work. I worked most Sundays from 12-4, but on that particular day, Mr. Stevens decided to take inventory. I didn't tell my mom about the change in my schedule; I hadn't wanted to go Sunday driving since I entered high school. Visiting relatives was okay when I was a kid, but like most teenagers I thought I knew everything. I was mature and sophisticated. Why would I want to sit on the dilapidated front porch of Uncle Earl and Aunt Ethel's ramshackle old house while DV and Marie spit tobacco into a spittoon?

After my family was safely out of town, Randall and I walked the four blocks from church to the Calico Café, where we ordered the Sunday special—a big plate of baked ham, mashed potatoes and gravy, green beans, and banana cream pie. Randall dug in with gusto. I was too excited to eat much at all. I had worn my newest Easter dress for this special occasion, and I was worried about getting gravy on it. We talked about Kent State. We talked about our assignment for Honors English. Even then a wannabe filmmaker, I was shooting an experimental short based on Marullus's first monologue in *Julius Caesar*. *Run to your houses, fall upon your knees, pray to the gods to intermit the plague that needs must light on this ingratitude.*

All the while we were sitting there, I could feel myself getting wetter and wetter imagining the threshold I was about to cross. I was afraid there would be a big puddle on the seat of the chair when I stood up.

After lunch it took fifteen minutes to walk to my house. When we arrived, we went straight to my bedroom. I unpinned the rose on my chest before it could get crushed. Our family custom was to always wear a rose on Mother's Day, which seemed to fall right after the roses in our front flowerbed started blooming. Red for a living mother, white for a dead one. At that time both of my grandmothers were living, so everyone in my family wore a red rose.

I laid the rose on top of my dresser, pulled my panties off, balled them up, and threw them in a corner before Randall could see how horrible and ratty they were. I pulled my slip and the navy A-line skirt of my dress up over my hips and sprawled back on the bottom bunk with legs spread. The bed was Kathy's, but we weren't going to crawl up on my top bunk and risk banging Randall's head on the ceiling.

Up to this point, Randall and I had never discussed birth control. My friend Desiree had been on the pill after she came back from Atlanta, but that wasn't an option for me. I couldn't tell anyone I was sexually active. After the fact, I read up on the rhythm method, and set guidelines about what time of the month would be safe. Like most teenagers, we believed we were invincible. Getting caught happened to other people, not us.

I patted the bed. Randall seemed nervous. He reached up to remove his glasses but changed his mind. I decided to keep mine on, too. I wanted to make sure I could see what I was getting into, or more like it, what was getting into me.

"It's okay, baby," I reassured him. "We've gotten this close before."

Randall smiled and seemed to relax. He unbuckled his belt, unsnapped and unzipped his Sunday pants, and pulled out his cock. He held it like he was going to the bathroom. I had taken care of my little brother for years, so I knew what a penis looked like, but I expected it to be a lot harder.

I thought Randall might take his pants off, but he didn't. He just got on top of me, and tried to stick his cock in. We weren't having much success because Randall didn't have a full erection. On the playground in fourth grade, I heard an older and much wiser sixth grader say that trying to have sex when a guy's "thingie" wasn't hard was like pushing a rubber band down an ant hole.

Randall and I started kissing, and he was getting harder. As he began to push his cock into me, my vagina began to hurt like hell. It seemed like an eternity passed before I felt him in me all the way. But after all the trouble of getting his cock in, he just lay on top of me for a few minutes until he came. I felt like singing along with Peggy Lee, "Is that all there is?" No in and out, no back and forth, no coming and going, no stars and fireworks.

"You finished?" I asked him.

"Yeah, I think so." Randall rolled to his side and sat up, careful not to hit his head on the top bunk.

Not much for a first time. I changed clothes and we walked over to David's to hang out. It's pretty sad when banana cream pie is better than sex. But even though it was kind of a letdown at first, Randall and I kept at it until, eventually, we figured it out. We couldn't keep our hands off each other. We became part of the same song. I was his electric guitar and he wailed away on my body like Duane Allman on "Whipping Post." He pulled notes out of me I didn't know I had. We screwed anytime and anywhere. Phone calls and love notes were our foreplay.

In the summer we dragged a rough drab-olive Army blanket out to the field behind his house. This blanket, the color of my dad's fatigues, became a nest. I began to feel like I was on fire, always on fire in the deepest, darkest, most secret reaches of my body. I only had to imagine for just the tiniest quarter of a second Randall's hand or tongue on me, and I would be bathed in fire, fire raining down from above, fire running over my head and down my back. I was a volcano, erupting fire and lava from my gut and it spread across my breasts and down my arms until it dripped through my fingertips into molten pools at my feet.

Randall and I balled our way through the rest of 1970, through the breakup of the Beatles in the spring, the deaths of Janis Joplin and Jimi Hendrix in the fall. We made love as if nothing could ever happen to us. I thought I was blessed, but boy, was I wrong.

My dad sipped his coffee. "I'm 'bout ready for a refill," he said handing back the top to the thermos.

I couldn't believe I was sitting next to my dad and fantasizing about Randall. Did I look flushed? I poured more hot coffee in the cup and handed it back. My hand shook.

"Watch what you're doing." My dad's raised voice cut through the remains of my lustful thoughts. My dad could be so quick to anger. On one Sunday visiting afternoon in Holdenville I thought he was going to beat the life out of me.

It was the fall of fourth grade just before he shipped off to Vietnam. A cute boy walked by the house while we were outside playing. I'd never seen him before. That boy must have just moved to Holdenville, I thought. "Uh, oh, he can't see me like this," and I took off my glasses.

I had just started wearing them because I had the most awful headaches. In school the other kids thought I was teacher's pet because I always wanted to sit up front. But it was the only way I could see the blackboard. I got my glasses out at Tinker, the Air Force base where my father was stationed. The eye doctor said they were the latest style—cat's eyes he called them—but they were big and thick and clunky, pointing up at the sides like the fins on the back of Nellybelle. I thought they made me look stupid, but I'm no slow leak. If there's one thing I've always hated, it's being taken for stupid.

That Sunday was a perfect warm Indian summer day, closing in on Halloween. The leaves in the few trees around the yard shimmered in red and shades of gold. I wore shorts with a back pocket, and I stuck my glasses in there. The boy walked by the house a second time; I guess he noticed strangers in the neighborhood, too.

His name was Andy and he was eight. I thought he was older, but he was just big for his age. We talked and played and soon it was time to go home. I always dreaded this part of the day, slobbery kisses from old uncles and aunts with scratchy chins. I hurried to get into the car, and as soon as I sat down, I knew I broke my glasses.

I kept quiet about it until we got down the road a piece. Then I whispered in my mom's ear. "Mom, I broke my glasses. I broke 'em down the middle. We can fix 'em, can't we?"

I was really hoping she'd keep quiet about it until we got home, but she started wringing her hands.

"John, what are we going to do? Lani broke her glasses and she can't go to school without them."

My dad's face turned red. His hands clenched the steering wheel tight, and he jerked the car to the right stopping just inches from a ditch, where we might have looked for crawdads on a better day. Before I even took a breath, my dad reached over the back seat and started slapping my face and hitting me on my head.

"Little Miss High and Mighty, Little Miss Smarty Pants." Those were just a few of his pet names for me.

"You prance around all uppity, but you're nothing but a sorry piece of work."

Mom pulled on my dad's arm, Billy was crying, my sisters were screaming, and me, I just tried to melt into the upholstery.

Now that this memory had replaced lustful thoughts of Randall, my face was less flushed. My dad listened to the radio as he sipped his coffee, but after a while it was hard to get any reception. We heard a garbled version of "Act Naturally," the Buck Owens version, and my dad turned the radio off.

The coffee seemed to loosen his tongue, because as we piled on the miles my dad started talking about family. Some of the stories I knew from staying up late and listening in the corners while the grownups talked.

I heard how all the boys around wanted to do nothing but play baseball all the living day, especially after the Dean brothers from Spaulding got picked to play for the Cardinals.

How when Uncle Earl and Aunt Ethel still lived on the farm outside Gerty, the house was used for running bootleg whiskey.

How when my Daddy was just a baby, and they lived in Arkansas, Pretty Boy Floyd hid out on their farm overnight and Memaw fixed him supper and breakfast. But unlike Woody Guthrie's Robin Hood description, the outlaw didn't leave my Memaw a thousand-dollar bill underneath the napkin, let alone the money to cover the biscuits and gravy she fed him along with some pork belly.

Around Broken Bow we stopped to eat lunch at a roadside picnic table. Eastern Oklahoma doesn't look anything at all like the flat prairie where I grew up. This corner of the state is pretty, with rolling hills, lots of water and pine trees that soar up a hundred feet.

I unwrapped the brown wax paper packages. The liverwurst smelled like cat food, but at least my mom didn't put mayonnaise on the sandwiches. When she made them that morning, the liverwurst had been hard and cold and spreading it had shredded the bread, so now the softened liverwurst squeezed through ragged seams and covered my fingers.

Not long after lunch we stopped for gas just over the border in Arkansas. The town was just a bump in the road with a single pump in front of a general store, much like our Seven Corners. Except this store looked like it was built for the set of Petticoat Junction or Hee Haw—a wide wooden porch, a bit of lean to the left, rockers and old men in overalls, waist-high barrels full of pickles.

"You can get yourself a piece of that penny candy," my father told me, but I couldn't decide between Mary Jane's or the Chick-O-Stick nuggets, so I elected to have a pickle instead. When I bit into the crisp skin, juice dribbled down my chin and my nose was overwhelmed with the scent of garlic and dill. It was better than any pickle I had ever eaten.

Daddy refilled his thermos with hot coffee. When we were back in the car, I poured him another cup, and he started telling stories again.

Some of them were new. The story of how his Uncle Tony's oldest boy, four-year old Eddie, drowned in the pond on Uncle Earl's farm. Ronald, my dad's brother, was supposed to be watching him, but he weren't much of a swimmer himself, and Eddie went in too fast and too deep. For all of Ronald's hollerin' the grownups didn't get to him in time. They pulled Eddy out of the water covered in thick red mud, and you could hear the women screaming as they ran down across the field. Ronald was just a kid himself at the time, couldn't have been more than nine, but dad said that Uncle Tony never forgave him.

My dad told me he was no more than six when his Uncle Newton took him to meet some fellas out by Route 75. Two men drove up in a '36 Chevy Coupe, and without saying a word, both men shot his uncle right through the heart and drove away. My dad waited for what seemed like hours while his uncle bled out on the ground. "They never got who did it, either," my dad said. "He mighta got murdered over some gambling debt, or maybe it was a woman. Who knows after all this time?"

He told me he stuttered when he was a boy and got picked on. Then he told a story I already knew. He was 12 when WWII erupted for the US with the December 7th bombing of Honolulu. Right after that, most of the men in Hughes County joined up, even those as young as 16. My Uncle Haskell, his older sister Alice's husband, risked life and limb on the beaches of Normandy. My dad really felt like he was missing out on something. As soon as he turned fourteen, he ran away from home and joined the Navy. I always thought that he ran away from home because he had trouble with his own father, but the way he told it, he just wanted to taste adventure and be part of something much bigger than himself. Before he could ship out, Memaw got him back, only to have him leave again at sixteen for the Air Force.

I handed my dad coffee whenever he asked for it. I was glad my mom had given me a fresh box of saltines; these and the stories distracted me from any nausea.

    I didn't understand at the time why my father was talking to me like that. It wasn't a conversation. He wasn't expecting any response from me. I always had the feeling that my dad knew as much about me as he cared to. But maybe he felt like I didn't know anything about him. Maybe he was hoping my baby could hear his voice, his stories, and somehow know where he came from.

    We stopped for dinner outside of Shreveport. I ordered the fried chicken liver special and a cola. When my mom fried up a chicken at home, there were only a few innards—the gizzard, the heart, the liver—and we fought over who got to eat them. Now I had a whole plate all to myself. They didn't serve Coke, only RC, but it was just as good, just a tiny bit sweeter.

    It was another three hours to Alexandria. In the dark, my dad kept his thoughts to himself.

    We found an inexpensive motel, a room with two double beds. I undressed in the bathroom and fell asleep the instant my head hit the pillow. In my dreams, I was standing outside our house in Moore. Randall was there, my sisters, the entire neighborhood, and we were looking up into a starless night sky. The moon was huge and bright. Thick, billowing smoke poured out of jagged horizontal seams across its landscape. The seams glowed red and molten like the lava that poured out of my body every time Randall touched me. I stood there watching the moon on fire, wondering if we could live without it.

Babylon

The room was still dark when I heard my dad's crack-of-dawn snorts. He quit smoking years ago, after he came back from Vietnam, but every morning he woke up with a throat coated in phlegm and he coughed and hacked for a month of Sundays. To hear my Memaw tell it, he started smoking in the cradle, but my dad always laughed and said he started when he was about ten. With one last humungous *Hrrrrrrmph*, I heard my dad's feet touch the floor and the bed creaked as he stood up. I was on my left side facing away from him, but the itchy, twitchy twin bed was next to the bathroom. I closed my eyes tight against the blinding light that shone on my face when he opened the bathroom door.

I really needed to pee, and I cursed myself for succumbing to laziness and not being quicker to the draw.

I was eleven—the summer after fifth grade—when my dad quit smoking. We were on vacation in Noel, Missouri, a backwater town in the most southwest corner of Missouri near the Oklahoma border. Even in the middle of summer, Noel's Main Street was decked out in Christmas lights and plywood candy canes. The town is situated right on the Elk River, which flows alongside and through the Ozark Mountains. Being a girl from flat Oklahoma plains, those small peaks might as well have been the Swiss Alps. Every summer, in the blistering heat, I tried to imagine what they looked like covered in snow.

When my dad was overseas, we never went anywhere, so Noel was our big get-away vacation whenever my dad was home. And we didn't camp in tents like we did at Great Salt Plains Lake in Oklahoma. We rented a cabin on Indian Creek, which runs straight into the heart of the Elk River. The water was shallow, and it flowed fast and clear. All day we sat on the rocky banks of that creek, reading, playing, but never really swimming. My mom was terrified of water, and we were only allowed to wade in up to our knees, and even then, we wore heavy safety vests.

In the evening back at our cabin, under light from kerosene lanterns, we played cards way past our normal bedtime. My dad was partial to Rook.

It's played in teams, and in Noel I partnered with my dad, while Kathy teamed up with my mom. There's lots of counting, cards to bid, cards to deal. My mother never cared when Kathy screwed up, but my father would get meaner than a wet panther when he wasn't winning.

On those hot summer nights, after a few losing hands and throwing the cards down in disgust, he would stomp off under the trees to smoke cigarettes. After chain-smoking at least three, my dad would come back to the cabin reeking of tobacco, and he and my mom would start to bicker. My sisters and I got used to covering our ears. Back then it seemed like our parents were always fighting, and we never left the dinner table or a card table without someone bursting into tears.

I never ever stood up to my dad about anything. As children, Kathy could become a pit bull, but it didn't take much to beat it out of her, out of all of us. Without even trying he could knock us into the middle of next week.

But that summer in Noel, I must have been feeling my oats, because I threw a hissy fit about his smoking. "You didn't die over there in Vietnam, but you're gonna let this kill you?!"

Right then and there he went cold turkey.

My dad was still coughing and hacking in the bathroom. It was a good thing he quit smoking when he did. I wondered how much longer he would monopolize the bathroom. I was feeling really uncomfortable; I needed to pee so bad. My sisters and I always joked about how long my dad could take, but I wasn't laughing then.

I finally heard the water running in the sink, and my dad came out of the bathroom still in his pajamas.

"You awake?"

"Yes, sir."

"Hurry up and get dressed then. We need to get a move on."

I gathered my clothes and my small bag of toiletries. The toilet seat felt hot to my thighs, and I wasn't sure if it was morning sickness or the stench that made me gag. I hated using the bathroom after someone else.

I put on the pink pantsuit my mother made me for my birthday and decided against putting on my face. I didn't think I would cry, but bawling was most certainly a possibility, and I didn't want my mascara to run.

When we left Oklahoma, winter was having itself a party, and not a Baptist punch and cookies party, but a Kappa Alpha party with beer snuck in from the 7-11. Randall had been right. We did get snow, and tons of it.

In fact, the blizzard that hit on February 20 brought some towns in the panhandle twenty-foot snow drifts. Even Moore had about five inches of snow, along with howling winds and temperatures in the low to mid-thirties. But that morning in Alexandria it was almost balmy, and I carried my pea coat over my arm, hugging my shoulder bag.

My dad and I ordered breakfast from a small café around the corner from the motel. The waitress's hair was a beehive plastered to her head, and her skirt was so tight, my Memaw would have said, "If she had a nickel in her back pocket, you could tell if it was heads or tails."

The waitress filled my dad's thermos with coffee, and he left her a decent tip, which was out of the ordinary.

He left the café whistling an upbeat, unknown tune.

We drove through the Louisiana countryside—soft, cool, dark. Birds were waking in the marshes. I heard their cries while the sun rose over my dad's shoulder. In the dim light, I could see how different Louisiana was from Oklahoma. Spanish moss dripped from cypresses. Leaning willows hid sleeping ducks and swamp chickens. Wind ruffled pampas grass. Water was everywhere, marshy bayous running alongside the road. Concentric waves of heat shimmered and threw back colors I had never seen. On the trip to New Orleans the previous summer, I was probably talking to my friends too much to pay attention. Now I was in a waking dream. A half-sleeping alligator with half-lidded eyes, conserving energy, naively treading water in a whirlpool.

I fiddled with the radio. All that came through was a preacher. I stared out the window and the sound of his voice buzzed around the car like a fly.

> *My sisters, brothers, I'm here to tell you the handwriting is on the wall. Just like back in Babylon, the people were so smug, so secure in their evil doing they didn't consider harm could ever come to them. They had the world in the palm of their hand. Or so they thought. Because who really has got the world in His hand? That's right. It's God and God alone.*

All my life we sang that song. "He's got the whole world in His hands." Sisters and brothers, sun and rain, oceans and seas, you and me. You and me. In His hands. I wanted to believe that.

> *Babylon was a great empire; it had whipped the entire known world into submission; all the world was paying*

> *tribute. It had the latest chariots, the hottest designs, the most powerful armors, the best metals. The king back then was Belshazzar. He had taken over after Nebuchadnezzar, the Babylonian king who took the Israelites captive, including Daniel. You remember Daniel, don't you? A man of God so strong in the Lord that he could be plopped down in the middle of a lion's den, and not get a single scratch. Nebuchadnezzar understood that Daniel was a righteous man. But Belshazzar was a wicked man. He didn't care.*

They said Daniel stuck his head right in the lion's mouth like the lion tamer at the circus. I liked the other story of redemption in Babylon, too. Shadrach, Meshach, and Abednego were tossed into the fiery furnace, and Jesus walked around in a circle with them. Not a hair on their heads was singed. I wanted to feel that Jesus was walking around with me, but on the road I was traveling, I felt like I was gonna burn up or get eaten alive.

> *So, all the people felt safe, felt secure inside those Babylonian gates. Gates that towered two hundred feet, gates eight feet thick. But just remember this. No matter how secure you think you are, God will find you out when you sin. There is only one security, and that's in Christ Jesus.*

I didn't feel secure. God and the whole world knew I'd sinned.

> *The Babylonians felt important, being the leading nation of the world. They were just like the one we live in, this fabulous America. I'm kind of disturbed because I'm afraid we're taking the same attitude they took. We've got the atomic bomb, jet planes that break the sound barrier. And we feel safe. But are we safe without God? You see, God never changes. He hates sin as much today as He did in the time of Babylon. And there's no hiding place down here. Only in Christ are you secure.*

Was the world really so unhappy because of sin? The war, the riots, the unrest? Could it be as simple as that?

> *So, the Babylonians closed their gates. They thought they could live in revelry because they were protected.*

> *Belshazzar thought he would have him a great big time. He invited all the celebrities, all the soldiers and men around town, all the wives and concubines. And he called in the best liquors he could find for this great rock-and-roll party. He got showgirls to come in to entertain the soldiers. I imagine they struck up the band, maybe it was the Rolling Stones, and they had music, maybe they're playing "Sympathy for the Devil," and the little teen-agers were wiggling all over the garden calling it dancing. And the soldiers, drunk, grabbing the women and throwing them over their heads, kissing them and then sitting down in chairs, and thinking they were safe. Oh, America, the God that looked down on that drunken, rock-and-roll party is looking on you tonight.*

It was hard for me to believe that the world's ills were due to music, sex, drinking and drugs.

To be honest, God and I hadn't been on the best of terms since the previous December when Sean died. In church school the Sunday after his funeral, Mrs. Bodine, our pastor's wife, led the lesson with the scripture for the day from Ephesians, Chapter 6.

She began reading, *"Be strong in the Lord and in the strength of his might. Put on the whole armor of God that you may be able to stand against the schemes of the devil."*

I wasn't paying attention until she segued into the proclamation that Sean went to hell. "You have to realize that Catholicism is a scheme of the devil. I'm not saying the Pope is the anti-Christ like some people, but he's not the head of the Church, either. Only Jesus is the Head of the Church. If you look back at Ephesians, Chapter 1, it clearly states that God hath put all things under Jesus' feet, and gave Him to be head over all things including the church."

"Catholics don't believe in Jesus," she continued. "They worship idols. Jesus said that unless a man be born again, he cannot enter the kingdom of God. Catholics baptize infants. They are never born again. That's why it's a false religion, and that's why they'll go to hell."

I couldn't believe what I was hearing. I grew up with the understanding that Baptists didn't really consider Roman Catholics Christian, but that kind of thinking never made sense after I met Sean. Sean's funny puns deserved no place in hell. Besides I had felt close to God in St. Andrew's, the church where Sean's funeral was held. Nothing the priest said seemed un-Christian in any way. We prayed in the name of the Father, Son and Holy Ghost. A layperson read a story that I knew well—the one of Lazarus being raised from the dead. The crucifix was gruesome, but it also made Jesus' suffering more tangible. Was heaven really an exclusive country club with certain people not allowed in?

"If you truly love your friends," Mrs. Bodine persisted, "you've got to be a better witness for God. Be strong in the Lord. Put on His armor. Talk to your friends. Make sure they're saved. It's not enough to be a good person, the only way you can get to heaven is to bring Jesus into your heart."

I was born again. Washed in the blood of the lamb. On a Sunday night when I was eight years old. Pastor Hart came down from the pulpit and started the altar call. "Sinners, come to Jesus. He's here waiting for you." We sang, "*Just as I am without one plea*" and I heard Jesus talking to me. The church deacons sat in the front pew, waiting to see if anyone wanted to get saved. "*Thy blood was shed for me. Thou bidst me come to Thee, O Lamb of God, I come.*" I knew we were singing those words for me. Jesus wanted me to come down to the front, kneel with a deacon, and ask Him into my heart.

I heard a roaring in my ears. The sound of my heart bursting inside my chest. I didn't have far to go, but the walk down the aisle took hours. Deacon Tyler came up to me. I whispered, "I want to be born again."

"Speak up, Lani," he said.

I didn't have enough breath to carry my words over the sound of my heart or the congregation singing. I said it again, louder. "Deacon Tyler, I want to be born again."

"All right, child. Repeat after me. I want Jesus…"

"I want Jesus…"

"…to be my Lord and Savior."

"…to be my Lord and Savior.

"Amen."

"Amen."

And that was it. I was saved. Born again.

Jesus loved me, and I loved Jesus, but I wasn't so sure about God. Like Jeremiah said, "*The heart is deceitful above all things, and desperately sick. I, the Lord, search the heart to give every man according to the fruit of his deeds.*" God knew all about my inside life. I wasn't as white as snow. I got baptized and still I worried about the fires of hell and the devil, the only monster I ever had under my bed.

One of Pastor Bodine's catch phrases was "God said it, I believe it, and that's the end of it." I couldn't think of a time when I didn't believe in God, but hearing what Mrs. Bodine said about Sean, I wasn't sure what I believed any more.

I thought back to that end-of-year party at the Duck Pond. Sean sharing the Chianti, the easy smile on his face, hair thick and coarse, the color of straw bales, his eyes bluer than Elizabeth Taylor's. If Sean wasn't in heaven, then I didn't want to go there either.

Besides now that I was seventeen, pregnant and unmarried, I was probably damned already, and nothing really mattered any more.

I glanced over at my father. He didn't appear to be listening, so I fiddled with the dial again. If that was God, speaking to me, then the conversation was over.

The gravelly tones of Johnny Cash replaced the stridency of the unnamed preacher. "Sunday Morning Coming Down." Finally, someone who knew how to speak for God. I had never spent a night drinking, smoking or pickin' a guitar, but I recognized the sound of loneliness, and I understood the need to escape the realities of each day. Who needed church when there was chicken frying, bells ringing and children kicking cans?

Outside the car window, shacks leaned in the lavender dawn. On hand-lettered signs, country stores advertised alligator boudin, crawfish and possum. We stopped for another bite to eat in Baton Rouge and got into New Orleans by two. I had almost forgotten how big New Orleans looked to a girl from a small Oklahoma town. The previous summer on the Girls' Auxiliary trip to Knoxville, we were in New Orleans just one day. They kept us on the bus except for the stop at Sellers, a walk in Audubon Park, and a beignet at Café du Monde. I'm sure they figured we'd get corrupted if they let us loose in the French Quarter. Little did they know that "corruption" happens anytime and anywhere.

Suddenly the brakes groaned, and my father pulled the car to a stop.

2010 Peniston. We'd reached the end of the road.

Stuck-up

The place hadn't changed any; it looked like I remembered it. The two-story red brick building took up most of the block. White shutters on the windows. A short wrought-iron fence. Bushes with sweet white blossoms that for some strange unknown reason conjured up the Lesley Gore song "Sunshine, Lollipops and Rainbows."

I grabbed my coat and bag from the backseat while my dad got the suitcase from the trunk. The wrought-iron gate creaked—a fence for looks, not protection. I took a deep breath as we climbed the few steps to the semi-circular concrete porch. I stood shaking from the inside out.

My dad rang the doorbell, and within a minute a pretty, young woman opened the door. She had a dark complexion, and straight shoulder-length dark hair.

"Hello, Mr. Lassiter?" The woman extended a hand to my father, and then turned to me. "I'm Marie Doucet. You must be Lani." I nodded, and involuntarily the "someone's walking on your mother's grave" shiver ran up and down my back.

"Let me take your coat. You're not going to be needing that." Her black doe eyes were kind. I laid the coat across her arm at the same instant she closed the door behind us. Rather than being dark, the foyer and adjoining living room were filled with light from two nine-pane windows.

Miss Doucet ushered us in and pointed to the blue brocade covered couch with an oil painting of a beach at sunset taking up most of the wall above it. I took a seat on the edge, clutching my shoulder bag like a lifeline. My dad stayed standing, staring at his feet.

"I'm sorry, Mr. Lassiter, but Mrs. LaPrairie was called away on business with the Home Mission Board, and can't meet with you today." Hearing her speak, my ears pricked up. Her accent sounded nothing at all like folks in Oklahoma.

"I can handle any necessary paperwork, and of course, if you need to speak with Mrs. LaPrairie for any reason, you can always call or write."

My dad glanced out the window and shifted his feet. He was always an in-charge kind of guy. No matter where we went, he never seemed too out-of-place or uncomfortable. Standing in that room, it looked like he'd gotten the short end of the stick. It was strange to see him unsure of himself.

"Would you like to meet Mrs. York? She's the housemother."

My father nodded, and he and I were alone while the minutes stretched between us like a spider's web across the branches of a bush. He cleared his throat, and stared out the window.

Soon the door opened and we were joined by Miss Doucet and an older woman. Introductions all around. Handshakes. Mrs. York. Housemother.

She reminded me of my grandmother—dressed in a plain cotton farm dress with sensible shoes. Her hair was tucked up in a hair net like my grandmother's, but it was much longer, and it perched on top of her head like an empty bird's nest. She wore glasses too, with lenses so thick that her eyes appeared wide and piercing, like a Great Horned owl hunting at night. She leaned over to pick up my suitcase, and although she had a gentle expression, I felt like a baby cottontail alone on a frozen field.

My dad seemed distracted and he reached to take the suitcase from her hands. "Don't bother with that. I'll carry it to Lani's room."

Mrs. York clutched the handle and shook her head. Her reprimand was sharp and quick. "No, Mr. Lassiter, we need to protect the other girls' privacy. I'm sure you understand. Lani, say your goodbyes now, so Miss Doucet can finish with the paperwork."

I turned to hug my dad, and dropped my handbag on the white carpet. The contents spilled across the floor and a tube of lipstick rolled under a side table next to the couch. In a second glance at the painting on the wall, I noticed the footprints in the sand, and remembered seeing one just like it hanging on the wall of the funeral home where Sean was laid out.

My dad knelt down to pick up my wallet and the hankerchief my mother had tucked into my purse before I left. It still smelled like her favorite perfume, Channel No. 5. His hands shook. When we stood up, he gave me a quick peck.

"Take that suitcase, now, you hear me. Don't be making extra work for nobody."

I nodded, and Mrs. York handed the suitcase to me.

"Your Mama and me, we're gonna try and get down here to see you. Once the kids are out of school."

I worked hard to keep my tears in check, and simply nodded.

Mrs. York shook my dad's hand once again. "We'll take good care of her, Mr. Lassiter. You and your wife can rest assured. And if you come down for a visit, when would that be—late May, early June? —we'll arrange for you to have a tour of our home and you can see Lani's room."

Miss Doucet handed Mrs. York my coat. I rearranged my shoulder bag.

"Bye, Daddy."

His lips were set in a hard, thin line. "Bye, Lani, we'll be down to see you soon. Write your mother. Don't make her worry."

"I'll write, Daddy."

Miss Doucet took my father's right arm and led him across the room. I followed Mrs. York through the door on the left. I felt like I ceased to exist. I could have been blown away by a puff of wind. The only thing of substance in my life right then was the weight of the suitcase in my hand.

We walked down a long hallway, and Mrs. York briefly described the rooms we passed. Chapel, Rec Room, Dining Room, with the kitchen just beyond. I could hear girls' voices, and the sound of a television. In a moment we reached stairs leading to the second floor.

Mrs. York clutched the banister. With each step, her knuckles showed white.

"Are stairs hard for you, Mrs. York?" I was sure if I took a look beneath her skirt, I would see knees swollen and red like my grandmother's.

"Just a touch of arthritis, Lani. The humidity here doesn't help much."

We reached the top of the stairs and turned right down a short hallway.

"My grandma's got arthritis, so does my mom. I guess it runs in the…" Mrs. York interrupted me and gestured to her left.

"The bathroom is here. There are two others, but this is the one you can use right now."

"My grandma drinks a bit of pectin in grape juice. Maybe about a teaspoon of pectin. She swears by it. Have you ever tried that? And she soaks in Epsom salts."

Mrs. York ignored my suggestions. On the right side of the hall she pointed to a small room containing two single beds. An unopened blue suitcase sat at the foot of the bed against the far wall.

"This is your room for the next few days—just while you're getting adjusted. We'll assign your permanent bedroom in the next day or two."

Mrs. York motioned to the bed directly across from the door. "Betty came in on Friday, and she's in the other bed. There's no place for you to unpack in here, so live out of your suitcase for a few days. Did you bring everything on the list?"

I nodded and set my suitcase down by the bed nearest the door.

Mrs. York laid a hand on my shoulder. "You're probably tired. Why don't you rest a while? Supper's at five. I'll make introductions then."

As she turned to leave, a girl stood in the doorway. With long black hair and wild violet eyes, she looked like Elizabeth Taylor eight months in the family way.

Smiling, Mrs. York nodded. The bird's nest on top of her head had begun to unravel. "Oh, good, I can introduce you now. Betty, this is Lani. She just arrived, and she'll be sharing your room a few days."

Betty stuck out a lovely manicured hand. The nail polish was the color of the Queen of England roses in our front yard back home. "Nice to meet you, Lani. Don't worry, Mrs. York, I'll take good care of her."

Mrs. York headed out the door, and down the hall. I could hear her speaking to other girls. Betty sat on the edge of her bed and rifled through her handbag. She pulled out a crumpled, half-empty pack of Virginia Slims and a silver lighter. I looked at her seeking reassurance, but she smiled at me in the awful fake way popular girls do, with the corners of the mouth going up about halfway only to freeze.

At dinner I sat at Mrs. York's table, and Betty made a point of sitting all the way across the room. Not that Mrs. York could see enough to care.

After we had finished eating, Mrs. York stood up with a grimace, and her knees made popping sounds. "Ready for a tour now, Lani?"

"Yes, ma'am." Unlike the previous summer when I toured with my Girls' Auxiliary group, no one needed to run and hide.

Mrs. York's steps were slow. I couldn't understand why the Southern Baptist Home Mission Board thought she was a suitable caretaker for twenty-four pregnant girls and women.

"So, how'd ya come to be here, Mrs. York?"

"I was in South Dakota with my husband on the Ute Indian reservation. We were there for forty years. John was the pastor and I taught school. Raised a lot of native children to be God-fearing men and women."

"Do you have children of your own?"

"No, the Lord never saw fit to bless us with children. But we were blessed in other ways. We had a rich life. Then a few years back John had a stroke and never recovered. So, the Mission Board sent me here to minister to you girls."

"I'm sorry about your husband. But we're lucky to have you. We must be quite a handful sometimes."

"No, you're no trouble as long as you obey the rules."

"Yes, ma'am."

Mrs. York opened a door in the center of the long hallway.

"Here's the clothes closet."

Clothes of every type, size and color sat jumbled on three wide shelves that stretched the length of the small space. Pillows, bath towels, bed sheets and other linens lined the shelves on the opposite side.

"It's kind of a mess right now. Someone got the sizes all mixed up. But you'll find pants, tops, some dresses, underwear."

She closed the door quickly, embarrassed that this unsightly mess occurred under her watch.

"When girls go home, they generally leave whatever they don't want, if it's still in good repair. If you need something, check in here. No sense spending good money on something you'll only wear a few months."

Next to the clothes closet, a phone booth was cut into the wall. Its open sliding door revealed a small wooden bench seat.

"Here's the phone. No calls out or in after nine o'clock at night. Nothing before eight in the morning. Unless of course, it's an emergency from home, but then the call should come to our administrative number."

The phone reminded me of the one in the *Stage Door* boarding house where crazy wanna-be showgirls talked to their gentleman callers. I could almost imagine Katherine Hepburn hanging up on her father, or Eve Arden making fun of Lucille Ball and her lumberjack boyfriend. I tried to focus my attention on Mrs. York. I was sure she must have been saying something important.

"If you hear the phone ring, always answer it with the phone number. See, it's right there in big block letters so you won't forget. Never, under any circumstances, identify this place by name. You'll generally know if someone's expecting a call, but some girls may not welcome any contact from the outside. Don't ever admit that someone is here. Your security and privacy are of the utmost importance. Understand?"

"Yes, ma'am."

Mrs. York pointed to a set of heavy metal doors that opened with a bar across the middle. They seemed to belong in an institution. A hospital, a school, but more likely, a prison.

"That leads to the smoking porch. Do you smoke?"

"No, ma'am."

"Well, I don't recommend taking it up, though a lot of girls do. If you change your mind, or just want some fresh air, this is the place for it. The only other place you can smoke is downstairs in the courtyard."

"Yes, ma'am."

"Have you been to the nursery yet?"

"No, ma'am."

She opened a door at the end of the hall. The nursery took up most of the north side of the upper floor. Inside the room was lined with more than a dozen cribs. In the back, a large black woman scrubbed out a white diaper pail. A pregnant girl probably a year or two older than me sat in one of four wooden rocking chairs with a baby across her left shoulder. A pregnant girl standing against a crib reached in for a toddler.

"Lani, this is Cheryl and Amy. And that's Shirlene in the back there."

Shirlene waved, a white rag in her hand, looking for all the world like she was ready to surrender. "Hi, shug," she said before turning back to her scrubbing. Her deep voice bounced off the walls and settled down in my chest.

Cheryl patted the baby's bottom in rhythm with the back and forth motion of the rocking chair. "Audrey's a mite colicky today. Can't seem to get her to relax."

Judging by its size, the baby couldn't have been more than a week old. Its eyes were tightly closed. A pink flannel cap covered a Lilliputian head, and the bottom of the white gown was drawn tight with a pink ribbon hiding the baby's tiny feet.

A few more pats, and Audrey let out a loud belch. We all laughed.

"There. That's better," Cheryl said. She turned Audrey so that she was cradled in the crook of her left arm and held her out to me. "Would you like to hold her?"

I glanced at Mrs. York. She nodded. I gingerly picked up Audrey with both hands and leaned her against my chest. I moved my right hand quickly around the tiny body before the head had a chance to wobble on the fragile neck like some pulled-over drunk walking the line. It had been a while since I'd held an infant so small. I was eight when my brother, Billy, was born, and I remember my mother asking me to sit very still and hold out my arms. I was petrified. Protect the head, she said; make sure it doesn't fall backwards. After that I'd held a few babies in the nursery at church, but their parents usually didn't bring them in until they were at least six weeks old. I felt as frightened as I did when I first held Billy. Audrey was teensy—a beautiful porcelain doll—and holding her I was afraid I might drop her, and she would break into a million pieces.

As if she could read my mind Cheryl said, "Babies are a lot tougher than they look. Pretty indestructible in fact."

I didn't believe her and handed Audrey back.

Amy came up with a little boy on her hip. I had no idea how she could perch him there since her belly was humungous. She looked like she could drop any day.

"Lani, this here's Jason."

Jason looked to be almost two—a towhead with piercing blue eyes.

"Go ride," Jason said, pointing to the door.

Amy sat down on an adjoining rocker and picked up a magazine from a wicker basket. "Let's look at some pictures."

"Jason has a heart murmur," Mrs. York said in response to my puzzled expression. "He can't be adopted right now."

"He looks fine. Why…"

Mrs. York interjected before I could complain. "The Lord will find a perfect home for him in His time. Until then he'll stay here under our care."

Jason wasn't interested in the magazine and he wiggled off of Amy's lap. With a few uncertain steps, he toddled over to where Mrs. York and I were standing. "Go ride," he repeated, lifting up his arms.

Suddenly I was so tired I couldn't see straight. I was grateful when Mrs. York concluded the tour. As she left for her apartment in the south hallway, I made a short right into the temporary bedroom I shared with Betty.

I had so much to take in and process. I kicked off brown penny loafers and fell onto the bed without removing my clothes. A small reading lamp was on the wall above my head. I flipped it on, placed my right hand on my belly, and squinted in the lamp's glare. The elastic waistband of my homemade pink polyester pants cut into my skin, and the round white buttons of the matching short-sleeved jacket tugged at my breast line. I was an Egyptian mummy in a tomb—bound, gagged, powerless.

I turned on my side. The pillowcase underneath my head was scratchy from too many washings, and it carried the strong smell of disinfectant.

I glanced over at the empty bed next to mine, and then rolled over to face the wall. The twin bed seemed narrower than my bed at home. I didn't move, playing possum, when Betty came into the room.

"You asleep, Lani?" Betty sat on the edge of her bed and I heard her unbuckle the straps of her leather sandals.

"No, I'm not sleeping. But it's just as well since you'd wake up the dead with all the noise you're making." I rolled over to face her. I avoided Betty's eyes and glanced down at the floor. Betty's ankles had swollen to the size of a can of green beans, and her fat toes were painted the same pretty pink as her nails.

"Listen, don't be so touchy. I know it's your first night here, but don't take it out on me." Betty crossed her left leg over her right knee and rubbed a swollen foot with both hands. "We're in the same boat. Well, maybe not exactly the same boat. When are you due again?"

"August."

"That's right, August, and this is what? March?" Betty switched legs and began rubbing the right foot. "Suit yourself, but you better learn to get along with people, or you're gonna be one mighty unhappy camper."

I didn't like it, but Betty was giving good advice. I got off the bed, opened my suitcase and took out my mother's nightgown. I turned my back to her, trying to undress with a modicum of modesty.

Betty's voice drifted over my shoulder. "You're making more work for yourself."

"What do you mean?" Underneath the polyester top, I tugged at the clasp on my bra, until I remembered I was supposed to leave it on.

"Well, take it from me, before this is over, you'll have a lot of strange hands in you and on you. You're going to have to get over being a Miss Priss."

I turned to face her. Almost defiantly I unbuttoned the top of my pantsuit until it gaped open exposing my plain white bra cupping ample breasts.

Betty laughed. "You do realize it's only six-thirty. Didn't Mrs. York tell you? We're not allowed in our jammies until eight o'clock."

I sat back on the bed. "What kind of rule is that?"

"They might tell you that they don't want us laying around in bed feeling all depressed. But mainly they want us to know who's boss." She slipped her feet back into the sandals and leaned over to buckle them. She groaned on the way back up. "Do you smoke?" Betty picked a pack of Virginia Slims from off the nightstand and held it out to me.

I shook my head.

"No matter. You can sit out there with us if you want. Tomorrow you'll meet with the Powers-that-Be, but you'll find out more of the real dirt on the porch."

I buttoned the white circus ring buttons, slipped my feet back into my loafers, and followed her out the door.

Outside the air was sticky and smelled sweet like Hershey's chocolate syrup poured out on vanilla ice cream. About eight girls, clumped in groups of two or three, leaned against a wrought iron railing that surrounded the porch on three sides. From there I could tell we were situated above the rec room downstairs, overlooking an inner courtyard.

"Hey, Betty," a girl called out. "You brought fresh meat."

The tall, skinny girl had hair so black it could only come from a bottle, and it was teased so high at the crown it looked like a diadem. Thick eyeliner came to a sharp point in the corner of each eye giving her the cat-eyes of a Jezebel. After taking a deep drag on her cigarette, she threw the still burning butt to the porch and ground it under her heel. She was trying hard to play it cool, but it seemed a bit ridiculous when, judging by her belly, she was at least six months pregnant.

"So, who'd you fuck to get here?" she drawled in a high nasal voice.

I turned around to head back to my room. "Nice to meet you, too," I said over my shoulder.

From across the porch, Betty shot words in my direction like bullets. "Don't mind her, Janice. She's got her ass on her shoulders."

"Hey, don't be so touchy." The skinny girl's words reached me before I reached the door, and I turned around. She held out a packet of Newports. "Sorry. That was a lousy introduction. I'm Janice. Want a menthol?"

I shook my head. "No thanks, I don't smoke."

Janice laughed. "Well, I didn't either when I got here. Amazing what you'll do when you're bored out of your skull."

I shrugged. "Yeah, I guess."

Betty came over, and she lit another cigarette. "You two making nice?"

"Sure." The night air was moist and velvety, but I felt cold, and I wrapped my arms around my shoulders.

Janice took a long drag on a new cigarette. "You'll get used to us eventually. But form no attachments. I've been here six weeks, girls come, and girls go. Just a bunch of ships passing in the night."

The embers on her cigarette burned bright, the color of the red planet. I looked up, but no stars were visible in the night sky. "When's your baby due?" I asked.

"In three weeks." Janice flicked some ash over the rail and into the courtyard below. "Yeah, I know, I'm small to be in my ninth month, but I'll be back to my pre-preggers weight in no time."

Betty nudged Janice's arm. "And back to doing what got us here, too, I bet."

Janice's smile was sly. "Maybe. Jim that son of a bitch can go to hell for all I care, but who knows what'll happen. Get a good job, save up some money, move away from Shelbyville. Go to college in a couple of years." The corners of her mouth froze. "A year from now I won't even remember what happened here."

The moisture in the air felt like it weighed a ton—no, every particle of hydrogen and oxygen weighed ten tons, and I was carrying them all around my neck. My head and back ached, and I wanted to crawl into bed and not move.

"Betty, I'm going back to the room. I had to get up really early this morning, and I'm just beat."

I turned to leave, reached the door, and then came back to where Janice and Betty were standing. "Listen, I'm sorry I was such a pain before. Don't worry about bothering me when you come in."

I don't know who I missed the most—Dayna, Randall or my mother. What I wanted, what I desperately needed was a hug—a great big, never-let-me-go hug; a lay-my-head-on-your-shoulders hug; a go-ahead-cry-your-eyes-out hug, but I didn't know who or how to ask for one.

Deep in the night, the sound of crying entered my dreams. I was on a ship, and its masts creaked from the force of the wind. A raging storm with twenty-foot gales rocked the boat from side to side. I couldn't get my balance; I was slipping, falling on the deck. Then the sails ripped, and I was afraid the main mast would soon break into the sea. I woke with a start. A baby was wailing down the hall. In the bed next to me, Betty was sobbing.

"Betty, you OK?" I asked quietly.

"Yeah, this just stinks." She choked on her words, and then took two deep breaths. "Every night the babies in the nursery cry. Maybe they're hungry or they want to get held, maybe they got gas and need burped, maybe they need their diapers changed, I don't know, but they cry, and cry and it never stops. It just breaks my heart to think about leaving my baby here."

The bed creaked as Betty rolled over to face me. Her voice sounded less hesitant. "You know, I had two abortions before I came here. The doctor said I might not be able to have kids if I had another one, so my mom sent me here. But I don't know if I ever want a baby after this. I don't think I could ever stand to hear it crying."

"Want a hug?" I asked in a whisper.

"Naw, I'm fine. How you doin'?"

"OK, I guess." I heard the stiff sheets scrape against each other as Betty rolled away from me.

I remembered the T. S. Elliott poem we read in Mrs. Massenger's class right after I found out I was pregnant.

> *So runs my dream: but what am I?*
> *An infant crying in the night:*
> *An infant crying for the light:*
> *And with no language but a cry.*

Newborn babies in the nursery crying in their cribs. Pregnant girls crying in their single beds. Sometimes we have no words for loss. I had never really thought about what the loneliest sound in the world might be, but that night, I heard it, and it never, ever left me.

The Powers-that-Be

At breakfast, I was at Mrs. York's table again. Cheryl, the girl I met yesterday in the nursery, sat next to me so I had one friendly face nearby. Betty was across the room, laughing like she didn't have a care in the world. Remembering her sobs from the previous night, I knew differently.

Just like dinner, breakfast was a family style affair. Each table held a little bit of everything and the girls and staff, if they were present, passed overflowing bowls and platters from left to right. I was in no danger of starving. In fact, it looked like they were trying to fatten us up. From the nearby kitchen girls traipsed back and forth, and that morning they carried bowls of oatmeal and scrambled eggs, platters of toast, pitchers of milk. Cheryl handed me a lumpy substance of indeterminate origin. It looked like institutional gruel in a Dickens novel, and I stared at her wide-eyed.

"Lani," she laughed. "Don't y'all have grits where you come from?"

I shook my head, placed a small amount on my plate, and watched as the others added butter, salt and pepper. I followed suit, hoping the added flavor would make the grits more palatable, but it didn't. The smallest bite made me gag, and this time I knew it wasn't from morning sickness.

Talk around the table was light-hearted. Plans to walk down to Woolworth's. The latest project in the crafts room. What pieces were coming out of the kiln later that day. No one talked about boyfriends or families or the reason we were there. Mrs. LaPrairie, the Sellers director, sounded like someone I should stay away from. Out of Mrs. York's hearing, I heard her referred to in whispered tones as the Powers-that-Be. Betty had called her that before we went out on the smoking porch. I didn't know what it took to run a maternity home, but whatever it was, Mrs. LaPrairie had it. She kept everyone's knickers in knots.

Mrs. York's powers of hearing were either greater than anyone suspected, or she was a mind reader. Before she left the table, she leaned over to speak with me. "Lani, finish your breakfast, and head straight to Mrs. LaPrairie's office. It's on the other side of the front room. Don't worry. She won't bite."

Sellers was a built like a large rectangle with a square cut out of the middle for an inner courtyard. Downstairs on the left side of the courtyard was the Living Wing with our rec room and a meeting room that also served as our chapel. The dining room and kitchen were across the back of the building. In the front was the formal reception area where my father had left me the previous day. To the right side of the courtyard the Working Wing held administrative offices, an examination room, and at the end of the hallway a couple of one-person bedrooms for girls who had delivered their babies and were waiting to go home.

Sometime during my introductory tour Mrs. York relayed that it wasn't safe for newly delivered girls to climb the stairs. The doctors believed it could cause complications, and so post-delivery the girls stayed downstairs. The living side was filled with people all hours of the day and into the night; on the working side, folks only showed up for regular office hours—nine to five, Monday through Friday. I wondered if the just-delivered girls felt deserted at night but knew I would discover it for myself soon enough.

I dawdled on my way to Mrs. LaPrairie's office. I hadn't done anything wrong, but I felt like I was being called on the carpet. Sent to the principal's office. I was a good student, often the teacher's pet, and in high school I had only gotten in trouble once. That was my sophomore year when Randall, Buzz, Lori and I skipped school on May Day, took a bus to Norman and hung out on the South Oval. First period the following day, Mr. Adler called us down to his office for a severe talking-to. No suspension, not even a threat of one, but lots of forced guilt and shaming. "How could you? What kind of an example are you setting? We expect more from you." Blah, blah, blah.

When I passed through the formal living room and opened the double doors that led to the Working Wing, I saw Miss Doucet at a desk just outside Mrs. LaPrairie's office.

"Hello, Lani, finding your way around?" She looked up from an electric typewriter and smiled. Her voice was as pretty as it had been the day before, but now I noticed she had a bit of an overbite that gave her face a horsey expression.

"Mrs. York said Mrs. LaPrairie wanted to see me after breakfast."

"Sure, just knock, and she'll call you in." Miss Doucet started typing again, and I continued the few steps down the hall to Mrs. LaPrairie's closed office door. There was a fancy nameplate on it. *Mrs. Allegra LaPrairie, Director*.

To my ears, Allegra sounded like a musical term. "Hello, I'm Adagio." "Pleased to meet you, Adagio. I'm Allegra, let me introduce my friend, Fortissimo."

I was sure with a name as pretty as Allegra, Mrs. LaPrairie couldn't help but be nice. All that Powers-that-Be stuff was just a load of hooey. As my Memaw would say, some folks can gripe with a ham under each arm.

My first knock was tentative, almost as if I had never knocked on a door before. I was nervous, and it felt like the butterflies in my stomach had gotten all liquored up. I knocked again, this time a little louder.

"Come in." The voice was soft and lilting, like silver bells rung by the Salvation Army Santa Claus outside the doors of Montgomery Ward. Clearly, Mrs. LaPrairie had a voice as lovely as her name. I pushed the door open and walked into a room of white. White carpet, white furniture. A clear glass vase of white flowers perched on an empty desk with Mrs. LaPrairie behind it.

Mrs. LaPrairie didn't stand when I entered the room. She didn't even bother to look up from the book she was reading. Her hair was white like the rest of her office, pulled tight behind her head in a chignon. It was hard to tell her age. She was older than my mom, she might even have been as old as my grandmother, but her skin was unlined except in two places. The first was a deep crease in the middle of her forehead, and she had wrinkles on either side of her mouth that kept it pinched in a forever frown.

"Good morning, Mrs. LaPrairie." I stared at my feet, fighting the urge to shuffle back out the door. I felt underdressed in my first store-bought maternity outfit—green polyester pants and a black and green plaid shirt with black grosgrain ribbon around the neck and sleeves.

"Please take a seat, Lani." Mrs. LaPrairie closed her book and motioned to one of two high-backed chairs in front of her desk.

The chair was upholstered in milk-colored fabric with pale blue scenes of eighteenth-century picnics and hayrides where courting couples mingled, and peasants picked apples. I sat on the edge and crossed my legs at the knees.

"Lani, young women of good breeding *do not* sit with knees crossed."

Without warning, the tinkling sleigh bells I thought I heard earlier in Mrs. LaPrairie's voice disappeared into the piercing air raid that disturbed the silence of my hometown every day at noon. Mrs. LaPrairie's bearing was imperious, regal. I quickly uncrossed my legs and stared at the hands in my lap. Lying in bed the previous night, I had ripped some of the cuticles out with my teeth, and the left thumb was red and looked infected. I was sure the hands were my hands, but they looked unfamiliar.

"Thank you, Lani, much better." Mrs. LaPrairie smiled with such effort I worried that her face might crack.

"Welcome to Sellers. I trust you are finding your way around."

I looked up from the ragged cuticle long enough to meet her severe gaze. "Yes, ma'am. Mrs. York gave me a tour yesterday. She's been real helpful."

Mrs. LaPrairie was impeccably dressed in a gray business suit and mauve silk blouse. As I glanced back down at my hands, I took a quick peek under the desk. Even in the sticky early morning heat and humidity, she wore stockings and high heels.

"Good, Lani, glad to hear it. Now, as to why you are here and what is expected of you. It may seem like you made a mess of your life, but at Sellers we are dedicated to helping you rebuild it."

I heard a strange buzzing in my ears. It wasn't the sound of a swarm of bees—it was more like the sound of wind in the trees at my Aunt Ruby's farm when the siren would send us scurrying for the storm cellar.

I couldn't look Mrs. LaPrairie in the face; I had trouble paying attention.

"We provide you with complete confidentiality. You can fully count on the discretion of our staff. Our only aim is to have you return to your home to live happily as a good citizen and a good Christian."

I knew I needed to stay present, so I would occasionally nod my head in agreement.

"Relinquishing your baby is the only choice in cases like yours. Rest assured that I am here to help you plan soundly for the future of your baby." Her voice was sharp as she launched into a long list of Sellers dos and don'ts.

I found it far too easy to slip away in my mind, so I decided to focus on her chest. Mrs. LaPrairie's blouse had a built-in cravat, and in the center at the base of her throat she wore a pin the shape of fleur-de-lis, inset with sapphires.

My family was working class—we couldn't rub two nickels together most of the time. My mother had one piece of fancy jewelry, a star sapphire ring my dad brought back from Thailand, which she wore on special occasions. Mrs. LaPrairie's sapphires were the color of the deep dark water surrounding Monet's lilies. My mom's sapphire was the steely blue-gray of Oklahoma skies when a tornado is coming.

Everything about Mrs. LaPrairie looked expensive. The chair I was sitting on, her fleur-de-lis pin, her impeccably made-up face. Ever class conscious, I often felt cowed and angry around the rich.

"Lani, I asked you a question. Do you understand what is expected of you here?"

I realized I hadn't heard a word Mrs. LaPrairie had said for the past few minutes. Someone else at Sellers needed to explain the dos and don'ts.

I nodded. "Yes, ma'am."

The wind roaring between my ears lessened when she mentioned school. Margaret Haughery School for Expectant Mothers. "Attendance is up to each individual girl. We will not force you to go, and we cannot hold your hand. Your social worker, Mrs. Stafford, will help you get enrolled if that is your decision. You can go see her now."

With that I was dismissed. Mrs. LaPrairie looked down at some papers on her desk, and from that vantage point I could tell her hair was thinning on top.

Mrs. Stafford's office was around the corner and down the hall. Through the open door I saw a large bookcase crammed full of books, folders and tchotchkes of every stripe. The plain wooden desk faced the hallway, and she smiled as I walked up.

"Hi, Lani, I'm Mrs. Stafford, your social worker. Please come in." The woman behind the desk stood and held out a perfectly manicured hand. Pink nails the color of cotton candy at the state fair. It seemed a somewhat formal gesture given the circumstances, but I shook it anyway.

"Nice to meet you, ma'am."

She beckoned to the chair in front of her. "Are you settling in all right? Starting to find your way?"

This time, determined to show I was a product of a good upbringing, I pulled the back of my blouse down over my butt, and sat, crossing my left ankle behind my right and pointed clenched knees in what I believed to be the direction of the Mississippi River. "Yes, ma'am."

Mrs. Stafford was much younger than Mrs. LaPrairie. Her face was kind and she had Marilyn Monroe curves and blonde hair—though this blonde, the color of new-mown hay, was not from a bottle. Aryan in every way except her eyes. Instead of blue, she had hazel eyes like mine, with gold flecks shining like the sun. Unlike Mrs. LaPrairie's office—stark, empty, white—Mrs. Stafford's desk was covered in papers, photographs, and an

IBM Selectric, much like the one used in my typing class sophomore year, sitting front and center.

"I understand you want to go to school."

Her velvety drawl was Southern but not twangy. Most certainly not from New Orleans. Or Texas, Arkansas, or Mississippi for that matter. Since the girls at Sellers came from all over, I quickly learned there wasn't a single way to talk southern.

"Yes, ma'am. I aim to go to school. It's real important I get all my credits for this year. Otherwise I won't be able to graduate with my class."

"Did Mrs. LaPrairie explain the situation?"

Mrs. Stafford appeared to be looking out the door to something or someone in the hallway. I heard sharp voices, the sound of a girl crying. Ever the nosy parker, I had to struggle with Jacob's angel to keep from turning around. "Yes, ma'am. She said I'd go to a special school. Margaret Haughery, she said."

The worry line in Mrs. Stafford's brow lessened and she redirected her gaze at me. "Yes, the school system here isn't set up to accommodate pregnant teenagers. They're not equipped to handle any medical emergencies that might arise."

"Yes, ma'am."

"Margaret Haughery also enrolls young women who've delivered their babies."

"Yes, ma'am."

I sounded like a parrot. Yes ma'am, no ma'am. Ever dutiful, as if I was without a single original thought in my head. Growing up an Air Force brat, I was required to answer my elders like that. A simple response "yes" was met by my father's "yes what?" And then it was "yes, ma'am" or "yes, sir" or we'd get backhanded mighty quick. Heaven forbid we ever responded with "yeah."

The crying in the corridor started up again. I couldn't tell what was being said, but the distress in the voice was palpable. Mrs. Stafford got up to close the door. She sat in the chair next to mine. "Lani, this probably seems overwhelming. I'll take you to school on Thursday and help get you enrolled. We have transcripts from your high school. But you have to realize they can't offer all the classes you were taking at Moore."

"Yes, ma'am."

"And it's not what you're used to I'm sure. The schools in New Orleans are integrated. Do you understand what that means?"

No black families lived in Moore, but I wasn't brought up to be prejudiced. Once, my dad brought a black airman and his wife home after work, and Mr. Parker from across the street yelled, "John, get those n—— out of our neighborhood." My dad yelled right back at him, "Devlin, their shit smells the same as yours." We were more shocked at hearing my dad cuss than at having black people over for dinner.

"Yes, ma'am. I understand what integrated means."

"And you still want to go?"

"Yes, ma'am. I'm determined to finish the year out."

Mrs. Stafford sighed. "As long as you understand the situation. The school is on the other side of town. I'll drive you on Thursday, but after that you'll need to make your own way there. It could take up to an hour each way. Any questions?"

"Do any other girls go to school?"

"No, you're the only one." Mrs. Stafford stood up and walked back around to sit behind her desk. "At Sellers each girl decides for herself what she wants to do about her education. Still up for it?"

"Yes, ma'am."

"Ok, then. I'll see you Thursday after breakfast."

When I reached the door, I stopped and turned back around. "Mrs. Stafford?"

"Yes, what is it, Lani?" Mrs. Stafford was looking down at some papers on her desk, but she raised her head and her eyes held mine.

"Last night Mrs. York gave me a tour. We went into the nursery." I hesitated.

"Yes?"

"Well, there was a little boy there who was almost two. Mrs. York said he has a heart murmur and can't be adopted." I looked down at my hands and started picking at the cuticle again, another nervous habit that well-bred young women should never take up. "It just seems wrong, somehow. Different caregivers every few hours, the girls who watch him changing every few weeks or months." Mrs. Stafford's eyes felt as if they could bore a hole right through me. "What if something's wrong with my baby? I don't want him to waste away in a crib at Sellers. Would you tell me so I could come back and get him?"

The gold flecks which had lit up Mrs. Stafford's hazel eyes earlier now fell through the center of the earth and disappeared. "Lani, Jason is none of your concern. Now excuse me, I've got work to do."

The third and final person I was instructed to see was Miss Popwell, the head nurse. Her office was down the hall next to an examining room. A cross between Mrs. LaPrairie's office and Mrs. Stafford's, the desk was devoid of any clutter, except for a single picture in a frame, but the bookcase behind her was filled with all sorts of books. Heavy medical textbooks, slender volumes of poetry.

Miss Popwell had the most beautiful brown eyes I had ever seen. I felt like I was looking into a deep, dark well, empty and bottomless. She had brown hair, too, lighter than her eyes by at least eleven shades. She wore it short, much shorter than anyone I knew back home, except my mom, though she would never think of going out in public like that. Because she had a bad case of dry scalp, she always covered her hair with a wig.

Miss Popwell had just a touch of gray at her temples and although she was tall, everything about her was small—small teeth, small hands; her breasts were almost nonexistent. She wore comfortable and unfussy clothing. Black polyester knit pants, a white short-sleeved sweater with a matching cardigan that hung across the back of her chair. The skin of her hands was red and chafed, but the fingers looked strong. The veins on the back of her hands bulged electric blue.

Without giving me a chance to sit down, Miss Popwell started speaking rat-a-tat-tat.

"OK, Lani, here's the drill. You'll take a pre-natal vitamin every morning with breakfast. You have to drink a glass of milk with every meal you eat here. Once a week we'll get your weight and blood pressure. Once a month the doc will come, and we'll check the baby. Listen for the heartbeat and how much your belly's grown. But unless there's a problem like bleeding, you won't need a pelvic exam until the last month and then we'll check you every week. I understand you're planning on going to school. I've never been there myself, but I understand it's a ways away. You still getting morning sickness?"

"Yes, ma'am, but not too bad."

"The best thing you can do is eat saltines. Carry them with you in your purse."

"Yes, ma'am, that's what my mama told me."

"Well, your mama's right. You should always listen to your mama. Now, there's a nurse on duty twenty-four hours a day. And I live right next door in the yellow house. It's above the crafts room. You been over there yet?"

"No, ma'am."

"After lunch, come over for a visit. Meet my cat, Tigger. I've got a porch in the back off the kitchen. I'll show you around the crafts room. It's really Mrs. York's domain, but I've been known to find my way around a pot or two."

I don't know what it was about Miss Popwell that captivated me. Maybe it was her eyes, which held me and drew me in; maybe it was the no nonsense tone of voice that stayed soft and without an edge. Maybe it was because she was a nurse, and someone who was there to care for me. All I knew was that for the first time since arriving at Sellers I believed I had found someone I trusted.

Forget-Me-Nots

On Friday I moved to my permanent room. "Hi. I'm Lani." I stood outside the bedroom doorway, holding my green suitcase in one hand, and my coat and purse in the other. "I'm your new roommate."

"Well, don't stand on ceremony. Come on in." The girl in the corner bed against the wall waved her hand, inviting me into the room. "We know who you are. Sometimes I pay attention when Mrs. York is speaking. Not always, but sometimes." The thickness of her southern accent surprised me. Betty, coming as she did from Texas, had an accent similar to my own.

"So, which one do you want?" The other girl, also in a corner but underneath one of the two windows in the room, had a voice right out of Hee Haw. She pointed at two empty beds. "That one's right next to the bathroom. Are you still getting morning sickness?"

"Yes. I'm usually okay if I keep saltines close by. As my Memaw always says, 'Better sure than sorry.'"

I dropped everything on the bed, thankful that it was under a window *and* close to the bathroom. I scanned the room. This would be my home away from home for the next six months. The walls were covered in a bright, floral pattern much like the small blue flowers on my mother's everyday housecoat. I recognized the room as the one we had visited on our tour last summer. The flowers weren't bluebells. They were forget-me-nots.

In each bedroom, every girl had a closet for some hanging clothes with a few drawers at the bottom for underwear, pajamas, t-shirts and polyester pants with forgiving stretchy panels. I hung up the coat I was wearing when I left the Oklahoma winter, and never wore it again during my time there. I learned all too well, "This is New awlins y'all, and it is damn hot."

I glanced across the room at the shorthaired girl lying back in the bed catty-corner to mine. "If we're not standing on ceremony, or sitting in your case, then who are you? Apparently, I wasn't paying attention when Mrs. York made her introductions."

The girl's cropped hair was the color of scrub oak leaves left in autumn to rot at the side of the road. Hair-coloring boxes call it ash, certainly a kinder description than rotting leaves. Ash, soot left behind at a youth group wienie roast, mixed in with brown. The girl was slender, no hips to speak of, with narrow shoulders. Without a baby belly she easily could have passed for a boy.

"I'm Jo. I come from Vicksburg, Mississippi."

The longhaired girl sitting on the bed next to mine piped up. "I'm Georgina. Georgie for short. But it's not my real name. I just like the way it sounds."

Georgie smiled; her mouth wide-open displayed top teeth slightly crooked. Something quick and light about her reminded me of a sparrow. I had seen her around the home the last couple of days; she would have been difficult to miss. She hardly seemed to touch the earth as she walked. Her most amazing attribute, however, was her hair, thick and curly, which reached way, way down below her butt. It looked like it had never been cut. Like Jo, Georgie's hair was brown, but hers was rich and dark like the color of ground cloves.

"Oh, and I'm from Star City, Arkansas." Georgie picked up a handful of hair and started to chew on the ends. "I'm fourteen. My baby is due in July."

"Oh." I was taken aback by this revelation. Fourteen? Holy Moly, how did she ever get in this predicament?

"Well, I'm seventeen, and I'm from Moore, Oklahoma."

Jo stood up and walked toward the bathroom. "Sorry, a girl's gotta pee when a girl's gotta pee."

Over the next few hours and days and weeks we learned a lot about each other. I had already heard about Vicksburg, a mid-sized town in Mississippi not too far from New Orleans, right on the Mississippi River. Cheryl, the nice girl from the nursery, hailed from Vicksburg, and she and Jo even went to the same Baptist church. They knew each other only in passing though, since Cheryl was almost twenty and in college. Jo described Vicksburg as beautiful, with streets lined with magnolia trees and southern mansions. Azaleas of all colors bloomed in spring, and the magnolias flowered into the summer.

Jo was fifteen and a freshman in high school. Her parents arranged for her to keep up with her assignments from school; every week a packet arrived filled with Geometry worksheets and lessons in Civics. The story they told everyone was that Jo was recuperating from a contagious disease at her great-aunt Alma's. She showed up to Sellers a few weeks before me, and her baby was due in late June.

Jo was definitely the boss of our room, even though she was almost two years younger than me. In that respect she reminded me of my sister Kathy, who, in our band of four sisters, always ruled the roost. Jo could only tolerate so much of anyone. Lots of people got on her nerves, and she had no problem letting them know it.

Like me, Jo was still in love with the father of her baby. His name was Danny and he was also a freshman. Everyone involved in both families believed Jo and Danny were too young to get married and care for a child. In Jo's case it made sense since she was fifteen and just finishing up ninth grade. Since I was seventeen, it was hard for me to believe that Randall and I couldn't have managed our senior year somehow but dwelling on that didn't do me any favors. I kept reminding myself of what everyone said: I was unfit to be a mother; adoption was the best thing I could do for my baby. Keeping my child would be pure selfishness.

Georgie had just turned fourteen and was the youngest resident of Sellers. She should have been finishing up eighth grade, but she wasn't in school and she didn't get class work from home. She wasn't worried about being held back, though. Her hometown in Arkansas had fewer than five hundred residents, and Georgie said more people were in a bother about forced bussing than anything else. Lots of people from town were keeping their kids home from school. Her parents were divorced, and she lived with her mom. The father of her baby, Larry, was almost twenty-two and married. When they started going out, Georgie thought he would get a divorce and marry her, at least that was the story hinted at in the back seat of his car. Then his wife got pregnant, and he made a quick about-face. Like a good Baptist, he told Georgie he was in his marriage for better or worse until death. It didn't matter who got hurt.

Georgie was young in other ways. She kept a big stuffed dog on her bed and slept with it at night. She said Larry had won it for her at the State Fair the previous September when they first started dating. I didn't understand why this asshole wasn't arrested for statutory rape, but I never criticized him in front of Georgie, who defended him at every turn, "Really, he's a good guy. Everyone in town looks up to him."

Jo loved magazines and her nightstand was covered with stacks and stacks of *Teen Magazine* and *Tiger Beat* and *Young Miss*. When she finished devouring them from cover to cover like a snake swallowing its food, she left them in the rec room for everyone else to read. I had the right of first refusal, but I could not have cared less what Bobby Sherman and David Cassidy were doing. I never saw Georgie read anything. She spent hours upon hours watching television. Sellers offered only a few other diversions, and in the craft shop next door, Georgie made ashtrays for Christmas gifts. She tried her hand at some paint-by-number kits, and she propped up the final products on her nightstand. A kitten playing with a ball of yarn. A canoe on a placid lake. Mostly, though, Georgie liked animal coloring books. She had one of the big 64-crayon boxes. At home I helped my brother Billy with his coloring. He liked cowboys and Indians, and he was partial to brown. Brown horses, brown leggings, brown hats. Since he never wanted variety, I don't think we ever owned a box bigger than 24 crayons. It was fun to color with Georgie. I could use periwinkle, aquamarine, or blue violet, even on a zebra.

As promised, I wrote to my mother right away.

March 5, 1971

Dear Mama,

I've been here five days now and I'm through the probation period. They've moved me into my permanent bedroom. It's real pretty with walls covered in blue-flowered wallpaper, much like the ones on your housecoat.

They've also assigned me some chores to do every day. All the girls have jobs until their last month. Of course, some girls don't come until the end of their term, so they get out of it all together. No matter. I don't mind doing my fair share.

I've been assigned to help cook in the kitchen. It's quite a bit different fixing food for thirty mouths than helping you at home, but I'm learning some new recipes. First off, we cook a thing called grits every morning. It's really nothing more than corn meal mush and why anyone would want to eat it for breakfast is beyond me. But we make oatmeal every day, too, so I'm happy.

G is the girl in charge of the kitchen (we're only supposed to use initials to protect each other's privacy). Anyway, G is real sweet and not bossy at all. Her baby is due in May. She's a senior in high school—from Georgia—but she's going to finish up in summer school and not bother going to school here. In fact, I'll be the only one going to school. I'm a bit nervous about getting there on my lonesome since it's on the other side of town, but Mrs. Stafford is going with me the first time, and I'm sure I'll manage after that. Speaking of Mrs. Stafford, I gotta run. I've got another meeting with her in a few.

Give the girls and Billy a big hug for me.

I love you. Please don't worry.

As always,

Lani

My new roommates, Jo and Georgie, seemed so different from me, and I hoped we could be friends. But I knew they would never take the place of Dayna. Dayna and I had been joined at the hip for more than four years. Before Randall came along, we did everything together. In 9th grade, when our Jr. High marching band played at the Oklahoma State Fair in September, we were excused from school for the entire day, and Dayna and I rode on the merry-go-round, oohed and aahed over handmade quilts, and got a sugar high from eating too much cotton candy. Later that fall we purchased tickets in advance for the movie *Funny Girl* as a surprise for our mothers. The screening was at the State Theater in downtown Oklahoma City, and I had never been anywhere so palatial. All four of us got all gussied up in stockings and heels. It was the best Christmas present I ever gave my mom. The following Christmas, just for a hoot, we stood in line with cranky children and their stressed-out parents just to drape ourselves on the lap of the Montgomery Ward Santa Claus for a photo we would later publish in the school newspaper. In the spring my mom drove us to Stillwater to see Three Dog Night—our first rock concert.

Besides being in band together, we loved journalism, and in ninth grade we were reporters on the *Lion's Cub*. David was the editor and Kip covered sports although he didn't have an athletic bone in his body. We started the year with a celebrity for a teacher, Mrs. Mae B. Axton, famous in some circles for writing the song "Heartbreak Hotel," Elvis Presley's first big hit. Mrs. Axton had even met Elvis Presley—been to his house and everything. She told us lots of stories of hanging out at the Grand Ole Opry, and to hear her tell it, she ran in rarified circles of other illustrious country singers. Her son, Hoyt Axton, was a minor celebrity in his own right. He wrote "Joy to the World," made famous by Three Dog Night, and it could have been considered our eighth-grade theme song and anthem.

Mrs. Axton was a total kook. She broke her leg before the start of the school year, and with her left leg in a cast up to her mid-thigh, she draped her arms around unwilling young men as if they were crutches. She was probably in her sixties, but she wore miniskirts, breaking even a teenager's sense of decorum, along with the school dress code. Mid-way through the year, at the State Journalism Awards luncheon held at the University of Oklahoma, when another school was awarded the top honor, she made a scene and forced us to walk out as a kind of "fuck you" to the establishment, and so she was thrown out on her ear. The school replaced Mrs. Axton with someone forgettable, but Mrs. Axton had been an inspiration about what storytelling could be. Dayna and I both signed up for journalism in high school and competed for the spot of Feature Editor at the start of our junior year. I got the position, but I didn't think there were any hard feelings, especially now that I was out of the picture and Dayna could take over for me.

We competed for Randall's affections, too—Dayna even had a crush on him, back in tenth grade before he started dating me. She was upset when she found out we were an item, but decided it didn't matter, no skin off her nose. But she lied when she said she never gave him another thought. After I told her about the baby, we hardly spoke—no more sleepovers, no late-night phone calls, no shopping trips, no more drawn-out lunches in the cafeteria, but I chalked it up to her own pain and distress over my predicament. Here I was, leaving high school just when everything seemed to be going so well for us both. I needed to believe that she was still in my corner, my no-matter-what-happens, I'll-stand-by-you friend. I decided to write to her as if she was still that for me, and I hoped that she would respond with the love and support I needed.

March 5, 1971

Dear Dayna,

I'm here at Sellers now. I'm sorry I didn't get a chance to talk to you before I left. I tried calling, but I'm sure you were busy—you still have your life to lead.

I'm finally settling in, and I'm so glad I've gotten moved into my permanent room. I didn't like my first roommate, B, much. (I'm using initials, because we're supposed to protect each other's privacy.) Any way, B's in college and she always makes fun of me—I guess it's just my goofy personality. She's also from Texas and you know how they can be. She acts like the sun comes up just to hear her crow. My permanent roommates, J and G, are SO much nicer. J is from Mississippi and G is from Arkansas, and as far as I can tell, there's not too much to brag about in either state, except for maybe the azaleas in springtime.

I'm gonna need you to write and tell me what's going on in the world. We don't watch the news much. There's a TV down in the rec room, but it's usually blaring "Get Smart," "Mod Squad," "Mission Impossible," or "Hawaii Five-O." Of course, G always wants to watch "The Partridge Family," but she's only 14, so what does she know? (I know, 14!?!)

I brought the little marble egg you gave me, and it's on the table next to my bed. Every time I see it, I feel close to you.

I'm gonna miss getting out to the movies. We aren't confined to the house during the day, so I guess if I found a theater nearby, I could make a matinee on Saturday or Sunday. I would just hate going alone. Most everyone here doesn't venture out too far.

My social worker, Mrs. Stafford, took me to school yesterday to get enrolled. No school paper, imagine that, but hopefully I can figure something out. I'm worried about losing my credits and not being able to graduate on time. Mrs. York is our housemother, and she's kind, but older than my grandma and a bit out of touch. I love Miss Popwell. She's our nurse and she talks a mile a minute.

We all have to do chores until our last month, and I'm helping out in the kitchen. Washing dishes, scrubbing pots and pans, peeling potatoes. Not too different from home, just for lots more people.

I wouldn't wish this on you in the world, but I so long to have you here. There are so many times in this last week I've needed a shoulder to cry on, someone I can pour out my heart to, but I just have to keep it all bottled up inside. Well, the tears are welling up just writing that, so I better call it a night.

Give Randall a big hug from me.

Your best friend,

Lani

Audubon Park

Saturday morning, I set off with Jo and Georgie on a day trip bound for Audubon Park. This was my first adventure outside the Home since I arrived on Monday, other than the trip I took to school Thursday with Mrs. Stafford. I was surprised at how easy it was to leave Sellers. As long as our chores were done, we could sign out with Mrs. York and take off for who-knows-where as long as we were back in time for supper. Somehow, I had imagined the Powers-that-Be would keep us on a short leash, but maybe they figured we had already committed the gravest sin, and there wasn't much more trouble we could get into.

Even though it was the first week of March, the sky was cloudy with temperatures that hovered in the high eighties. My body wasn't acclimated to the heavy, humid heat, and sweat dripped from every pore in my body. Jo looked as dry as the talcum powder on a baby's bottom, but then she was used to living and breathing in high heat and humidity. Georgie hailed from a small town in the middle of Nowhere, Arkansas with a climate similar to Oklahoma, but she had been in New Orleans for more than a month and gotten used to moving through air that could have passed for mud.

We waited for the St. Charles trolley on neutral ground, what the locals call the wide strip of grass in the middle of an avenue. They also call sidewalks "banquets," and as a lover of words I felt I was learning a new language. Besides grass, the neutral ground on St. Charles held trolley tracks and worn-down patches of dirt made by the feet of waiting passengers. Lucky for us, we had a trolley stop right on the corner of Peniston and St. Charles, only three blocks south of the Home. On Monday, when it was time to head to school, I would take the trolley in the opposite direction downtown to Canal Street.

I took a seat on the right-hand side of the trolley. Jo and Georgie sat next to each other on the bench across the aisle. On the back of the wooden seats in front of us were the carved initials of long-ago lovers.

S. A. + T. M = ♥ 4ever. I wondered if "S" and "T" were still together. Still in love.

I glanced over at my traveling companions, struck by how young they looked, and how pregnant.

The trolley rattled past a large hotel, not even a block from our stop. The glass windowpanes were cracked. Large columns held up a wide veranda, and peeling paint revealed the tattered remnants of a glorious past.

I pointed. "Look, you guys. It's Tara from *Gone with the Wind*."

Jo laughed. "That's no southern mansion. You gotta go to one of the plantations to see that."

I turned to face her. "I don't mean Tara from the beginning of the movie, when it's all fixed up, gleaming white and beautiful. It's more like Tara before intermission when it's ravaged by five years of neglect."

"You have a funny way of talking, Lani." Georgie squinched up an adorable and tiny nose sitting in a sea of freckles.

"What do you mean?" I worried I had offended her in some way. Since we would be roommates for the next three or four months, I really wanted both Jo and Georgie to like me.

Jo leaned over and patted my hand in a motherly fashion. "She means you use some highfalutin words."

"It's just that the porch of the hotel is so grand. But rundown at the same time. Kinda bohemian like. I can just imagine Tennessee Williams sitting up there on the porch, sipping mint juleps. And look over there." I pointed over their shoulders to a gentleman with a cane and a straw fedora waiting for an eastbound trolley. "See the man in the blue seersucker suit with the slanted grin? It's none other than Truman Capote. On his way to the hotel for afternoon cocktails. He'll surprise Tennessee, who's quite sloshed by now. 'Tennessee, my old friend, he'll say, care if I join you?' And Tennessee will slur his words and hold up a half-empty glass. 'It's great to see you, Truman. Pull up a chair.'"

Now Jo and Georgie both laughed at me. "My how you carry on," Jo said. "I haven't the faintest idea what you're talking about."

"*Streetcar Named Desire? Breakfast at Tiffany's?*"

I sighed. There was no reason to pitch a fit just because we didn't read the same books or have the same appreciation for American literature. I laughed with them and shrugged my shoulders. "No matter. It don't make me no nevermind."

Georgie smiled. "Now that's something I understand."

I turned back and stared out the window. I wanted to be a writer someday. Dayna and I always talked about going to work for *The New Yorker* after college, but I wanted more than that.

I wanted to write down all the stories that got caught in the cracks of my brain. All the stories that stirred up the blood in my veins. Like the story about Pretty Boy Floyd. Or when my dad was in a plane over Enewetak, waiting to see what would happen after the hydrogen bomb was dropped. Maybe it was a story as simple as my mom and grandma taking in laundry to make ends meet, or the time they killed a chicken in the front yard just as my school bus pulled up.

Watching those strange and magical streets from the trolley, I felt full of something close to joy, or hope. If I breathed the heavy Gulf air, and drank muddy Mississippi River water, then maybe, just maybe the New Orleans writer magic could happen to me, too, just like Williams and Capote.

The trolley ride to Audubon Park lasted about thirty minutes. St. Charles Avenue was the most charming boulevard in the world. Beautiful homes lined the street, each with its own story to tell. Some houses were ablaze in light, and we could get glimpses through windows of elegant people and crystal chandeliers. Some were ruined palaces with shuttered windows. And in the lost homes shaded by banana trees, the swaying couples were ghosts.

Along the footpath in Audubon Park, massive live oaks dripped with Spanish moss. I imagined them standing sentry for decades, shading all manner of people—children, lovers, seekers, the despondent, and those filled with joy. The park was filled with attractions like a miniature railway, the enormous Whitney Young public swimming pool, swan boats in the lagoons, and a carousel. The park housed the Audubon Zoo, too, but I thought it was a disgrace and an embarrassment to the city. The zoo in Oklahoma City had large, open enclosures that tried to mimic the animals' natural homes. It wasn't the vast plains of the Serengeti or an Arctic ice flow, but the animals could do more than pace back and forth over a few feet. At the Audubon Zoo, animals were packed into tiny filthy cages, even the bigger mammals like bears and lions.

A rickety Tilt-a-Whirl stood near a miniature Ferris wheel. I'm terrified of heights—it's difficult to walk across bridges or look out any window above the second floor—so the Ferris wheel was out. A Tilt-a-Whirl, however, I could do.

"Come on, you guys, let's ride it," I begged Jo and Georgie.

"No way, what are you crazy?" Georgie pouted and sat on a nearby bench.

Jo shrugged her shoulders in her best "don't make me no nevermind" manner, and we both ponied up a quarter and climbed aboard, completely ignoring the admonition against riding it while pregnant or with heart or back problems. Surprisingly, even though I had seen plenty of kids puke on the Tilt-a-Whirl at Springlake, the small amusement park to the east of Oklahoma City, I didn't feel nauseous at all. Spinning, spinning, all the fears that clogged my brain flew out and nestled with the herons on Oschner Island. All I could see was the smile on Jo's face, and for the first time in a long time my laughter felt genuine.

Margaret Haughery

Leaving home in March really screwed up my junior year. The New Orleans school district didn't allow pregnant girls in regular high schools, so instead the district provided a special school, one just for pregnant girls—the Margaret Haughery School for Expectant Mothers. In the early 1800s Margaret Haughery was a beloved New Orleans benefactress referred to as the "Angel of the Delta." Herself an orphan and a widow, she devoted her life to caring for the poor and hungry, and she built orphanages throughout the city. Margaret also knew the pain of losing a child, as her infant daughter died within a few months of her husband.

At least New Orleans had a school for pregnant students. If I had been in Moore, as soon as it became common knowledge that I was pregnant I would have been expelled. I didn't understand why schools ruled that pregnant girls needed to be kept away from other students. Pregnancy isn't contagious. Maybe they thought our big, swollen bellies served as overt reminders of rampant and unrepentant teenage sexuality, and it would be distracting for other students. Didn't they realize that nothing and everything could turn a teenager's thoughts to sex? I didn't go a day without thinking about it at least a gazillion times. And distracting? I got hot and bothered just looking at mini-skirts and hip-huggers plastered on the covers of glossy magazine covers, and I was fit to be tied when these sexy clothes were worn by the warm bodies I passed each day on the streets. Thankfully, mini-skirts and hip-huggers were not allowed on the bodies of the girls at school.

The school itself was a ramshackle collection of three old houses and a couple of outbuildings—each with no more than four rooms. The wood siding was weathered, the paint peeling, and I was sure the slightest wind could knock them over. I was thankful I would be back in Oklahoma before the worst of the hurricane season hit. Back there I only had to worry about the occasional tornado. Hurricane Camille pounded New Orleans in 1969, but two years later signs of her destructive power were everywhere, and folks still said the name with reverence and awe.

Margaret Haughery used one house for administration; the other buildings were for classrooms. The classes were small—maybe eight or ten girls in each—and each class covered multiple grades. Since Margaret Haughery was for all pregnant school age girls in New Orleans, the faculty provided lessons and assignments for freshmen through seniors at the same time. One of the young girls at the school was in sixth grade.

I called Margaret Haughery "MHS" for short, which I found amusing since my old high school was also MHS—Moore High School.

Moore, Moore, school we all adore.
M-O-O-R-E!
Red, royal blue, faithful, always true,
We'll be together whatever the weather
Lions and Lionettes, too.

Unsurprisingly, Margaret Haughery didn't have a mascot, sports teams, or a fight song.

Getting to high school in Moore was a cinch. Some mornings Randall picked me up in his '67 yellow Impala—the scene of many a wild ride and one too many midnight trysts. Sometimes I took the bus with my sister Kathy, and all I had to do was walk out my front door to catch it.

To get to the New Orleans MHS, I walked south down Peniston, past the corner grocery store where neighborhood girls stood outside smoking. They never spoke to my face, but they called out "ho" to my back. Then it was a four-block walk to St. Charles Avenue, where I caught a trolley downtown.

The trolley was always crowded—hot, pungent people on their way to work, or school, or out shopping. Everyone dripped with sweat. Even at eight in the morning, I could feel sweat slip under my armpits, down my neck and between my thighs. The trolley was not only crowded, but the aisles were tight, and the bodies seemed huge and the center was filled with butts overlapping the wooden bench seats. Old ladies grasped packages, businessmen clutched briefcases, shoppers clasped shopping bags. Even though I was only finishing my first trimester, I felt as big as an elephant, and I kept a chokehold on the book bag I held in my lap.

I've always been a big eavesdropper, but on the trolley, I couldn't understand half of what people said. I was sure the other passengers were speaking English, but sometimes it seemed mixed up with French or Cajun, or maybe it was Creole. It didn't matter that I didn't understand enough to carry on a conversation—no one bothered to talk to me directly—so the chorus of voices sang in a cacophonous harmony that could rock me to sleep, and if I stopped paying attention, I might have easily found myself heading around Lee Circle and back to the Garden District.

It took a half hour to get downtown, and on Canal Street I located my bus in a long line of other city buses. Then I climbed onboard, grabbed a seat, and rode for more than twenty minutes to Elysian Fields. From there it was another five-minute walk to reach the school. During the few months I attended Margaret Haughery, I still had morning sickness until mid-afternoon, so I kept my saltines close at hand. I was grateful, however, that I was walking with my pudgy little belly; I couldn't imagine doing it with Amy's eight-month waddle.

I wasn't the only school age girl at Sellers. Of the twenty-four girls—give or take a few depending on who was in the hospital or getting ready to go home—probably 1/3 were teenagers. We were grouped by age in our dorm rooms, and both of my roommates should have been in school. My boss in the kitchen, Glenda, was a senior, too. Most said they could make school up when they got home over the summer, but the unspoken sentiment was that they didn't want to go to school with black girls.

I didn't live around any black people. Not a single black family lived in Moore when I was growing up. But I watched television—it was all on there—the riots, the marches, folks being set upon by dogs and blasted with water, Dr. King's assassination, the ugly rhetoric, stupid Governor Wallace. It seemed to me that most of the nastiness came from the white side of the argument. The black leaders were articulate, eloquent, while the whites, when they weren't covered in hoods, were red in the face, spitting profanities. Regardless of the racial makeup of the student population, I didn't have an option to stay back at Sellers instead of going to school. The girls at Margaret Haughery could have been green for all I cared. Regardless of their skin color, I needed to go and get all the credits I could.

My Memaw always said, "Blessed are those who have low expectations, for they will not be disappointed," and she was right. I didn't expect much from MHS, and I wasn't disappointed. The classes were OK, but not challenging. I took Geometry, History, Earth Science and English, but, unsurprisingly, they didn't offer French or Choir. I could live without those subjects, even though I desperately missed singing, but when the guidance counselor said, "No Journalism," I thought I would die.

I loved journalism. Our first Jr. High teacher, Mrs. Axton, had a passion for rooting out interesting stories, and she made me believe that journalism was a noble profession.

"Lots of great stories out there," she said. "Just dig around and you'll find them."

I couldn't imagine a more courageous way to live my life than by talking to people—rich, poor, black, white, Christian, Jew, American, Russian—listening to their stories and sharing them with the world. With my Pollyanna optimism, I thought if we could only understand that deep inside we were all the same, then maybe the ugly divisiveness would end. The world seemed like it was going to hell in a hand basket, and I was so sick of it all—the Vietnam war, weekly demonstrations, riots burning down cities. I wondered every day what kind of a world my baby would grow up in.

Telling stories helped me stay sane, and I knew I had to keep doing it, even if it was only at Margaret Haughery School for Expectant Mothers. So, after the guidance counselor told me there was no journalism class, I came early to school the following Monday and headed straight to Principal Caffrey's office. The door was closed, and I didn't hear a peep, so I knocked and waited.

"Yes, what is it?"

I pushed the door open and peeked in. Mr. Caffrey was younger than I expected, thin with dark hair that brushed the top of his collar. He looked in my direction, eyes piercing blue.

"Mr. Caffrey, I'm Lani Jo Lassiter. I'm new here. I live at Sellers." My voice was soft and weak. I grabbed courage with another lungful of air and continued. "If I put out an issue of a newspaper four pages long every few weeks, will you give me credit for journalism?"

Mr. Caffrey smiled. His bottom teeth were crooked.

"I'll have to OK it through the district, and I'll need to get one of the teachers to work with you on this, but I think it can be arranged."

Thus, *The Stork's Gazette* was born. I started working on the first issue right away. Favorite baby names, which turned out to be much different than the ones my girlfriends and I imagined for our babies. I, for one, couldn't hear the name "Precious" without thinking of *Lord of the Rings*. I added stories about the teachers—how they ended up at Margaret Haughery helping all of us "troubled" girls. Some articles about nutrition and pre-natal care. A recipe or two, a book review of *To Kill A Mockingbird*. I even faked my way through a column for the love forlorn. Kind of like *Dear Abby*, but for pregnant teens, and named after the voice actor for the stork in *Dumbo*.

Dear Holloway,

I'm sixteen, six months pregnant, and my boyfriend wants to sleep over at my house. My mom says no, but what kind of trouble can I get into? Besides, I'm not even sure if I want to have sex with this big belly. I would really just like someone to cuddle with.

Needing Affection Teen

Dear NAT,

If you're still living at home, then you need to follow the rules of the house. Your mom is providing you with a roof over your head and food to eat. When you are living on your own, you can make your own rules. If affection is what you need, talk to your mom about your boyfriend coming over to watch TV. The couch is a great place for cuddles. Just don't get too carried away and create an embarrassing situation for everyone. Believe it or not, your hormones are raging, and it's easy to have a desire for sex even with a big belly. You may think you wouldn't know how to do it, but where there's a will, there's a way.

Sincerely,

Holloway

I was still waiting for a letter from Dayna. I hadn't heard from anyone back home except for Randall. True to his promise, he did call on Thursday nights, but the conversation never lasted more than three minutes—long distance calls were too expensive. The calls usually went something like, "Hi, how are you?" with the simple response, "I'm fine. How are you?" To anyone listening through the keyhole, it probably sounded more like we were in a first-year language class, learning the most rudimentary way of speaking to strangers. Randall never inquired after my health, or the baby's, and when I wanted the latest gossip from school, he said it was silly and distracting—the very reason I wanted to hear it. I wanted normalcy in my life again, but as each day passed, I began to understand that life as I knew it was never going to be possible. I asked after Dayna, but here again, Randall seemed to find the topic of our other friends too offensive to discuss. I wondered if our happy band had disbanded. Sean was gone and never coming back, I was a million miles away, and Dayna seemed like she had up and disappeared. I tried writing one more time, and decided if I didn't hear back, then I would wait until September for a long and hard heart-too-heart.

March 12, 1971

Dear Dayna,

Two weeks down. This is going to be a long, long six months. Would you believe it? Pregnancy's reached epidemic proportions in New Orleans. We're the mecca of maternity homes. Besides Sellers, there's a VOA home down the block, a Presbyterian home, Methodist, Catholic. Everywhere you look you see pregnant teenagers.

I'm going to be able to keep my journalism credit after all. I'll publish four issues of The Stork's Gazette between now and the end of school. The first issue will be out in a week. I know, I know–it's a cheesy title, but I couldn't think of anything else. It's certainly not as classy as The Lion's Roar, but this school isn't about the Mighty, Fighting Lions; we're just a bunch of pregnant girls trying to get through each day. I'm still working on the first issue, but so far, it's been fun. Of course, I don't get to set type, paste it up, and send the layout to the printer like you do. It's back to typing up mimeograph sheets and running them off in the office.

When I'm not at school, I stay up in my room reading. There's a library about a half a mile away on St. Charles Avenue, and I went there yesterday after school, and got my very own library card. I've decided to work my way through the novels of Thomas Hardy. First up, <u>Far from the Madding Crowd</u>.

No one really talks to me at school, but that's okay. I can spend all of my dead time reading. The girls here are really different, and I don't fit in, so it's best if I keep my head down. I am making a few friends at the Home. There's my roommates J and G (I told you about them in my last letter), and I adore my boss in the kitchen. We've got girls here from all over the south, and I never knew there were so many different southern accents. One of the funniest expressions is "Bless your heart." When you say it, it means that you think the person you're speaking to is a complete and utter idiot.

How is everything there? Wish I could be in Honors English with you. Everything here is too easy. I miss you bunches. Say hi from me to those in the know.

Your Best Friend,

Lani

A. Wilson, Stalker

I had been attending school about three weeks when on one morning ride I caught the bus driver staring at me in the rearview mirror. I could have sworn it happened every time I looked up. At first, I chalked it up to my over-active imagination, but when it happened again and again, I was sure I wasn't imagining it. The guy was really giving me the creeps.

He had a nice enough face, and although he wasn't bald like my father, I was sure he was as just as old. His bus driver's uniform was *so* dorky looking he might as well have been wearing a great big letter "D" on his shirt pocket instead of his name.

A. Wilson.

I wasn't showing, but the clothes I wore were *so* ugly they could only have been maternity clothes. Silly Peter Pan collars, lacy ruffles and big pink bows—maternity clothes made *us* look like babies. I looked like what I was—an unwed teenage mother. He had no reason to be interested in me.

The bus driver glanced at me again, and a shudder ran across my shoulders and down my back. I decided to ignore him like I did most of my problems. What a jerk. My Memaw would have said he was lower than a snake's belly in a wagon rut.

The next morning, A. Wilson was again at the wheel. I avoided his knowing looks in the rearview mirror, and thinking I might throw him off my scent, I got off one stop early. I kept my head down and didn't answer when he called out, "You have a nice day, hear?" As I turned to walk down the tiny residential side street Abundance, the long city bus began to follow me. Under heavy tires, oyster shells crunched like the breaking of a baby bird's bones. I wasn't the last person to get off—there were still lots of folks on the bus—and I couldn't imagine what the other passengers must have been thinking.

The bus seemed to be moving in slow-motion, and I could feel the driver's eyes boring into my back like he had Superman's x-ray vision. What did he want from me? Even though I was fully clothed in a ridiculous maternity outfit, I felt like he could see through my clothes to my bare body. My dry mouth filled with an unpleasant metallic taste. Could it be blood? Heat flushed my neck and face. Nothing more than a featherless, motherless baby bird, I scurried away, still looking down at my feet, fearful of any impediment that might trip me up and keep me on that street. Go away, leave me alone, I screamed in my head, but he kept following me all the way to the school. I entered the administration building breathless. My palms were sweating; I could barely hold on to my books, but I felt safe and relieved.

That feeling was short-lived. When I left school in the afternoon, Mr. A. Wilson sat across the street in a black Mercury, much like the one my father used to drive. He had changed into street clothes and was no longer wearing the dorky bus driver's uniform with his name on the chest.

The car engine was running. He rolled down his window and I could hear the air conditioner fan blowing. He poked his head out of the window. "Let me give you a ride. It's too hot to be out walking."

Clutching the book bag to my chest, I shook my head and bolted back into the building. Like Cinderella fleeing the ball at midnight, I almost lost a penny loafer in my mad dash to the principal's office. This time I didn't bother knocking on the door, and my voice came out in short, sharp pants.

"There's a man following me, Mr. Caffrey. He's sitting in his car outside the school."

Mr. Caffrey quickly stood and came around to the front of his desk. "It's OK, Lani." He pointed to a chair outside the office. "You just sit here while we sort this all out."

The next thirty minutes seemed like two hours. I heard him calling Sellers, speaking to the Powers-that-Be. Then he offered to walk me to the bus stop.

As we exited the main building, A. Wilson sat in his car with the engine still running. He glared at me, and I got the same grave-walking shudder I felt earlier in the day.

Mr. Caffrey took my hand. "Lani, I'll wait with you until your bus comes."

We turned left and walked down the block towards the bus stop. In a few minutes, we heard the car speed off.

When I finally got back to Sellers, Mrs. Stafford told me that she would ride the bus with me on the following day "incognito" to see if he tried to follow me again. At the very least, she would take down his license number and other identifying information and talk with his supervisor.

Calls must have been made to the transit "Powers-that-Be," because Mr. A. Wilson never drove my bus again that spring. Each day when it came time to board the bus on Canal Street, I panicked that he might come back. Yet every day I was able to breathe a sigh of relief. I knew that if I didn't finish out the year, I wouldn't graduate with my class. I didn't even want to begin to think about the ramifications of that. So, come hell or high water, crazy bus driver or no, I had to get to school.

As much as I hated being away from home, I loved New Orleans. I loved its sounds and smells—everything was bigger, brighter, bolder. But sometimes, New Orleans was an ogre squatting on its haunches taking a shit. I felt like a little kid, scared to death, not knowing how in the world I could go out and manage on my own.

Toothpicks

In the dining room a buffet cabinet stood along the wall closest to the kitchen, and it held a fancy set of dishes, tablecloths, silverware. On top, a Suggestion Box sat next to a vase of blue and coral artificial flowers and a bowl of fresh fruit, if week-old mealy apples could be considered fresh. Mrs. LaPrairie read the suggestions once a week, usually Wednesday after lunch.

Most of the time the suggestions were food requests like bacon more often, oatmeal less often, pork chops once a week, Brussels sprouts never. Sometimes there was a suggestion to extend pajama hours on Saturday or to limit tour hours during the week. Every new girl always suggested that they find a way to let us take baths though we were told time and time again that baths could give us an infection. Once in a while a brown-noser would request extra Bible study like "Why don't we read through the book of Job," as if we needed to get more in touch with the "woe is me, what ever did I do to deserve this, shut up and quit complaining, God is with you anyway" crap. At least Esther and Daniel were heroes. Job was simply pitiful. We might as well have been reading through Revelation and contemplating the end of the world. Mrs. LaPrairie feigned empathy for our suggestions, especially the ones that requested more Bible study, but in the few weeks I had been there, nothing ever changed.

One Wednesday after the long commute back to Sellers from school, I went upstairs to my room and plunked my book bag on the bed. I looked over at Jo. She was writing on a piece of tri-fold stationery with brown and gold leaves covering the back and a bright orange pumpkin in the bottom right corner.

"My dogs are barking," I complained, sitting on the edge of the bed and sliding off my penny loafers, pushing toes against the opposite heels. "I think I'm starting to get a blister. Does Mrs. York keep Band-Aids?"

"Don't know. Probably," Jo mumbled.

I picked up my left foot and laid it across my right knee, then pulled off a white anklet. I rubbed my toes. The nails were getting long and ragged.

If I didn't cut them soon, I would have an in-grown nail, and from past experience, I knew it caused pain comparable to Job's boils.

"Your paper's not very spring-like. And shouldn't you be using a book or a magazine instead of your lap? It would make it easier to write."

Jo looked up and finally acknowledged my presence. "What? This? What are you, my mother? I don't care if it's ugly. Someone left it behind in the rec room. Free is good. Besides I'm writing Danny, and he doesn't care what I use as long as I promise to love him forever."

"You're right, sorry. I'm just kinda tired." I switched feet. My left foot looked even worse. I had rough calluses along the bottom of my heels. In Moore I never did much walking. "Anything exciting happen today?"

"Yeah, Mrs. LaPrairie went ballistic over one of the suggestions in the box."

"Really?"

"Yeah, someone asked if we could have toothpicks on the tables in the dining room or at least a dispenser on the buffet. And she just went off on how we were young ladies and she wasn't going to have us picking our teeth in public like some yee-haws. I thought she was gonna bust a gut."

Suggestions were submitted anonymously, so no one knew it was mine, but I could feel my face getting red.

"You all right, Lani? You look flushed."

"I'm fine. Just wishing I could take a nap before dinner, but I gotta get downstairs and cook. What's on the menu?"

"Well, if it's Wednesday, it must be meatloaf. That means you've got potatoes to peel."

"Did you think toothpicks were such a bad idea?"

"Naw, when me and Danny used to go to the Calico Café..."

"Calico Café? We've got one of those in Moore."

"Well, we never left without grabbing a toothpick. I like the mint flavored ones.

"Me too. I never thought about toothpicks being uncouth. Everyone in my family chews on a toothpick after a meal."

"Everyone? Even your grandma?"

I laughed. "Especially my grandma. Didn't you know Okies are nothing but a bunch of yee-haws?"

"Then I guess it's a blessing you were sent here so Mrs. LaPrairie can school you how to be a proper young lady."

Jo always knew how to get me laughing. "You're so right. Every night I thank God and my lucky stars. Now I hear a sack of potatoes calling my name. Say 'hi' to Danny for me. I'll see you at dinner."

Were You There?

A few weeks later, I sat cross-legged on my bed, against a wooden headboard, propped up by two pillows. Keeping a small, white Bible in my hands, I looked up and glanced at my roommate in the bed catty corner from mine. "Jo-Jo, which version of Easter do you think I should use for the pageant?"

Jo was reading the latest issue of *Tiger Beat*. I smiled back at David Cassidy whose luminous chocolate eyes peered out from the glossy cover. Knees bent, Jo stretched back on the blue and white chenille bedspread, and the magazine rested squarely on top of her ample belly.

"What do you mean, which version?" Jo dropped the magazine against her thighs. "There's only one Easter story, right? Jesus dies for our sins on Friday, and then by Sunday he's alive again."

"That's the basic story, but there's four different versions. So, do I work from the story in Matthew, Mark, Luke or John, or do I write something using all four perspectives?" I stuck scrap paper between the thin parchment pages of the Bible, a baptism gift from my grandmother nine years ago, and flipped back and forth between the four gospels, looking for similarities and differences. "This is so frustrating."

I leaned over to the small side table next to my bed and took a small notebook and Bic pen from the top drawer.

"OK, from Mathew, we've got Mary Magdalene, another Mary, guards, one angel, or it could be a man, and Jesus."

Jo shook her head. "Wow, I never knew that about Easter. How can there be four different stories if every word in the Bible is true?"

I switched to the Gospel of Mark and shrugged. "I don't know. That's just the way it is."

Jo shook *Tiger Beat* in my direction. "But Lani, the Bible wasn't written by humans. The Bible's God's own words. He just used people to write it down 'cuz they spoke English."

I laughed and dropped my pen. "Jo-Jo, I don't know how to tell you this, but the Bible wasn't written in English."

Jo scrunched up her face. "Well, Miss Smarty Pants, I know it wasn't written in *our* English. It was written in that other English—what is it?—yeah, Shakespeare English—the one with thees and thous."

I uncrossed my legs, stretched them out along the bed, and shook them on top of the bedspread that was a perfect match to Jo's. I was officially in my second trimester and my belly had a slight visible bump, but I hadn't felt the baby move. I was beginning to feel the effects of the pregnancy in other ways, however. "Whatever you say, Jo. My legs are cramping, and I gotta pee." I set the notebook on its spine between a small desk lamp and the egg made from marble the color of midnight. With its tiny, swirling flecks of silver, it had become my nightly wishing star.

Standing up, I slid my feet into blue terrycloth slippers. They seemed to wait patiently by my bedside much like my collie, Patton, used to do when I was eight, when we lived in my Memaw's house on Chestnut Street. I bent over to pick up the Bic and placed it next to the notebook.

Jo laughed. "Bet you won't be doing that in a month. I can't remember the last time I saw my toes."

"Yep." I began singing, "Bye-bye waist, bye-bye happiness."

When I returned to our room *Ingenue* had replaced *Tiger Beat*, and Jo studied the style feature—"Mini shorts: How and Where to Buy Them." Summer was just around the corner in most of the States, but in New Orleans, summer had already arrived.

I had never worn mini shorts, but I wanted a pair of bright red ones. I could hear my mother's voice inside my head. "Heavens to Betsy, Lani Jo, do you think those shorts come in 3X?" I slipped out of the blue mules and climbed back onto the bed next to my Bible. My belly may not have been big, but my butt and breasts were humungous.

I grabbed the notebook and pen from the top of the nightstand and turned my attention to Luke. "Luke might work. It's got eight people in it."

Jo opened the drawer of her nightstand to cram in the magazine. "How many girls have signed up to do this?"

"Maybe eight. So, Luke would work. I was just hoping to have the resurrected Jesus in the play, too, and he doesn't show up in Luke."

"So, make something up, Lani. It's not like anyone's going to know the difference." Jo stood up and turned to fluff her bed pillow.

"I suppose you're right. It's not like God got His facts straight anyway."

Jo raised her eyebrows. "Lani, I don't think you can say that sort of thing—it's blasp—it's blasp—it's making fun of God. You can go to hell for that, you know."

"You're right, Jo-Jo. I shouldn't blaspheme." I flipped to the fourth Gospel.

Jo stopped by my bedside on her way out the door. "I'm going to the rec room to watch 'Gilligan's Island.' See you later?"

"Sure, I'll be down soon. I'll keep working on the script now, and we can have our first meeting after dinner."

"Sounds fine by me. I'll put a note up on the bulletin board."

After dinner, nine of us gathered around the game table in the rec room.

My eight actors were in various degrees of pregnancy. Amy was due in two weeks. The pageant was Easter Sunday, April 11th—a little more than a week away—so there was a chance we could lose her. If she delivered her baby before we had the pageant, then I would fill in.

"First off, I want to thank you for agreeing to be in this year's pageant." I looked up from my notebook and smiled at the faces around the table.

"You mean they have one every year?" Georgie asked.

"No, I think this is a first, so maybe we're starting a tradition. Or maybe I'm the only one stupid enough to think it's a good idea. No matter. I'm just grateful that you're willing to be part of this production."

I had only been at Sellers a little more than a month, and I was amazed that anyone wanted to help out at all, but with little to do and a lot of time on our hands, we expanded the meaning of a captive audience to include the performers as well.

"Now, does anyone know what time the church service is scheduled to begin? Do we want a sunrise service?"

Unanimous groans erupted from the table. "Oh, my God, no," Jo exclaimed.

Glenda put out her hand to silence the moaning hordes. "Lani, it's bad enough that they make us go to service in the first place. A ten o'clock start will be just fine." Glenda was not the oldest resident, nor had she been at Sellers the longest, but it was apparent from my first day that she was our little mother, like Wendy was to all of the Lost Boys in Peter Pan. If two girls got into a scrap, she was the one we came running to for mediation. When we got a hard letter from home, or we were feeling sad or scared and lonely, she had the perfect ear.

I wrote "No Sunrise Service" in my notebook. "I understand. Ten it is. I was thinking we could have the service out in the courtyard, unless it's raining. We could move the chairs from the chapel. And with the French doors open, we could still hear the piano."

The few girls paying attention nodded. Georgie was distracted by the television. Of course, "Mod Squad," her favorite show.

I referred back to my notes. "I thought we could start first by singing the third verse of "Were You There?" We could even do it a cappella all quiet like."

I pitched my voice soft and low. "Were you there when they laid him in the tomb? Were you there…?"

Before I sang another note, Anita started in with "Oh, O-O-OH, O-O-H" loudly and off-key. "I hate that song."

Amy poked her in the ribs. "Well, it's probably because you sing it like a cat in heat. That's a fine start to the pageant, Lani. What's next?"

"We've got the actual play. There's eight parts, but only four of them speak. So, who wants what?"

Anita piped up before I had even finished speaking. "Well, I ain't talking in this play. Give me one of the silent parts."

Georgie turned her head away from the television. "Give me something where I don't have to talk. I can't memorize for squat."

"You want to be the guards? They don't speak."

Georgie and Anita nodded, and Georgie turned back to "Mod Squad."

I glanced over at Amy. "How about you? If you don't deliver before then, would you mind being Jesus?"

"Those are pretty big shoes to fill. I don't know how believable it's going to be with me in this condition, but I'll give it a shot." She rested both hands on a belly that could hold a dinner plate.

"It'll be fine. Not that I don't wish you out of here sooner, but you'll make a great Jesus."

I looked around at the other girls sitting at the table. "Glenda, if you don't mind, I'll assign you the part of Mary Magdalene since you have red hair; then there's another Mary…"

"Wait a minute." Jo reached up and straightened her headband. "Wasn't Mary Magdalene a whore?"

"No, she wasn't a whore. I looked it up in at the library. The *Encyclopedia Britannica*, in fact, and for your information, she's a saint."

Glenda laughed. "Well, the girls at the corner store call us hoes, so anyone of us could fill the part."

Exasperated I pursed my lips. "We're not whores, or hoes, and neither was Mary Magdalene. Only three things stay the same among all four gospels—Jesus was buried in a tomb, Easter happens at sunrise, and Mary Magdalene was the first person to see him alive."

Jo was the only person I had told about the four different Easter versions, so everyone else looked confused.

"What the fuck are you talking about?" Renee asked. She arrived at Sellers less than two weeks ago, and unfortunately for me, Jo and Georgie, she now occupied the bed across from mine. Her potty mouth was nothing new; she cussed like a sailor. Nevertheless, Cheryl rolled her eyes and covered her ears.

"Renee, there are children present," she laughed. "Oh wait, you're one of the children."

There was always a bit of a rift between the high school girls and the college-age girls, so before Renee left in a huff, I jumped in. "It's a long story, but it doesn't matter. I'm just trying to let Glenda know she has the most important part after Jesus. And back in the Middle Ages, when they painted Mary Magdalene, she had red hair, just like Glenda."

Glenda's hair was the color of the cinnamon I shook out on my oatmeal in the morning, and it cascaded in thick curls to the middle of her back. She took out the rubber band tying her hair back in a ponytail and ran her hands through her penny-colored mane, shaking it out. "I kind of like the idea of playing a ho."

Cheryl sat next to Glenda, and she leaned over to whisper loudly in Glenda's ear. "I bet Dale might like it, too." Dale was the father of Glenda's baby, and as Glenda's best friend, Cheryl could make comments like that. Glenda smiled a Mona Lisa smile.

Cheryl turned to face me. "What do you want me to do, Lani?"

"How about if you're Peter, and Janie, I'll assign you the part of John. Neither one speaks."

"Sure, fine," they chimed in unison.

"I don't care if I have a speaking part," Jo offered. "I can handle it."

"You can be the Other Mary, and Renee, you're the angel. How's that for type casting?"

Renee made a fist and held it up in the air. "Why, you…"

Jo came to my defense. "Hey, you're an angel, remember?"

I went back to my notebook. "I've got the script mostly written along with the stage directions. Now that we know who's playing who, I'll write up a copy for each of you and highlight your parts. We can do a run-through tomorrow night, OK?"

Glenda came around to my side of the table to give me a hug. "It's great. I bet there won't be an Easter pageant to rival ours anywhere in the world."

Cheryl got up and stood behind her chair. "Yeah, where else can you see this?" and she did the pregnant penguin waddle all the way out the rec room door.

Peggy Lee Was Right

With less than a week to go before the Easter pageant, at breakfast, over a bowl of oatmeal mixed with milk, butter, raisins, brown sugar, cinnamon and maple syrup, I felt the baby kick for the first time. Right under the third button of my pink polyester pants suit.

Sitting in a dining room with twenty-three other pregnant girls and women, no one was going to get too excited for me, but I didn't care—feeling the baby move made me happy. I had been trying to imagine what it would feel like ever since I first learned I was pregnant in January. Would it hurt? Would it tickle? I felt Glenda's baby kick, and even icy Jo let me touch her belly, but now that the movement was inside my own body, it was nothing quite like I imagined. In a single moment, with a hard foot pressing against my belly, the baby seemed so substantial and real.

I wanted to celebrate this red-letter day and decided to play hooky from school. All I needed was to finish my chores and then head to the Quarter, but everyone seemed to linger over breakfast. Impatient, I stood, hands on hips, next to the bussing table, until the dining room was finally cleared. Then I quickly wiped up sticky messes left on tables, put the first load of plates and bowls in the dishwasher, and scrubbed the big pot. Good thing I had elbow grease. Sandra had forgotten to put the pot in hot water to soak, and its sides were caked with oatmeal as hard as concrete.

When the kitchen was presentable and Sandra had stacked the last load of dishes, I ran upstairs to the room I shared with Jo, Renee and Georgie. I couldn't leave the house without making my bed. The Powers-that-Be handed down rules about everything, and room presentation was a big one, especially if there were tours scheduled. I wasn't sure how they would enforce any of their silly rules; what was important was exercising control over our lives. So I made my bed—nice, tight military corners, just like my mother taught me.

Jo rifled through a copy of *For Teens Only*. Its glossy cover promoted articles like "Sally Fields: How She Wins Her Boys," "Those 'Bluesy' Feelings—How to Make Them 'Rosy,'" and "Our Summer Kisses—Too

Sweet to Last." The magazine might have been right about summer kisses, but I doubted it had any magic formula for curing the blues.

After our one big excursion to Audubon Park, my roommates hardly ever left the house except to walk to the Woolworth's down on St. Charles. I thought about asking them to join me on my red-letter, playing-hooky day, but I decided to be selfish—this was a special day for me and my baby.

Georgie was flat on her back staring at the ceiling. Her belly had grown exponentially since I had arrived, and now it was almost as wide as she was tall.

"You off to school? I'll walk you downstairs." She slowly lifted herself to a sitting position. "I figure I'll go watch my shows. Did you know that Laura and Mark are going to adopt a baby? But Laura's crazy—she's still seeing that psychiatrist."

I nodded. "Yeah, that's a bummer. Hope they don't find people like that for our kids."

I had no idea who Laura was. Georgie was a soap opera addict and she threw around the names of characters like they were real people. At least she kept the drama on the television set. Not like Renee, whose drama took up way too much space in our bedroom. Her family, her boyfriend, Kenny. Everything was a trial of the greatest proportion.

I grabbed my book bag from the side of my bed. "You guys need anything from downtown?"

Jo shook her head, and Renee didn't look up from her letter writing. Maybe she and Kenny were back on good terms.

I headed downstairs with Georgie, left through the kitchen—the front door was for visitors—and walked the four blocks down Peniston to St. Charles Avenue. The trolley was crowded this time of day, full of white men in suits who lived in a nicer part of the Garden and probably worked in one of the huge skyscrapers filling up downtown. Plenty of black folks rode the trolley, too, dressed in white uniforms to dish out burgers from behind the lunch counter at Woolworth's or black uniforms to clean the rooms of Maison Dupuy.

A spot opened up near the back. I squeezed in and jingle-jangled on the hard-wooden seats all the way downtown. At Canal Street, instead of transferring to the bus that would have taken me across town to Elysian Fields, I set my sights on Jackson Square. It was a fine morning to sit and drink a cup of coffee at the Café du Monde. On the Girls' Auxiliary trip last summer, the coffee shop was our only stop in the French Quarter. Woolworth's had plenty of postcards with pictures of the world-famous chicory coffee and the beignets lightly dusted with powdered sugar, and since arriving at Sellers in March, I had sent some to Randall, Dayna, and my mother, even though I had never been there. It was about time I paid the place a visit myself.

The rain began as I neared St. Louis Cathedral. When viewed from the riverfront, the cathedral looked more like Sleeping Beauty's castle than a church. I peeked through heavy, wooden doors that faced the square. The sanctuary looked as big as a football field.

The black and white tiled floor belonged in a kitchen, although it was marble and not linoleum. Just to the left of the door, a statue of a baby angel with outstretched hands held a large seashell full of water. Inside, the air seemed still and soft, unlike the bottomless, unyielding air that filled every crack, pore and crevice everywhere else in New Orleans.

It had rained pretty much every day since I arrived in March. In the morning, when I was on my way to school, the air was sticky and wet and like cement, so thick you couldn't swim in it if you tried. As the air got deep and heavy, the whole world started moving in slow motion. I always thought I should be feeling sleepy, or lazy, but I didn't. It was like some kind of strange electrical current was moving in and around the heavy molecules of air, and it kept building and building until the skies emptied out pounds and pounds of rain. Then, through the rest of the day and into the night it was like the world was running a fever. In the morning, poof, the fever would break, and the skies cleared along with my head. For a few brief hours everything seemed normal.

But normalcy never lasted long. Every night another fever brought colors bright and neon, laughter and music that pierced each strand of my hair and made it stand on end, and disturbing thoughts that left my skin prickly to the touch. Why had I been abandoned at Sellers? Did Randall still love me? Why didn't Dayna or my mom write? How could I ever live with myself if I left my baby to be adopted by people I would never meet?

Maybe the church was immune to New Orleans and its fever. I slipped inside to get out of the rain. I thought about lighting a prayer candle but decided against it since I didn't want to be found out as an imposter.

The only time I had been in a Catholic church was at Sean's funeral. There were lots of differences between Sean's church and mine, but only superficial ones. At First Baptist the aisles were carpeted in red—the color of the Holy Spirit, but at St. Andrew's, my high heels made an unfamiliar clicking noise on the wooden parquet floor. A large wooden crucifix hung from the ceiling, and I had never seen a crucifix up close, only in pictures.

We didn't have statues at First Baptist. We were taught that Jesus was raised from the dead; he was certainly not still hanging on a cross. I didn't like the grimace on Jesus' face, or his almost naked body. He seemed so broken and vulnerable.

In the front of Sean's church, an unadorned altar dominated the space. First Baptist, like most other Protestant churches, had a huge pulpit up front and center. When I was little and we attended Shields Boulevard Baptist Church, Pastor Hart stood behind the pulpit with his gray hair and booming voice, and I confused him with God. Especially when he bellowed, "Trust in Jesus. Come to Jesus or face the fires of hell."

First Baptist didn't have stained glass, but at St. Andrew's a small stream of light shone through one of the stained-glass windows that covered the wall behind the altar. It was a fishing scene with Jesus and several men. One of them was Andrew, since the church was named after him, and one of the others was his brother, Peter. The wooden ceiling was high and arched, like the inside of an upside-down boat. When it was time for the funeral to start, deep, large bells began to toll. First Baptist didn't have bells, although sometimes we sang about them. Golden bells, wedding bells.

The priest wore a collar and cassock, a far cry from the plain suits worn by Baptist pastors. A stole the color of winter wheat stretched down to his knees. The funeral mass for Sean was unfamiliar and formal. It began with a psalm, and the priest instructed us to use a worship book in the pews for the hymns and prayers. I flipped back and forth between the pages and lost my place more than once.

When it was time for communion, a quiet murmuring rose from the front of the church as the priest moved down the rail, dropping small wafers into open hands and mouths. At the Baptist church we only had communion every couple of months, on a Sunday night. We stayed in the pews and passed silver trays down each aisle. One tray with wafers, one with grape juice. No wine—never any wine. We ate the wafers and drank the grape juice together. We even set the tiny tumblers down at the same time in little cup holders on the backs of the pews. All around the sanctuary you could hear the plink, plank, plunk of glass against wood.

At the close of Sean's funeral mass, the priest circled the casket, all the while sprinkling it with water. Then he took an incense burner from a white-robed boy and circled the casket again. This time he swung the burner up and down and from side to side. Nothing was rushed; every movement seemed part of a choreographed dance. Soon the whole sanctuary was engulfed in the sweet, pungent aroma of billowing smoke.

I felt uncomfortable not knowing what to say or when to kneel or what to do with my hands. I liked the service though—no yelling—and the music calmed my troubled heart. When Sean died, I felt like I was in some kind of nightmare. I couldn't fathom why Sean was dead. It wasn't the first time our high school class had experienced death. In tenth grade Rob wrecked his motorcycle and died from blunt force trauma. In the fall of our junior year, just a few months before Sean died, Sharon broke her neck when the car she was riding in hit an embankment. But I knew Rob and Sharon only in passing. Sean was different. He seemed like a brother to me, a male friend without any sexual tension. I loved his sense of humor; he could crack me up over the smallest thing. He had a unique way of viewing the world, and I felt like we were kindred spirits—curious, hopeful, bright. And like me, Sean seemed destined for a life far from the constraints of Oklahoma. I knew some of the kids from high school would live in Moore until their dying day, and then there were others—me, Sean, Randall, Buzz, Dayna, David—that I knew would be gone with the wind at the first chance.

Now, in the cool muted light, I pulled down the small footrest in front of me and fell to my knees. Since childhood I had been cautioned repeatedly about avoiding all things Catholic. Baptists don't kneel; even when I was saved I did it standing. But here in the cool, muted light of the cathedral, kneeling seemed like the only option. I hadn't prayed in weeks. We said grace at all our meals, and we prayed in the church services, but I didn't know what to say to God anymore. At night when I asked God to watch over my sisters or remind Randall of his duty to me, when I asked God to make sure my baby grew inside me strong and healthy, a knot of pain went from my throat to my chest. I wished Baptists got to make the sign of the cross on our bodies. Hand to head, to heart, left shoulder, right shoulder, back to heart. It seemed like a nice, quiet way to signal, "Hey, I know you're out there and I hope you know how much I need you right now." I wondered if I made the sign of the cross, would I feel like Jesus was with me again?

In that moment, kneeling in a foreign church in a foreign city so far from home, I felt truly abandoned, like Jesus had decided to stay back in Oklahoma. I was bereft at sea without an anchor. No friends, no family, no god. Kneeling, sitting, standing—it didn't matter—God had stopped listening to my prayers.

I turned away from the cathedral and walked through the center of the Square past two street musicians. Even in the rain, they were blaring out

"When the Saints Go Marching In" on a clarinet and trumpet. They smiled, hoping I had more than empty pockets. Since it was a weekday with Mardi Gras long past, there were few tourists in the Quarter to place coins in their coffee can. Feeling generous, I surprised them by dropping in a Kennedy half-dollar.

As I neared the statue of Andrew Jackson, it was obvious the rain did little to remove the years of built up pigeon poop. Cigarette butts, pop cans, and paper bags littered the street. The brewery was working overtime, and the stench of malt and hops was overwhelming. My stomach did a few flip-flops, and I gagged on the oatmeal I had for breakfast. I was in my fifth month, and I feared I would never be free of the scourge of morning sickness.

The Café du Monde sits catty-corner from the Square, and I scurried over hoping to replace the smell of hops with the more rewarding scent of coffee and fried dough. I found a table on the Decatur street side and ordered a café au lait and beignets. The coffee arrived hot and strong, the color of peanut brittle my mom made every year at Christmas.

I had begun to worry I would never feel the baby move. Those baby butterfly feelings started about a month after I first arrived at Sellers, but I wanted to feel something real and substantial–a foot or a hand pounding on the inside of me. *Here I am, mama. It's me!* As if on cue, the baby kicked again as I took a bite of the beignet. Powdered sugar flew up my nose and I resisted the urge to sneeze.

I wanted Randall to feel it with me. Somehow, I kept holding on to a hope that if he saw my belly getting bigger, if he could reach out and touch our baby moving just a hair's breadth away from my naked skin, then he would have a change of heart. I knew, however, that wishful thinking was unproductive and put me in a world of hurt. As my Memaw always said, "You can ruin your life with too many what if's."

I forgot to bring a book to read. I hardly travelled anywhere without a book. The previous week I picked up *Tess of the D'Urbervilles* from the library on St. Charles. I had always been an avid reader, and the library was a lifesaver. With little to do at Sellers, my brain was turning to mush—too much television and too few engaging conversations. I was determined that before the baby came, I would read all of Thomas Hardy's novels. Two down. Many more to go.

I cleaned up some of the powdered sugar mess. I decided to work on my geometry homework. I really wasn't any good at playing hooky. It certainly wasn't the same as the previous spring when Randall and I skipped school to attend May Day festivities on the South Oval. Had that really been only a year ago?

When the rain stopped, I walked back to Canal Street and caught the next bus out to Elysian Fields. So much for playing hooky. I needed to get to school and take advantage of the few clear hours I had left, before the New Orleans fever started again and I would be useless.

Cardboard Breastplates

Easter morning dawned with the typical New Orleans haze. The humidity was nearing a hundred percent. I knew it would pour all afternoon, but I hoped we could get through the pageant before the deluge.

The pageant was a truly ridiculous idea, and I didn't know why I wanted to do it. Everyone was helping out just to be nice. The staff didn't care, and the girls couldn't give a hoot. Sometimes I didn't have the sense God gave an ant. I was beginning to believe that God didn't give any kind of sense to anything—I wasn't sure I even believed in him anymore.

That was a scary thought.

What if there were no God? There had to be some reason we existed, but first Sean's death, then my pregnancy, then New Orleans and Sellers.

When I was twelve and my dad was stationed overseas, my mom and grandma took my sisters, my brother and me to see the Easter Passion Play in the Holy City of the Wichitas down near Lawton. Back in the 30s, WPA crews built life-sized buildings out of mountain granite. They still exist today—a stable, the Lord's Supper building, Garden of Gethsemane, Herod's court, Pilate's judgment hall. The Mount of Calvary with three stark crosses twenty feet high are there along with Joseph of Arimathea's tomb. Watch towers, rock shrines, and a snack bar complete the sprawling set situated on five rolling hillsides.

I had heard about this play for years. My mother went to see it when she was in high school, and she said it changed her life. The service started in the dead of night with Jesus' birth in the stable, and it ended at sunrise with the resurrection. So, we left our house around seven on Saturday night, with Billy and Janet sprawled sleeping across the back of the station wagon next to a cooler and bags of food. Bologna and bread for sandwiches, potato chips, hard-boiled eggs, grape pop.

No highways existed, and we took small county roads all the way from Moore to Lawton and arrived at the Holy City around midnight. Thousands of people were already gathered on the hillside. My mom and grandma got out of the car to join the throng, but my siblings and I were mostly in it for the food, and we stayed in our seats as quiet as field mice, the only sounds the crunch of chips and the slurp of soda.

I fell asleep after we ate, and I missed most of the play. I woke up just a little before sunrise. My sisters and brother were asleep, and my mother and grandmother were still gone. I could see a bit of light on the hillside near me. On cold ground, rocky and uneven, I stumbled toward it.

When I arrived at the spot I looked for my mother and grandmother in the packed crowd of worshippers. I didn't find them, but I saw several women standing next to a tomb, actors in long robes with scarves covering their hair and faces. A great, deep moaning seemed to come up from the heart of them. Maybe it was simply acting, I couldn't tell, but their moaning triggered an outpouring of emotion in all the people standing around me. The actor's tears tapped into the pain and sorrow we all carried, and men, women and children sobbed, letting out anguish like all hope was gone, and love with it.

It was hard to feel the mountaintop living in New Orleans below sea level. I kept trusting that my negative feelings about God would change. I held onto the belief that I was struggling through my own personal Valley of the Shadow, and that soon God would reveal His will for me. As the old gospel song says, "We'll understand it better by and by," and my comprehension of God's love or God's will for my life was so limited, the revelation could only come in the distant future.

After breakfast I gathered with my cast of seven in the rec room to make any last-minute adjustments to our costumes. The other girls were wearing bathrobes; I was wrapped in a white sheet. We were missing Amy, who went to the hospital on Good Friday morning. A girl, seven pounds, six ounces, named Belinda. So, as feared, I needed to direct *and* play the part of Jesus, too.

About thirty chairs from the dining room and chapel filled the small inner courtyard, a blue Baptist hymnal in each seat. Lined up in rows of ten, five to a side, with a wide aisle down the center, the chairs faced a small pink flowering camellia with a chair on either side. Its sticky sweet fragrance hung in the air, and I prayed that my morning sickness would hold off until we finished the play.

I looked around at the bodies filling the chairs. Most of the girls had arrived, but so far only Miss Popwell and Mrs. York represented the staff. I was disappointed. We put so much effort into this; I thought more of the weekday staff might attend. Of course, our simple courtyard pageant was no match for the fancy hat and glove festivities at New Orleans First Baptist.

We peeked through the curtains and watched as the last of the girls straggled in to take their places.

"Anyone getting nervous?" I asked looking around.

"Nah, I'm just hoping my breastplate doesn't rip." Anita adjusted the cardboard taped to her bathrobe.

"It'll be fine, Anita." Whoa, I didn't think I would get the jitters, but I was definitely feeling butterflies. "Glenda, if I give a short welcome, will you go out and start everyone singing? Do you know the song number?"

"Sure, no problem." Glenda turned pages in the hymnal. "It's page 179. You ready?"

I nodded and we pushed the sliding door to the left and walked out into the courtyard. All heads turned in our direction. Miss Popwell smiled, and the twinkle in her eyes calmed me. Careful not to trip on my sheet, I walked in front of the first row of chairs and stood in the center next to the camellia. With the first deep breath I was hit with a small wave of nausea. I could thank God for one more unanswered prayer.

I took a deep breath. "Welcome everyone on this glorious Easter morning. Our pageant begins with the singing of the third verse of 'Were You There?' found on page 179 of your hymnal." The girls thumbed through the songbooks in their hands. From the back, Glenda's melodious voice rang across the courtyard.

"Were you there when they laid Him in the tomb?"

I made my way back to the rec room, careful to take slow, solemn steps befitting the occasion.

"Let's keep the door cracked open so we can sing along," I suggested. Unfortunately for our meager congregation, I had commandeered all the best singers to be in the play. I could hear Glenda and poor tone-deaf Mrs. York, who belted out every hymn with the gusto of Ethel Merman on a Broadway stage. But no one else seemed to be singing. I was actually worried the play wouldn't have the same import if we didn't start out trembling.

Georgie whispered, "Lani, we don't have hymnals in here."

I gave her one of my mother's looks. "Georgina, you sing the same line over and over until you get to the tremble part. OK?"

She nodded. As the voices from the rec room joined those in the courtyard, a silvery sound seemed to caress the pink blossoms on the flowering camellia bush until they trembled along with the song. I knew it was only a small breeze, and not a sign of God's presence, but I felt relieved. Maybe we were going to pull off this pageant after all.

We moved into the last verse, and I began to pay attention to the needs of my actors. "Jo, where are you? Go stand next to Glenda. You got the props?"

Jo nodded, and picked up an empty jar of Noxema, still recognizable in brilliant sapphire blue, even though its label was defaced. In her right hand she clutched a fancy bottle of bubble bath, courtesy of Amy. She slipped out the door and stood at the back of the courtyard next to Glenda.

"Anita, Georgie, as soon as the song is finished, go stand next to the tomb."

Georgie shook her head, "Tomb?"

I sighed. "The camellia bush. Remember, we're pretending it's the tomb."

She nodded, and Anita fiddled with the breastplate one more time.

"Leave it alone," I told her, "or it will fall off."

Both Anita and Georgie had gold cardboard breastplates taped to their bathrobes to make them look like Roman soldiers. Janie and Glenda made them Saturday afternoon, out of a box brought in by Mrs. Anderson after she and her husband got a new television set. Glenda even went to Woolworth's on St. Charles to buy a can of gold spray paint. She was as handy with crafts as she was with food, so Anita and Georgie had gold butcher paper helmets on their heads, too. They looked like tall chefs' hats with mutton chop sideburns, but they were quite presentable even if they didn't have a feathered crest.

The song ended and I motioned Anita and Georgie out the sliding door. I tried to adjust the breastplates over their huge bellies, but they hooked to the left as crooked as my Grandma's feet. At least the hats were on straight.

As soon as they were in position next to the pink bush, Glenda and Jo made their way up the center aisle holding the Noxema jar and bottle of bubble bath.

"Renee, get over here, quick. You're up next."

I started to shove her out the door, but realized her wings weren't going to fit. I squeezed the two clothes hanger wings covered in glittery butcher paper—another creative costume idea of Glenda's—toward each other until Renee made it out the door. She moved across the front of the courtyard toward the pink camellia bush. The angel was supposed to arrive at the tomb at the same moment as the two Marys, but our tempo was off. Glenda and Jo waited a moment for Renee to appear, and when she did, Cheryl, Janie and I started banging pots and pans with wooden spoons, simulating the earthquake found in the Gospel of Matthew. Since most of us are only familiar with the Easter story in Luke, it probably didn't make much sense, but I thought it added needed drama.

On cue our two guards fell back into the chairs next to the bush like they were as good as dead. Of course, we didn't test the breastplates on chair-sitting guards, so the tape started to pop off over the girls' bellies. We should have used duct tape. And I shouldn't have expected a fourteen and fifteen-year-old to keep still under pressure. Anita squinted through her half-closed eyes, and Georgie tried hard to suppress giggles. My old collie, Patton, was much better at playing dead.

Ignoring the gigglers at their knees, Jo and Glenda held the props in their left hand and covered their faces with their right. They remembered their stage directions, shaking their shoulders to look upset and scared. It was time for Renee's first line. She looked over at me with wide eyes. I whispered through the door, "Don't be afraid."

She scrunched her face and whispered back, "Fffff, I'm not afraid."

I shook my head. "No, that's your line."

Renee nodded and turned back to the two Marys. "Don't be afraid. You're looking for Jesus, but he's not here."

She turned back to me.

"Look inside," I mouthed. "He is risen."

Renee, still looking at me, repeated the line. "Look inside the tomb. Jesus is risen."

She turned to face Glenda and Jo and said it once again with more volume. My two Marys were staying in character as much as possible, given they were confronted by a forgetful angel and two giggling guards. They took their hands away from their faces, stopped shaking, and stepped toward the camellia. Once there, they bent over and looked inside.

I told them to think of the woman in the "Long Black Veil," but they sounded more like the chorus of "Were You There?"

"Ooooooh, where is He?" Jo howled.

Glenda was a little more circumspect. "Oh, where have they taken Him?"

Renee had her next line down pat, and she interrupted the two Marys. "Aren't you listening to me? What's wrong with you? He's not here. Now go away and tell the disciples."

Way to go, Renee. My baby gave me a little kick. Maybe he agreed with me and was supplying a big thumbs up. This whole pageant was going much more smoothly than I had hoped. As Scene One ended, Glenda and Jo turned and came back down the center aisle and into the rec room. Renee moved across the front of the courtyard. Once again, she was stuck in the doorway, but she pushed her way in without any help leaving a trail of glitter in her wake. That left our two guards still on the set.

Great, now they've got their eyes shut tight.

I hissed and shot them an evil glare, and I didn't know which did the trick. Anita and Georgie opened their eyes as wide as Spanky McFarland and looked around. They were supposed to look terrified, but they were having trouble getting out of their chairs. Seven-month pregnant teenagers are most certainly awkward. They managed to stand with the breastplates hanging off their bathrobes and I heard tittering in the audience.

This embarrassing situation was not what I envisioned for my guards.

Once Anita and Georgie were safely in the rec room, I called for Cheryl and Janie. "You can't believe the good news, so run down the aisle if you can, OK?"

Cheryl stuck her tongue out at me, and she and Janie headed out the door. They were off like a herd of turtles—a slow, slow trot given that they were both due in less than a month and each walking with a ten-pound basketball balanced below their hearts.

"Mary Magdalene, it's your turn."

Glenda moved out the door and headed down the aisle. She paused about halfway to the camellia bush.

Cheryl and Janie, our dear Peter and John, arrived at the bush and bent over to look inside. When they stood up, they held their hands up in the air, and shrugged. I motioned for them to come back, and they moved across the front of the courtyard and into to the rec room.

Glenda moved to the camellia bush, bowed her head, and pretended to cry.

At the sunrise pageant in the Holy City of the Wichitas, I stood in the dark and the comforting anonymity of the crowd for what seemed like hours, quietly sobbing, until it seemed like no more tears could fall. Was I crying for Jesus because he was dead? Was I crying for my dad because he was in Ethiopia spending yet another Easter away from us? Was I crying for myself or my mom? I don't know. I was only twelve; I might have been crying because Billy ate all the baloney sandwiches. But when the sun began creeping over the mountainside, in the hushed voice of dawn, first an angel appeared to Mary, and then Jesus himself, and I felt happy. I didn't stop crying, but I felt happy.

Glenda looked up at me and then put her head back in her hands. Shoot, I had forgotten that I was Jesus. How long had I been standing there daydreaming?

I headed out the door and walked across the front of the courtyard, tripping on the white sheet wrapped around my body.

"Why are you crying, woman?"

I was confident that this part would go smoothly. Glenda and I had practiced it a million times.

Glenda didn't look up. "Are you the gardener? Do you know where they've taken Jesus's body? Please tell me where it is. I'll come and get him."

I only needed to say one word, "Mary."

At the sound of her name, Glenda looked up with sheer joy and amazement. She reached out her hands, "Teacher."

I looked into Glenda's eyes that were almost the color of the Noxema jar. "Don't touch me, Mary. I need to ascend to the Father. But go now and tell my disciples that you've seen me. Tell them I am alive. Tell them I am going to my Father and your Father, to my God and your God."

I let out a huge breath of air, then turned and walked off across the courtyard. I waited just outside the rec room door.

Glenda came half-way down the middle aisle. I was willing her to remember how we had rehearsed it. Pause, pause, then release.

She stretched out her arms. "I have seen him. I have seen the Lord."

A deep loving confidence stirred in my heart. I waited one perfect beat, a moment in suspended time that held all the unsaid prayers for myself and my baby, and then stepped into the courtyard.

"Let us sing 'Low in the Grave He Lay.' Please turn in your hymnals to page 182." Soon our voices filled the courtyard again.

> *"Death cannot keep its prey; he tore the bars away; up from the grave he arose."*

I felt goose bumps along my arms, and my body trembled, the same way it would tremble when Randall took me in his arms and kissed me. Was God finally letting me know I was in the palm of His hand? The sun started to break. Maybe God wasn't so far away after all.

Wiggling

A well-worn, well-read copy of *The Story of O* made its way around Sellers. Passed from girl to girl, it was hidden under pillows and in drawers, out-of-sight from prying eyes. By the look of its torn and tattered cover, patched repeatedly with Scotch tape, the book might have been thumbed with care by pregnant girls since it was first published in the fifties.

The book was obviously porno, and even though I would never admit it, some parts got me really hot. Like in the beginning when René, the lover, has O undress in the taxi. I imagined taking off my clothes with the possibility of someone else watching in the rear-view mirror. I had never considered myself an exhibitionist, but that was hot—really, really hot.

My confusion about God and sex started as early as eight. That's when I started wiggling.

In our grown-up world, my "wiggling" is officially called masturbation, but at eight, I had no idea that what I was doing even had a name. Even once I knew the correct term for it, the word "masturbation" sounded medical—like herniation or lactation—and I stuck with "wiggling" as a much better description. The act itself was pretty simple—lying on my stomach, I pressed my hand against my panties and wiggled my butt up and down. The feeling was wonderful and totally natural, so I did it anywhere. I wiggled while I wrote in my diary; I wiggled on the floor in front of the TV; I wiggled on the sofa reading *Little Women* and *Tom Sawyer*.

I even wiggled while I fantasized about Jesus. I imagined his long, brown hair. His large gentle hands. The sound of his voice. "Suffer the little children to come to me," he would say as I sat at his feet with my head in his lap. During an altar call when we sang "Jesus, lover of my soul," I was sure everyone could take one good look at me and know what I was thinking and what I wanted to do.

When I was ten, an older cousin caught me wiggling, and I learned that shame can come from acts of pleasure. She also told me how babies were made. What a revelation! This was how I was going to feel when I got married and did "it" with my husband. Wiggling seemed like good practice, so the next time I spent the night at my best friend's house I convinced her to pretend we were newlyweds. She was the blushing bride, and I played the part of her husband. In our pink flannel pajamas, I wiggled on top of her with all the passion of our wedding night.

My first encounter with pornography happened in sixth grade, one night while I was babysitting for the Petersons, and a whole new world of wiggling opened up.

The family dog had carried the three-year old's worn-out blankie into the parents' bedroom, which was completely off limits. But I knew unless I retrieved it soon, poor Mikey would never get to sleep, and he would cry all night for blankie and Mama. And as every babysitter knows, you gotta get the kids to sleep before you can raid the fridge and call your friends.

I stood at the doorway of the room. "Come here, Fluffy. Bring me the blankie."

Fluffy ignored me, but not wishing to cross a sacred threshold, a married couple's bedroom, where they had done "it" at least three times, I tried again, this time my voice a little higher, a bit sharper, and definitely louder.

"Bring me the blanket NOW, Fluffy!"

Fluffy responded by going under the bed and cowering in a corner. So, I did what any self-respecting, good babysitter would do. I ventured across that sacred threshold, got down on my hands and knees and peered under the bed. To my utter amazement I found magazines. *Playboy* magazines.

I retrieved the blanket, and after putting the kids to bed, I went to the bedroom instead of the kitchen. What was a ham sandwich compared to the chance to gaze in wonder at these photographs? Where did these women come from? I thought these creatures only existed in myths—Diana, Venus, Hera. They reminded me of the popular girls in school—pretty, bouncy, not too smart, pouty lips, faces reflecting sunshine and storms, exuding sexuality while at the same time appearing untouchable, unapproachable.

I longed for the roundness of their hips, the fullness of their breasts. I wanted skin that gleamed like alabaster. Of course, at the time I had no idea what alabaster was, but I had read the line somewhere in a book, and I knew without a doubt it meant unforgiving, eternal beauty.

I felt a special bond with Mr. Peterson. I imagined him looking at the pictures. I wondered if his wife knew they were there, and if she ever looked at them with him. I tried to imagine being one of those special women, a

Playboy bunny, the June centerfold, Playmate of the Year. I imagined Mr. Peterson looking at me. Did he desire me? Yes, all men desired me, and I was far from unapproachable. I was there, ready, waiting, just like O was always available for René and the purple robed masters in the chateau.

After seeing those photos, my wiggling took on a new dimension. Night after night I was a goddess, a princess, a being so gossamer fine that I could slip through the silk chords that chained me to my bed and red Oklahoma dirt. I made love with countless lovers in exotic locales. Men drove me to frenzied passion. I screamed in delight, but in the darkened room I always shared with one or more of my three sisters, I learned to muffle my satisfied cries.

The summer after sixth grade, I fell in love with my first stranger. My family had rented a cabin near Indian Creek in Noel, Missouri. We lounged by its banks, played cards every evening, and, of course, we went to church—a tiny white clapboard building situated in the center of town on a Main Street bedecked with Christmas lights and plywood candy canes year-round.

I spotted my soon-to-be first love in Sunday school. It was hard not to notice us—five new faces among just a handful of regulars. He was the preacher's son and had the air of privilege that seemed to come less from having money, and more from having educated parents in a town where completion of high school was a lofty goal. Brown eyes so deep I was sure I could dive in and never touch the bottom.

We flirted, which for prepubescent bewildered kids meant some kind of disagreement, anything to generate a passionate debate. Our first argument was over who was the best Monkee. Me, I liked the unflappable, irrepressibly quiet quirkiness of Peter Tork, though I did have to agree that Davy Jones was probably the best singer, and cuter, but only just a bit. After church we made plans to continue our discussion at that evening's ice cream social.

The late afternoon air was muggy, thick with mosquitoes that required constant swatting. No daylight savings time then, so even at seven o'clock dusk was settling in. We carried dripping ice cream cones to the yard in back of the church and sat on the crumbling cement steps that led to the children's nursery wing—his was chocolate and mine, vanilla—another topic for debate. Just as the sun began setting behind us, and with fireflies beginning to replace the mosquitoes in the dim light, he kissed me.

This was a movie kiss, no parted lips or probing tongues, just sweet, sticky pressure on my mouth. But I didn't feel the intensity of the moment in my mouth. A ring of fire raced around the top of my head and my stomach trembled violently from the inside out. The whole kiss lasted less than ten seconds, but in those ten seconds I felt like I had been transported to a parallel universe, and in it I was always kissing, always tasting the goodness of that hot August evening along with the flavor of chocolate ice cream.

My first French kiss came in seventh grade, the same year I got my period. Mitch was in tenth grade and the boyfriend of another girl at church. One brisk October evening after a Youth Group meeting to plan the annual Halloween hay ride and wiener roast, and with Diane conveniently away for the weekend, Mitch and I began fooling around in his parents' basement turned rec room. We sat close on the couch, his arm around my neck and his hand on my shoulder; each face intently turned toward the other, eyes locked, keenly observing each word spoken, each deliberate pause, each heightened breath. Then out of nowhere a large, slobbery, probing tongue was trying to reach the back of my throat. I could have been kissing a sheep dog. I was so disappointed. I had been sure that when I finally opened myself up to such sweet caresses, I would be transported to life's truest reality. I believed I would finally understand the suppressed passion that smoldered between my thighs and in the depths of my belly. But nothing was any clearer. I was no closer to understanding my sexuality and my lust for a deep physical connection than I was to understanding the workings of the atom bomb.

Throughout the rest of the fall and into the following wet and windy spring, boys were the most-discussed topic of conversation between Dayna and me. The air in the hallways shimmered; we walked with the hair on our arms standing on end. Every pore on our bodies was super-sensitized to a simple look, and we swooned with each body-bump near the lockers where the boys' thighs could oh, so accidentally graze our tight, round asses and their arms could unintentionally brush against our small, firm breasts. We could meet all of the world's deepest energy needs by harnessing the giggles and emerging sexuality of seventh grade girls. What did he say? Does he like you? Are they going steady? Isn't he cute? So much lust in such little hearts. And all the while, in church we heard the constant groan of chastity, chastity, chastity. Life continued with its complex onslaught of opposing viewpoints. Skirting round the edges of our fantasies—flirting, teasing, imagining the culmination of our sexual desires.

The confusion over sex and God, my inside/outside split, became even more complicated the summer after ninth grade. I worked at the Tastee Freeze on SW 4th right next to Moore Cemetery, where everyone on my mother's side of the family is buried. Mr. Sanders, our State Farm insurance agent, owned this palace of soft serve ice cream delights, but he had more important work to attend to, and the day-to-day management of the store was left to his son, Jeff.

Jeff was one year younger than me and just out of eighth grade. Big for his age, he played second string for the Moore Cubs, our Jr. High football team. We didn't run in the same circles even though we both went to First Baptist. Jeff hung out with the popular kids—the cool kids who didn't wear hand-me-downs, who were willing to make average grades, the kids who were cliquey and flirty and gossipy.

But despite our differences in taste and temperament, somehow that summer, Jeff knew what I was feeling, what I was wanting.

Sex.

On the list of Baptist "don'ts," sex is up at the top. Good girls don't have sex, but by the time I was fifteen, I thought about it all the time. It didn't matter where I was or who I was with. I fantasized about what it might be like to take off our clothes and rub our naked bodies against each other. It didn't even matter whether or not I liked the guy. Because I didn't like Jeff. I thought he was stupid and crude and mean. My attraction to him seemed to come out of nowhere, and it was like an infection or a Pentecostal religion.

On long, hot afternoons when the store was empty of customers, we went to the back, out of the line of sight from the big plate glass windows that surrounded the store. He leaned me up against the freezer, slipped his hand up my short-shorts and pulled aside my panties until he could insert one, two, even three fingers into my vagina. In all of my wiggling days, I had never thought about putting anything inside me. The first time he did it, I thought I was going to pass out from the pain and the pleasure.

I wanted to please him, too. I unzipped his jeans and jammed my hand between them and his underwear. I never actually touched his flesh the way he did mine. He made sure I kept my hand on the outside of his dingy white briefs, smelling of pee and sweat and eventually cum. He kept me pressing, only pressing, on the steel rod that appeared like a miracle while his fingers dug inside me like a cat scratching around in a litter box.

We never kissed.

Kissing might have meant we liked each other and that was far from the truth. At times it even seemed like he detested me, and I knew I truly hated him. What I liked, what I loved, was the way he made me feel.

Preachers sometimes talk about the God-shaped hole in our hearts that only Jesus can fill. I felt that hole. Felt hungry, left out in the cold, shivering, needing to be fed, needing to be enveloped in a big, warm coat. Even after I stopped wiggling over Jesus, I could sing "Precious Lord, Take My Hand" and believe that it was Jesus filling that aching hole. I could believe I was healed and shielded from all the sorrow and pain in the world.

What I didn't and couldn't understand was the way Jeff's fingers seemed to fill up my God-shaped hole the same as Jesus. At least for a little while.

I never told anyone about what happened with Jeff that summer. Not Dayna, and certainly not Randall. I liked and wanted sex so bad that I thought I was a nympho. I felt guilty all the time. And confused. Was I good girl or a slut? I never stopped believing that Jesus loved me, but I felt out of control. I was afraid, as afraid as a man on a gallows-tree that I would go completely crazy and do something I might regret for a lifetime. When it was time to go to church camp, I quit my job at the Tastee Freeze, and Jeff and I acted like nothing had ever happened.

The Story of O had plenty of insights into other sexual activities. I didn't think I was into spanking, but how could I know before I gave it a try? There was a passage about blowjobs, and O got nauseous and gagged. Girls talked about blowjobs on the porch, but at that point I had never given one. I had a strong gag reflex, and I worried I might throw up on my unlucky partner.

Would I enjoy bondage? At night O's arms were tied above her head. "The lips between her legs, her burning lips were forbidden her."

Reading it, all I wanted to do was find my way back to Randall and fuck like there was no tomorrow. But since that wasn't going to happen, I thought I needed to figure out a way to wiggle, but like O, I wasn't finding much of a way to relieve myself. Sleeping in a room with three other girls didn't provide much in the way of privacy, and with my ever-growing belly, I could only sleep on my back.

I wanted to touch my sweet bushy triangle. I wanted to come again. My orgasm. Up and down the full length of my body, an uncontrollable warmth, a shimmering fire that would leave me panting, breathless.

I decided to read no further and passed the book on to Renee. Sex had gotten me into my predicament in the first place, so I didn't have any business feeding that fire. Besides, what was the use of having beautiful burning lips, if no one could kiss them?

Lake Champlain

At school, I kept my head down and stayed inside my comfort zone. Most of the writing I did for *The Stork's Gazette* required little to no interaction with the other students. I got along fine with the teachers though, so my reputation as a stuck-up brown-noser followed me all the way from Oklahoma.

Most of the girls were black, and the few white girls at the school stayed together, arriving on the same bus every day and always heading out as soon as the last bell rang. Lunch was a solitary affair—no lunchroom, no outside patio where friends could gather for the latest gossip—and most days I brought a bag from Sellers with a tuna fish sandwich, an apple and a handful of potato chips, and ate alone sitting on the steps of one of the rickety wooden porches.

One girl seemed different. I could see her eying me in the classrooms and out on the lawn in front of the buildings. It was painfully obvious that I wasn't from New Orleans, and she seemed curious about why I was at Margaret Haughery all on my lonesome. After two issues of the gazette had been published, she approached me after class.

"Hey, you the one working on that newspaper, right?"

"Yeah, it's *The Stork's Gazette*. Did you read the last issue?"

"Glanced at it. It was okay. Pretty white, though."

I blushed. "Yeah, it is, isn't it? Guess that's because I'm white. I've tried to camouflage it, but it hasn't done much good."

She smiled showing all of her teeth and held out a hand the color of café au lait. "I'm Champlain. I can help you with the paper, if you like. I've always wanted to be a writer."

Champlain had her baby, a boy, in early March. Louis, named after Louis Armstrong, was staying with her mom during the day while Champlain was at school. She was a sophomore and hoped to transfer to a regular high school in the fall. Like me, she had big dreams of a better future for herself and her son, but unlike me, she didn't care if she ever saw the father of her baby again.

"Didn't know him," she said. From the tone of her voice, I knew not to ask any more questions.

One afternoon Champlain and I went to the foot of Canal Street to catch a ferry over to Algiers. The ferry had been operating since 1827, more than thirty years before the start of the Civil War. It held pedestrians and cars, and standing at the rail we could look deep into what appeared to be a bottomless cauldron of black ripples and strong currents.

I knew Mark Twain had been a steamboat pilot on the Mississippi River, had even taken his pseudonym from a river term, and I wished I could feel like he did—that this river was an unworldly dreamland, and I could float down it forever without a care or concern. In New Orleans, my life was also a dreamland, but only because my world had shrunk mightily—to my body, the baby I carried, my chores, the bedroom I shared with three other girls, the trolleys and buses that transported me to school each day, the transitory interactions with teachers at the school. Champlain was a part of my world now, too, but I knew our connection would be fleeting. She would go home to her mother and her son, and hopefully next year to a regular high school, and I would only have hazy memories of her laugh and her white teeth.

"Not to be rude, but Champlain is an unusual name. Does it have special significance?"

"Yeah, my folks went to Lake Champlain in Vermont on their honeymoon. Since I arrived about nine months later, they thought I was conceived there, so they gave me the name."

Black people were an enigma. I thought they lived in cities like New Orleans or Chicago or sharecropped on cotton farms in Mississippi. If I were doing word association for black Americans, I would come up with "hot, sultry, sweaty, passionate, angry, broken, long-suffering, and God-fearing." I knew that black people invented the blues and jazz. They were great dancers and athletes. I could only picture them in smoke-filled juke joints or toiling under a blazing sun. They were not a part of my white world. Although I had never been to Vermont, I assumed it was populated by whites just like Oklahoma. New England was an enigma, too, and I tried to imagine Champlain's young black parents honeymooning in a place I associated with Ethan Allen and Robert Frost, white clapboard churches with soaring steeples, maple syrup, deep winter snow, and stoic, independent-minded people. I couldn't imagine what they found of interest there.

"You didn't think blacks could vacation in Vermont, huh?"

I blushed, embarrassed to realize that Champlain could see right through me. But she continued as if my ignorance didn't make a difference. She probably encountered white folks with prejudice like mine on a daily basis. "Well, they were living in DC at the time, and they took the train up to Vermont. It was fall, and they wanted to see the leaves changing colors."

I didn't want Champlain to think that I had fewer brains than God gave a goose. I wanted desperately to find common ground.

"We mostly have scrub oak in Oklahoma, so I've never seen the leaves change the way they do in Vermont. I bet it's real pretty. My name is sort of a place name, too. I was born in Hawaii, and Lani means heavenly. It's used in all sorts of ways over there. My middle name, Jo, is the part that drags me back to Oklahoma. I'm named after my mother's cousin, Veda Jo."

I turned back to gaze into the water. Champlain didn't seem to judge me, even though I had so many preconceived notions of who she was. Since I hadn't connected with anyone at Sellers in a meaningful way, and since Dayna appeared to have written me off, I longed to have a friend who truly knew me. I wondered if Champlain might have misconceptions about my life, too.

"When I was in second grade, the school was right across the street. I could see the slide and the swings from our front porch. We were pretty poor, and my mom and grandma took in laundry to make ends meet. My mom packed me a sack lunch every day, but I didn't think it was good enough. I wanted the hot lunch that my friends ate. In fact, one day I was so embarrassed that I threw away my bagged lunch not realizing my Grandma had put a fried pie in there—apple, probably my favorite dessert ever. No matter, I talked with the lady in charge of the cafeteria and fixed it so that I could clean trays after lunch in exchange for the hot meal. But you know what? Those lunches weren't much to talk about, and I missed recess every single day because I was cleaning trays. My mama always said that I wouldn't be satisfied with my lot in life, and I started proving her right back in second grade. I guess I'm telling you all of this, because I'm an odd duck, and I speak when I shouldn't, and I never know when to leave well enough alone."

Champlain smiled her million-dollar smile and shook her head. "You're right. You are an odd duck. But I know no offense was intended and none was taken." She held out her hand. "Friends."

At Algiers we got off just to get back on. On the ride back to the ferry terminal we discussed the next two issues of the paper.

Champlain got her mother's recipe for chicken gumbo, and she wrote her own review of *To Kill A Mockingbird*. She had a completely different take on the racism in the book, and I realized that I didn't know the first thing about the life of a black girl in America.

Christy Makes a Different Choice

Near the end of the school year, I arrived at the end of a long day to one crazy brouhaha. Christy and Cheryl delivered their babies at the same time, and Cheryl had left for Vicksburg on the previous day. The big news at Sellers was a first for me: Christy had decided to keep her baby. Mrs. Stafford took her to the office to sign the relinquishment papers in the morning and Christy just flat out said, "No."

Not one of the girls had talked to her directly; they kept Christy quarantined downstairs in the Working Wing until her parents could come and get her. They didn't want us getting any ideas, I suppose. Renee sat at Mrs. Stafford's table at lunch, and she reported back that Mrs. Stafford said Christy was being selfish.

Renee was steamed. "Can you believe it?! What a load of shit. That was not called for on Mrs. Stafford's part."

I nodded. "Yeah, I wonder if we'll hear about it later."

Right as rain, Mrs. LaPrairie showed up before dinner. We were not eating until we heard her lecture.

"Some of you may have heard that Christy decided to keep her child." Mrs. LaPrairie looked mad enough to drown puppies. "Of course, that is your decision to make. But I think I speak for all of Sellers staff when I say that to do anything other than relinquish your children for adoption is not in your best interest and certainly not in the best interest of your child. Christy's parents are now under a significant financial burden to the Home Mission Board for the care Christy's received. Christy thinks her parents will help her raise her the baby, but she will soon discover this is not true. Think carefully before you make this mistake."

Mrs. LaPrairie turned to leave, her high heels click, clack, clicking on the wooden floor. Mrs. York cleared her throat. "Let us pray…"

I glanced around. Anita was fiddling with her silverware. Like any second she was going to burst out playing spoons. Glenda and a few others looked like they could cry. Keeping our babies was what most of us dreamed about at night. Being at Sellers was not our happily-ever-after ending, but we liked to believe that we had no other choice. Christy was going home.

She was keeping her baby. A choice I dreamed about but wasn't even willing to consider. Was she foolish or courageous? And what did that make me? Was I playing it smart, playing it safe, or was I a big coward?

I wanted to talk with Christy, find out what made her change her mind. Margaret, Christy's best friend at Sellers, said her folks came by the hospital, took one look at the baby girl, and said Christy could keep her. Like Christy, she had a thick head of dark hair, so maybe Heather reminded them of Christy as a baby.

After lunch I watched through our bedroom window as Christy packed her stuff into the trunk of her parents' Oldsmobile. She climbed into the back seat with Heather on her lap. I wished my parents would change their minds.

As they drove away, I thought to myself that Christy looked real good.

Voodoo Queen Marie

In a few short weeks, a lot had changed around Sellers. Cheryl's departure meant there was an opening in the nursery. I had been itching to get out of the kitchen for ages, so I asked Mrs. York if I could take Cheryl's spot, and dear ole Owl-Eyes said yes. Of course, Glenda was disappointed. She was hoping I might take over management of the kitchen, but the last thing I wanted was the responsibility for feeding all those hungry, pregnant mouths. Since we were stuck at Sellers with nothing to do and nowhere to go, not to mention the loss of love and affection, eating was one of the few pleasures left. When the food stunk, the kitchen staff certainly heard about it. Glenda, however, didn't need to worry about our food happiness much longer; her baby was due any day, and she had been removed from all kitchen duties.

I had my own set of changes, too. I took my finals, and the previous Thursday I put the last issue of *The Stork's Gazette* to bed. After three months of trudging to the other side of town, three months of spending my days alone with geometry and the history of World War II for company, it was almost June and school was finally out. We didn't have any end of school parties, and certainly no Junior/Senior prom, but now I only had three more months of waiting until my due date, and that was reason enough to celebrate. Champlain and I promised to stay in touch, but I knew it wouldn't happen.

Friday morning, I was up in my room, my bed covered in clothes. A few pairs of shorts, a couple of summer tops, two dresses. I was desperate. I had to find the perfect outfit. It was Memorial Day weekend and my parents were coming for a visit.

Jo was lying back in her bed, reading a letter from Cheryl. I looked over at her with the saddest puppy-dog face I could muster.

"Jo, my folks are coming tomorrow and we're going to Brennan's for breakfast. Can I borrow your green dress? Please? I don't have anything to wear."

Jo didn't take her eyes off the letter, so my puppy-dog look failed to move her. Cheryl had the prettiest little girl, Bethany, on the seventeenth, and this was the first letter Jo had received from her since she returned to Vicksburg.

"You mean the green dress with the rope belt? Brennan's is pretty la-de-da. And that dress makes your boobs look big. I'm not sure it'll work"

"Well, it's a heck of a lot fancier than anything I've got here. And green sets off my eyes." I swept the clothes from my bed to the floor, completely disregarding one of the cardinal housekeeping rules—floors must be kept clear at all times.

Jo looked up from the letter. "Sure, wear the dress. I don't care. If you want it, I'll leave it for you when I go home."

I smiled. "Thanks. What's Cheryl got to say? Can you share or is it private?"

"No, it's not private. But be on the lookout for Renee."

Jo shifted on the bed and turned to fluff the pillows before lying back down. "Why can't I ever get comfortable?"

I laughed. "Maybe because you're pregnant?"

Jo smiled. "Wanna hear this letter or not? And you better pick up those clothes before Mrs. York sees them."

"Yes, mom. You read, and I'll clean."

Jo cleared her throat and began reading in her endearing Mississippi drawl.

> Dear Jo,
>
> Hi! Your letter was so sweet, and it made me feel wonderful. It's great to be home. Things haven't changed much in Vicksburg since we left. But things haven't changed in Vicksburg in a hundred years.
>
> Your turn is coming up. When will you see the doctor? How are you feeling? How is Danny? I bet he'll be glad when you get home.
>
> Tell me all about Lani and Georgie! I don't care about Renee. She's a spoiled brat. Heaven help her.

> *I finally got a job. I'm working for Gav and Brothers Pharmacy. I like my job, but I have to work until 9 on Friday & Saturday night. Oh, well, can't win them all.*
>
> *Mark & I are very happy, but we aren't getting married until we save some money. I really think this is best. Don't you?*
>
> *It's hard to believe, but I miss working in the nursery. Has anyone taken my place? Tell Shirlene & Freddie I said hell-o. Don't forget!*
>
> *Oh: Please don't forget to tell Dr. Rutledge hell-o for me and please get his address for me. Thank you so much!*
>
> *Tell everyone hell-o for me especially Miss Popwell. Sorry I couldn't talk to you Sat. but I'll call you back. Gotta get some sleep. Love ya!"*

"She sounds good. I'm glad she got a job." All the clothes were off the floor and back in a pile on my bed. "You gotta write and tell her I took her old job in the nursery. And she's right. Renee is a brat."

"Shhh! She could come in any second. And we still gotta live with her." Jo got up and sat next to me on the bed. "You're really jumpy, Lani. You nervous about seeing your folks?"

I picked at a chenille tuft. It was nearly worn down and left a shiny patch on the bedspread. "Yeah, I guess. I haven't seen them since March. I wish you could meet my mother. She'd get a kick out of you."

Jo laughed. "Why? Is it my sparkling personality?"

"Of course. That and you usually manage to keep a civil tongue in your head, and, you know, you're a good friend to me." I left off picking at my bedspread and started to bite my nails. Jo shot me the evil eye.

"Stop that. You're gonna make them bleed. It's gonna be okay, Lani. Listen, if your mom is anything like you, I'd probably like her too. If you want, I'll take a peek out the window as you're leaving. I don't think anyone will care if you look up here and wave."

That night I worked my first shift in the nursery, and all was quiet. Besides Jason, we had Bethany, Cheryl's baby, and seven other little ones.

Freddie picked up Shawndra and took her to the changing table in the corner.

"I don't know what we been feeding this chile, but she's got the loosest stools I ever seen. Smells as bad as a dog fart, too."

Freddie was right; I could smell it from where I was sitting. "I'll get you some more rags, Freddie."

I headed to the sink in the rear of the room, next to the changing table. An open cabinet to the left contained everything needed for cleaning and diapering a baby. Washrags—nothing more than old diapers torn in half—were stacked in rows like pancakes. We had vaseline to soothe tiny bottoms, zinc oxide for diaper rash, talcum powder for the fresh baby smell. I grabbed a few rags and ran them under the hot water tap before handing them to Freddie.

"My folks are coming to visit me this weekend. Any ideas about where we should go?"

"Lawd, Lani. I don't reckon I frequent the kind of places your folks might like. You goin' to the French Quarter?"

Behind me Jason started rattling the sides of his crib.

"Down. Want down."

Poor Jason. Just looking at him from the outside, no one could tell anything was wrong. He seemed so healthy.

"Just a minute, sweetie, I'll be right there."

Jason was adorable, a real charmer. But he needed a mom. I didn't understand why they made such a big deal about his heart murmur. Why couldn't he get adopted?

I let down the sides of his crib, and leaned over to pick him up. He was getting so heavy. I wouldn't be able to hold him for much longer.

"Let's go find you something to play with."

There was a large rag rug in front of the windows, and I set him down. Jason toddled over to a milk crate filled with blocks, small cars, a few balls. He had gotten to be such a good walker. I knew it wouldn't be too long before he was running all over the place.

"Want to play with the ball, Jason?"

I got down on my knees.

"Roll the ball to me. Yeah, that's right."

Jason bent at the waist and leaned out to push the ball. When it rolled toward me, Jason lost his balance and fell on his hands and knees. He contorted his face like he was thinking about crying and then decided better of it.

"You all right, baby?"

I felt so bad for Jason. No one could ever convince me it was a good thing for him to grow up in that small room. Freddie had been taking care of Sellers babies for more than ten years, but caregivers like me came and went. The babies stayed at Sellers for at least six weeks before they could get adopted, and I prayed every night and day that my own baby would be hale and hearty and go to a good home as early as possible. I tried to strike a bargain with God. Listen, I'll keep believing in you, and at the end of six weeks you make sure my healthy, beautiful baby is living in the lap of luxury with the best parents in the world.

"Your turn, Jason. Get the ball." I rolled the ball in his direction. It made a little right turn, and then rolled toward of one of the rocking chairs. "Get the ball, Jason."

This was my dream for my baby. He would grow up a prince, in magnificent splendor, just like Moses in Pharoah's palace. And I would be like Moses' mother, forever nameless, but the only person who could set him free. I only wished I could go with my baby like Moses' mother went with him, and make sure my baby would be loved without fail and never, ever spanked.

Freddie came and sat in the chair closest to the window with a bottle and Shawndra. She kicked the ball with her foot and it rolled in the opposite direction. Jason headed for it. "Ball, ball."

"So, Freddie, any suggestions? We're fixin' to go to Brennan's for breakfast."

"Well, that's mighty fancy. Never been there myself, but I hear it's real nice." Freddie set the bottle down on the floor next to the rocker and put Shawndra over her left shoulder. For such a big woman, Freddie had the gentlest hands. Every pat on Shawndra's back was as tender as a dying rose.

"After you get done with breakfast, you should take your folks over to the old cemetery on Basin Street. It's a nice way to walk through the Quarter."

"I remember passing some huge cemeteries when my dad drove me down here last March. I had no idea folks got buried above ground."

Jason seemed tired of playing with the ball. "Are you hungry, sweetie? Would you like a cracker? Freddie, can I give him a graham cracker?"

"Sure, hon. Now, if you drove down Highway 61, you probably were looking at the cemeteries up in Metairie. They got some big ones up there. The one I'm talkin' about is much smaller, the oldest one in New Orleans. It's even got Marie Laveau buried there."

I rolled back on my knees, and gingerly got up off the floor. I felt like an old woman. The graham crackers were kept back by the sink, and I grabbed the box and filled a small plastic cup with water.

"Come here, Jason. I got you a cracker. Who's Marie Laveau, Freddie?"

"What? You never heard of Madame Marie? She's just the most famous Voodoo Queen in all of New Orleans. Most powerful one, too."

Freddie returned Shawndra to her lap, and the baby eagerly sucked down the formula.

I sat in the other rocker, and Jason waddled over and placed his hands on my knees. I offered the cup of water, and showed him how to hold it himself. "Voodoo?"

Jason dribbled water down his t-shirt, and it mixed with the cracker crumbs, making the front of his shirt look like crust for a chocolate chiffon pie.

"You don't believe that stuff, do you, Freddie? I thought you were Catholic."

"Lani, hold the bottom of the cup so he doesn't drop it. Course I'm Catholic. So was Marie Laveau. She was a devout Catholic. Went to Mass every day. You can be Catholic and Voodoo at the same time."

Jason drained every drop of water.

"Boy, you were really thirsty. Want some more?" I stood up and headed back to the sink. "I didn't know that. I mean about being Catholic and Voodoo at the same time. Did she die recently?"

"Lawd, chile, you don't know nothing now, do you?" Shawndra finished her bottle, and Freddie stood up and returned the baby to her left shoulder. She jiggled the baby up and down and paced between the two rows of cribs.

"No, Madame Laveau was born a long time ago. She knew that pirate, Lafitte. Even Layafette came to her for advice. Kissed the top of her head when he said goodbye even though she was colored."

We met in the middle of the room. Freddie laid Shawdra down, just as Bethany stirred in her crib and April start fussing. It wouldn't be long before all the babies needed feeding.

"Lafayette? That French guy from the Revolutionary War?"

I realized I should have gotten a rag while I was back at the sink. Jason had crumbled up the rest of the cracker, and it was all over his shorts, shirt, and the carpet. "I'm sorry about the mess, Freddie. I'll clean it up."

"Don't worry 'bout nothin', shug. Cain't have a baby without having a mess." Freddie headed to the small refrigerator and four-burner stove next to the sink.

"Madame Marie lived to be more than a hundred." Freddie turned on a burner underneath a small pan filled with formula, and stirred it with a wooden spoon. "Baby, she was loved by everyone. White folk and colored folk alike. She knew all about healing folks with herbs and things. When the yellow demon came crawling up from the river, killing so many with its fever, Madame Marie nursed lots of 'em back to life."

I brought the blue plastic cup back to the sink. "I'm such an ignoramous. I never even heard of her. Did she do spells on people? Make dolls and prick 'em with pins?"

Freddie filled two bottles with the formula, taking care to pour over the sink. "I don't know what she did exactly. She had a million different things she could do. She said prayers, mixed potions for you to drink or rub on your body." Freddie placed the pan back on the stove and started screwing on the nipples and caps. "Sometimes she might make you throw something over your shoulder or in the river. It just depended on what you needed done. She could keep someone from hurting you, but she could put the hurt on somebody that was givin' you trouble. Make 'em do what you want. She got most famous for granting love wishes. Go find her grave. She'll set that boy of yours straight."

Freddie handed me one of the bottles. "You wanna feed April?"

April was our smallest baby, although she was four weeks older than Bethany. She wasn't premature, but when she was born she weighed less than five pounds. Her mom, Joyce, didn't show up to Sellers until her ninth month. Even then she was hardly showing. April had to stay in the hospital for more than a week after Joyce came back to Sellers and then home, but I don't think it mattered much since Joyce wasn't interested in seeing her baby any way.

I set the bottle next to the head of the crib and picked up April with both hands. Once she was safely in the crook of my arm, I grabbed the bottle and headed back to the rocking chair. Jason came over and stood next to me. "Ball, ball."

"Jason, I can't play right now. I'm feeding April. See the pretty baby, Jason."

I daubed a bit of the formula on my wrist to make sure it was not too hot. Sometimes at first it was hard to get a baby to take the bottle. I had to poke it around in their mouth a little until they got the idea it was food.

"Freddie, you're pulling my leg about the wishes. She can't do anything now she's dead, can she?"

Freddie sat in the rocker next to mine holding Bethany and a bottle.

"No, chile, I ain't kiddin' you. The power of a Voodoo Queen doesn't end in death. The spirit world is smack dab next to ours, right here, close at hand. Someone like Marie Laveau is waitin' to listen to your heart's desire. I'm telling you, go ask her. If that boy's been fooling around, she'll make him behave."

Finally, April was taking the formula. I rocked back and forth, enjoying the sensation of the baby in my arms.

"Freddie, Pastor Bodine says Voodoo is the devil's handiwork."

Bethany in Freddie's arms was making loud slurpy noises as she sucked on her bottle. Unlike April, Bethany was a good eater, same as her mother, Cheryl. When she was at Sellers, Cheryl was always after Glenda to bake cakes and pies, and just like me, red velvet cake and pecan pie were her favorites.

Freddie caught me admiring Bethany. "She's a pretty little one, isn't she, shug? Now I'm not trying to be disrespectin' of your church, but Voodoo ain't got nothing to do with the devil. Just the opposite is true. It's a little bit of a guarantee that good things happen to good people and bad things happen to bad people. The power of Voodoo is real, and it works its magic whether you believe in it or not."

I stared at her. She wore a big gold cross around her neck.

Freddie shifted Bethany from her left arm to her lap. "Let's just say I'm not above asking for help. And I wouldn't want to cross anyone who might be connected. I walk a straight line."

Bethany had her mother's eyes, with enough of a upward slant on the corners to look a little like a pampered Siamese cat. She seemed to look at me real hard in a strange knowing way. I needed to write Cheryl and let her know how big Bethany was getting. I turned back to check on April. She had drained only a quarter of the bottle, and she was playing with the nipple instead of sucking on it. I wiggled it around in her mouth, frustrated.

"Freddie, Amy's never gonna get any bigger if she doesn't start eating more. When can we give her some cereal?"

"Hon, give her to me. I'll get her to eat."

Freddie placed Bethany over her left shoulder for a quick burp. Then she laid her back in her crib on her stomach. "Hand me Amy, and go pat Bethany on the back. She'll fall asleep in no time."

I did as I was told. Leaning over the crib, I sang an old lullaby under my breath, "I gave my love a cherry…" while my hand patted Bethany's back in time with its gentle rhythm.

"Freddie, Voodoo sounds a little bit like the spirit mafia to me. Ok, so if I find Madame Laveau's grave, what do I do?"

"First you got to bring her something, an offering of sorts. She really likes cigars; rum—white rum not the brown kind; and candy, any kind, don't matter. Probably not chocolate since it might get a bit messy. So you lay your offering on the grave and you knock on it three times. Then you gotta make your petition three times and focus real hard on what you want. Say you still want to marry that boy of yours."

"Randall."

"Yeah, say you still want to marry Randall. So you go to Madame Marie, ask her for help, then imagine yourself in your wedding dress with Randall standing next to you. Then ask for her help again, and imagine the two of you in front of the preacher and he's saying, 'Now you may kiss the bride.' Then you could ask for help and imagine you two on the church steps with all your friends and family throwing rice on your heads."

"I don't know where I could get cigars or rum, but I still have some candy I bought the other day at Woolworth's. I don't know how I'll mange to do it without my folks thinking I've lost my mind, but maybe I will talk to your notorious Voodoo Queen. I'm sure Randall's gonna marry me like he promised, but a little extra push in the right direction couldn't hurt."

On the Banks of Lake Pontchartrain

The following morning after breakfast, I waited upstairs in my bedroom for my parents to arrive. Saturdays were more relaxed. We could sleep in a little; we served breakfast a little later. We could even come downstairs in our pajamas and robes. Of course, schedules didn't change that much—we still had chores. In this way—maybe it was the only way—Sellers was like home. Beds must be made, food cooked, dishes washed, bathrooms cleaned, laundry done, babies fed, vacuuming, dusting—the list was endless—but at least on Saturday we mostly had the house to ourselves. The weekly staff was gone—no social workers or receptionist or office administrator. No nosy psychologist or the Ice Queen, Mrs. LaPrairie. And thank God, we didn't have to give any tours. Mrs. York even took a well-deserved day off, so we were pretty much left to the care of the on-duty nurse, just in case one of us decided to go into labor.

I looked up as Glenda wandered into our room.

"Whatcha doing here, Lani? I thought Saturday morning you went to the library. I'm headed that way now. Wanna come?

"No thanks, Glenda, but you can return this for me." I reached into to my nightstand drawer and retrieved *Jude the Obscure*. "Think the walk might help you go into labor?"

Glenda's due date came and went last Wednesday, and her anxiety took up a bigger space in the room than her nine-month plus belly.

She shrugged. "Well, walking can't hurt."

"My mom says she was late with all five of us. I was due at Christmas and my birthday's February 5th."

"Oh, don't tell me that. The thought is positively gruesome."

"Well, that's what I wanted to tell you. She said she was so miserable, she just started walking. My folks lived in Honolulu at the time, and she started out from their apartment around eight o'clock in the morning and she didn't stop walking until she was in labor six hours later."

"That's cool. I didn't know you were born in Hawaii."

"Yeah, I'm an Air Force brat. But I never got to appreciate the beauty of the islands. We left before I was six months old, and I've never been back."

"That's a drag. But maybe you and Randall can go there on your honeymoon."

"We can dream, can't we? Thanks for taking back the book for me. I'll see you later. No, better yet, I'll see you next week when you come home from the hospital."

"You got it, Lani." Glenda left the room, giving me a smile and a thumbs-up.

I picked up my shoulder bag, placed it on the bed beside me, and nervously rummaged through its contents. Wallet. Notebook. Pen. Lipstick. Mascara. A few pieces of candy for Madame Marie.

Margie's voice hovered at the top of the stairs. "Lani, you've got visitors." Margie was our oldest resident—32, with a five-year-old son staying at her mother's while she waited to deliver. When it came to men, being older didn't mean smarter. My heart started pounding. I grabbed the mascara and ducked into the bathroom. I was shaking so hard I thought I was having a seizure. My hands looked terrible. I'd torn my cuticles out with my teeth and chewed my nails down to the quick. Glenda always shot me the evil eye when she caught me biting them. She showed me how to use an emery board so my nails wouldn't look so ragged, and she brushed my nails with a coat of light pink nail polish. Glenda was so sweet to me—as much a big sister as a friend. I wanted to please her and stop biting my nails, but nothing seemed to do the trick. Bad habits were hard to break.

I leaned over the sink, opened my mouth and began brushing my lashes. What is it about opening your mouth and sticking out your tongue that makes putting on mascara so much easier?

I took one last look at my reflection. I was right. Jo's dress did look nice on me. The green made the color in my eyes pop. Georgie offered her green eye shadow, but since I had never worn any before it seemed silly to start now. Besides, my mom and dad might have thought I looked like a hussy.

I was definitely showing. When I left in March, I had no belly, but now it looked like I was hiding a basketball. Complete strangers seemed to feel like they had the right to touch me—strolling in Audubon Park, crammed next to me on the St. Charles trolley, looking for a tube of Crest on aisle four of Woolworth's. But what about my mom? What would she say when she saw me? Would she look at my belly? Would she reach out and touch it?

I adjusted the rope belt that fit snuggly underneath my boobs. They were certainly bigger than when I left. I wondered if my mom might notice that, too.

Back in the bedroom, Georgie was back from breakfast and lying on top of her unmade bed. Still in her robe, she had borrowed a pillow from Jo's bed and placed it under ankles so swollen they look like car wash sponges.

Georgie stopped staring at the ceiling long enough to turn in my direction. She almost looked like she could cry. "Going out with your folks?"

Georgie's parents hadn't been to visit once even though they lived only five or six hours away. I was lucky my parents kept their promise to make the trip down. Lots of times, parents or friends started out with good intentions, but once behind those red brick walls it was easy to forget we were there. I had yet to hear from Dayna.

"We're just going out for the day. Wish me luck." I dropped the mascara back into my shoulder bag.

Georgie lifted herself up on her elbows, her chin unable to rise above her belly. "You bet. All the luck in the world."

As I left the room she called out, "You look real nice, Lani."

Downstairs, I stopped before entering the living room. My heart was racing to the beat of "Wild Blue Yonder," the oh-so-familiar Air Force anthem. The baby started kicking in time. "Okay," I thought, "so off we go."

The room was flooded with light from the window, and my dad, in front of it, hands on hips with his face turned away, looked like a standing shadow. My mom sat on the sofa with her purse in her lap—the big brown leather one that always smelled like Juicy Fruit gum. I leaned over to kiss her on the cheek.

Before either she or I had a chance to cry, my dad walked over to us. "You 'bout ready to go?"

"Yes, sir," I replied. "Mom, did you meet Mrs. York? It's her day off, but she's in her apartment, and I'm sure she would be glad to meet you." My voice was tentative as I fought back tears. I began picking at the cuticle on my left thumbnail with my index finger.

My mother stood up clutching her purse to her chest like it was a life preserver. "Lani, stop that. I'd have thought you'd outgrown that by now. Yes. Mrs. York came downstairs to let us in. I was hopin' we'd get a tour of the place, but I guess they don't give them on Saturdays." My mom relaxed the chokehold on her purse and moved its handle to the crook of her arm.

"Yes, ma'am. They give us a break on Saturday. Tours are actually a pain in the butt."

My mother's face registered shock. "Lani, what a way to talk."

If only she knew some of the language I'd been hearing, I thought. That would really shock her.

"I only meant that we have to go hide out and it's disruptive, especially if it's my bedroom on show. And I don't like the idea of strangers looking at my things."

My mother sighed, "Well, I'm sure the tours serve a purpose."

I felt my shoulders tighten. My mother wasn't listening to me. Once again, it seemed like she was siding with the establishment.

"I hear that there might be a wait," my father interrupted. "If we're brunching at Brennan's, we best be goin'."

Along pink stucco walls, people lined up waiting to enter the fabled doorway that led to Brennan's world-famous turtle soup and Bananas Foster. I felt out of place. My mom and dad looked out of place. My mother's homemade polyester dress was fashioned out of the same material as my birthday pantsuit, and she could have blended into the Pepto-Bismol colored wall. Her frosted wig, a worn handbag, and scuffed Sunday shoes completed the outfit. Dad was dressed in a short-sleeved shirt, polyester pants belted high on his waist, utilitarian shoes.

Next door to the restaurant was an antique store, and while we waited, I stared through windows at statues of nymphs, paintings of the Madonna, and chandeliers that could have filled up the entirety of our living room. When we finally reached the small reception area, the hostess told my father that he needed to wear a jacket, so they loaned him a green one with a rooster on the pocket. Once inside we were seated near a courtyard dotted with fountains, each a majestic lion with water gushing from its open mouth. My dad ordered Eggs Benedict and Bananas Foster for all of us, and the Bananas Foster came to the table in flames. The dish had been doused in rum and set on fire, and my father reassured me that the alcohol was completely burned off. In truth, I would have appreciated a bit of a buzz. Anything to loosen our lips. I had so many questions I wanted to ask them. Did they tell my Memaw and the other relatives in California about the baby? Had there been rumors at church about where I was? Had my sister Carla forgiven me? Did Janet still rock and cry when she listened to my Rod McKuen album *The Sea*? What about Billy? I had always been his second mama. Did he miss me?

I wanted them to ask me about Sellers. Had I made any friends? How was school? I wanted them to comment on how big my belly had grown. I wanted them to ask me what it felt like to have a real, live, kicking baby inside of me. But the conversation was stilted. We discussed the food and the weather, but nothing personal. It was as if we were acquaintances who just happened to meet up in New Orleans for no reason at all. Nothing to see here.

After breakfast we walked up and down the narrow streets of the French Quarter. We peeked into the courtyard at Napoleon House, and then rested awhile on the benches in Jackson Square. The day was hot and humid, and sweat stains were visible on our clothes even in the most unlikely places. I hoped we could sit in the dark, coolness of St. Louis Cathedral, but my parents weren't interested in going inside. I was disappointed—I needed to say a little prayer for courage to make it through the day without bawling, but I put on a happy face, and held the memory of my April visit close.

I was still full from breakfast, but we stopped for coffee and beignets at Café du Monde, an obligatory visit for any first-time New Orleans tourist. Then we tramped all the way across the quarter to the oldest cemetery in New Orleans. In Moore my ancestors were buried deep in hard red dirt, but New Orleans was filled with cities of the dead. Family tombs housed generations on top of one another, forced to live together for eternity. These crumbling edifices were surrounded with their own wrought iron fences, such an integral part of New Orleans architecture that I hardly took notice of them anymore. The tiny city was crowded with tombs arranged smack dab up against each other on narrow streets. The place felt eerily familiar and I realized it was where the *Easy Rider* acid trip took place. My dad took a picture of us in front of a tomb, one of only three photos he took that day, despite being an avid photographer. He had me turn to the side with my mother slightly in front so she could shield my baby bump. They wanted to leave almost as soon we arrived. My mom said she was burning up. She said that the air was so thick and heavy she could hardly breath.

But I had unspoken business at the grave of a voodoo queen. "I'll meet you up front," I told them as I rushed around a corner. Although unmarked, the tomb wasn't hard to find. Vandals and petitioners covered the gray walls with "XXX" scratches, and the ground was littered with flowers, small trinkets and bobby pins. I was glad Freddie told me to knock three times—defacing the tomb seemed like such a disrespectful way to request help.

I pulled out the three pieces of Mary Jane candy I had dropped into my pocketbook earlier that morning. I placed my hand on the tomb's wall. Knock, knock, knock.

I dropped one piece of candy and sent my intention up to the heavens and Marie Laveau. As Freddie suggested, I thought of standing at the altar hearing the preacher say, "I now declare you husband and wife." Second piece of candy. I imagined our first home together—OU's married student housing. We're having a dinner party, and I'm making spaghetti for all our friends. Third piece of candy. I wasn't prepared for this request, and my mind flitted ahead to a distant future where I meet a young man who calls me "mama."

"Lani?"

I heard my mother call my name from a distance. By the sound of it, my parents were at the entrance to the cemetery, anxious to leave. I rested my hand a moment longer on the crumbling brick wall and knocked three more times, just in case the infamous Voodoo Queen Marie hadn't heard me the first time.

Later that afternoon we drove out to Lake Pontchartrain and had dinner at a seafood restaurant. Again, my baby wasn't talked about at all except for indirectly—"How are they treating you?" and "What does the doctor say?" They shared some stories from home—my sisters' summer activities, what Billy was up to, news from First Baptist—but nothing of substance. It was easier if we just stuck to what we were seeing or hearing or tasting in the moment—we couldn't discuss what had come before and we certainly weren't going to ponder what lay ahead. I knew that when my parents left, I wouldn't see them again until I came home, and my baby was gone. This was the only time we shared him as a real, tangible entity, yet neither my mother nor my father acknowledged my pregnancy, and neither of them touched my belly.

When I arrived back at Sellers, I discovered Glenda was in the hospital. She walked to the library and came back in labor. Miss Popwell took her, but then the news came that Miss Popwell's father was near death, so she left Glenda alone. I couldn't imagine how terrifying that might be.

That evening I thought back on the day, especially the trip to the shores of Lake Pontchartrain. Although it was a freshwater lake, in my eyes it looked as wide as a sea. In the muddy, red lakes of Oklahoma it's easy enough to spit as far as the middle. When I stood at the edge of Pontchartrain, I had no view of the opposite shoreline. All I could see were miles upon miles of empty water stretching out to infinity. For a short while I sat on the cold concrete steps they call the Sea Wall. Sitting there, the wind whipping white caps that danced like Flipper on his back, I could almost imagine I was Poseidon sitting on his throne. Could I paddle far away? Not likely. When we were little, playing in the shallow waters of Indian Creek, my mom kept us encased in orange vests and plastic inner tubes. It was her way of trying to keep us safe. Now instead of a plastic inner tube around my waist, I carried a baby. My mother didn't throw out a lifeline. She wasn't coming to save me. And I still didn't know how to swim.

Cotton Candy

The new girl stood at the doorway of the dining room. She looked like a human Bambi—afraid of hunters in the clearing and very much missing her mother. She arrived sometime in the early morning. Mrs. York brought her around before lunch and introduced her; she seemed as sweet as her name—Candy.

Fair, curly hair bounced above her shoulders. The color of honey when you hold the glass jar up to the sun. It looked as if a halo surrounded her face. She seemed nice, about my age, so I caught her eye and waved her over to our table. I was in my usual spot with Georgie, Jo and Anita.

I pulled out the seat next to me. "Here, you go. I saved you a seat." Up close, I was amazed at how tall she was. She must have been at least 5 foot 10. To this day I tell everyone that I'm 5 foot 5 inches tall, but I have never measured more than 5 foot 4 my whole life.

I scooted my chair closer to the table. The new girl slid into her seat and looked over at me with a half-smile. "Thanks. I guess the first few days are the hardest, huh?"

Something sweet floated from Candy's direction. She smelled amazing. I wondered if it was the soap she used.

"Yeah, they're hard, but I hear the last few days are killer. You're Candy, right? Is that a pseudonym or your real name?"

Jo laughed. "There you go again, Lani, getting fancy with your five-dollar words. Candy, Lani's the professor. My name's Jospehine, but everyone calls me Jo-Jo."

Candy glanced around the table unsure of all the newfound attention. Her eyes were a deep gray blue—the color of the ocean when a cloud passes overhead. I didn't want to look in too deeply; I had never felt that kind of physical attraction to a girl before, and it left me feeling vulnerable and confused.

I started again. "Candy, you know what I mean, don't you? Are you using your real name or a made-up one? I've never known anyone named Candy before."

Before she had a chance to answer, Mrs. York stood up at the head table. "Girls, we have a new young lady with us today. If I haven't introduced you already, say hello to Candy. Candy, will you please stand?"

Candy pushed her chair back from the table and got to her feet. Her hand was trembling, and she steadied herself by touching my shoulder. The touch itself was soft, almost imperceptible, but I felt a tiny tingle of electricity and for no known reason my heart seemed so heavy and full that a single kind word could have made it overflow.

Mrs. York continued. "Make a point of helping Candy get comfortable here. Let us pray."

Candy sat back in her chair. I was surprised at how sad I felt when her hand moved from my shoulder and into her lap. We bowed our heads, and Mrs. York droned on for longer than necessary about the food, the hands that made it, and the hands that served it. I wondered why in all those months of being on pots and pans detail, we never heard any thankfulness for the hands that cleaned up the caked-on mess.

When the prayer was over, girls began bringing in trays of food from the kitchen. Since we ate family style, each of the six tables was laden with a bowl of salad, a bowl of tuna casserole, a bowl of peas, and a pitcher of milk.

I took the pitcher and poured the cold milk into tall drinking glasses. I looked over at Candy. She was unusually pretty in a model/movie star kind of way. Like Peggy Lipton from "The Mod Squad," but with shorter, curly hair. "Hope you like milk, cause you gotta drink at least three glasses a day. Me, I detest milk with a passion, but Miss Popwell says it's good for my baby, so I force myself."

I placed the pitcher back on the table and picked up my glass. "Chug-a-lug."

Candy smiled and finished her glass in about three swallows.

"Wow, that's impressive." I handed her the bowl of salad. "They dress the salad in the kitchen. Less mess that way, and nothing to argue over. Usually it's Ranch or Thousand Island but on Sundays sometimes we get French."

Candy put salad on her plate and passed the bowl to Anita. "I don't care what they feed me. Nothing's going to seem like home anyway. I just gotta bide my time until this is over." I heard a catch in her throat. I was sure if someone looked at her crosswise, she would have burst into tears, which could have set the whole table to bawling.

"On the weekends we get chocolate milk. Doesn't that make all the sex worthwhile?" I joked.

Candy looked shocked at the mention of the "S" word, but if she thought that was bad, just wait until she went out on the smoking porch. There we had enough sex talk to make our toes curl.

Candy smiled. "I might miss out on the chocolate milk. My mom's coming to visit every Saturday. So, I guess I had all that sex for nothing."

I felt an inward sigh of relief, glad she wasn't uptight. With Cheryl and Glenda gone, and Jo and Georgie close to their due dates, I wanted a friend for the long, hot summer.

"So back to the earlier discussion. Is Candy your real name?"

"I know what pseudonym means." She glanced in Jo's direction. "And you might catch me throwing in a few expensive words myself. I'm one of those nerds who likes to read the dictionary for fun." Her eyes brightened. "Candy's my real name. It's short for Candace."

Georgie pushed some peas onto her fork with her knife. "I'm Georgie. But that's not my real name. Did you get teased a lot when you was a kid?"

Anita let out a little laugh. "Yeah, do the boys tell you they want to eat you up, you're so sweet?"

Candy blushed. "Yes, on both counts. And today I feel as inconsequential as spun sugar, if you must know."

Jo raised her hands to the heavens. "Lordy, Lani, now that there's a ten-dollar word. I think you've found yourself a soul mate."

I started to blush, but quickly switched into a playful pissed-off mode and glared at Jo across the table. I scrunched up my face. "Eat your peas, Josephina Colleen." I turned back to Candy. "Don't mind them, Candy. They're just ignoramuses. When's your due date?"

She hesitated while she finished a mouthful of tuna casserole. "August 28th. I've got about ten weeks to go. How about y'all?"

Jo piped up. "Can't you tell by the size of this belly that I'm down to my last week?"

Georgie moved the tuna casserole out to the edges of her plate. "I'm due on the Fourth of July."

Candy looked at Anita, whose plate was empty and so clean it looked like it had already been washed. "Sorry to embarrass you with that candy eating business. I'm Anita. That's my real name. I'm due in the middle of July, and it can't come soon enough, let me tell you. I got baby pigs at home."

I groaned. "Anita, you gotta stop it with the pigs." I swallowed my last mouthful of milk. "And I'm sorry, I neglected to introduce myself. I'm Lani and I'm due on August 28th too. We'll be having our babies at the same time, so we can wile away the long hot days of summer together."

Candy's eyes widened. "The 28th of August? What are the chances of that? So, are you pretty new here too?"

I picked up Candy's plate and scraped the leftover food onto my own. She had hardly eaten a thing—a case of first day jitters.

"No, I'm an old-timer. Been here since March. I can show you all the ropes."

I sensed pity in her eyes. I was sure she was wondering what kind of family I had that would leave me there so long. Sometimes I wondered the same thing.

Glenda Sends Cookies

"Lani, there's a package downstairs. It's from Glenda."
I didn't need to be told twice. Glenda plus package equaled cookies. I jumped up from my bed and nearly knocked over the half empty glass of water on my bedside table.

"Coming, I'm coming."

I really missed having Glenda around, but if I were honest with myself, I was a little jealous of her, too. Not because she was smart and beautiful, or because she could play the piano. I wasn't even jealous of her red hair. No, I was jealous because she was out and moving on—not stuck like I was in this uncomfortable pregnant pause.

At Sellers, especially after school let out, time seemed strange. I knew there were everyday changes in my body, but except for the stretch marks that crossed my stomach like the tributaries of the Amazon River, the changes were so small and insignificant I didn't always notice them. Until I looked at a picture of myself from three months ago, I would have been hard pressed to believe that time was marching on. Each moment felt stretched out like silly putty. I hung suspended outside the real world—insulated, separated. The news of each day never consisted of much more than what was to eat, whether or not the doctor was coming, who was going to the hospital, who was coming home. Because I worked in the nursery, I knew which babies had been adopted, but we were given the strongest admonitions to always push the thought of the babies, our babies, right out of our minds. I lost more and more of my sense of self—who I was and who I wanted to be. Every day began and ended with waiting—waiting for the baby to come, waiting for the day I could leave that place, waiting to go back home. More than anything I was waiting to believe that the tremendous hole that was tearing me up inside would someday close.

I met Jo as she reached the top of the stairs. We turned and went back down together. Her breath came in short pants. Her mouth was open, and she kept her tongue behind her teeth.

I slipped my arm around her. "Are you all right? You're breathing kinda heavy."

Jo pulled away from my sisterly embrace. "I'm fine." Even after almost four months of rooming together, four months of nightly confidences, four months of shared eye rolling over Renee's tantrums and Anita's pictures of pigs, Jo was still prickly and uncomfortable with public displays of affection. "Lani, I'm two days late. The baby hasn't dropped, and it's so damned hard to breathe." Her voice came out strangled, as if she had just run a ten-minute mile.

We entered the dining room. Mrs. York stood near the sideboard handing out mail, like she did every weekday afternoon around two. We were like the women in Cell Block C, so desperate for news from home, even a dumb Hallmark card would have been welcome—anything from the outside world.

I never expected to receive letters unless they were from former Sellers inmates. Randall still called every Thursday night, and my mom had called a couple of times and written letters in the first couple of months, but both her calls and her letters were now few and far between. I had given up hope on ever hearing from Dayna.

Some of the residents, like Jo, still had boyfriends who wrote, and those letters got catcalls. Later, after dinner, when it was dark and all the staff had left for the day or gone to bed, we read the juicy parts out loud on the smoking porch.

Some of us got a hot letter one week followed by a "Dear Jane" the next. My Memaw would say, "Why pay for milk when the cow is free?" I think she meant that if someone was getting something for nothing, then they didn't want to put in the work required for a relationship and might drop you like a hot potato if something easier came along.

Sometimes girls got hard letters from home—like when Anita's grandma had a stroke or Alison's dog died—but there was nothing any of us could do about it. Once you were at Sellers, there was no going back, especially in our condition. I never saw anyone punch a wall—usually the girl just broke down and cried. The rest of us felt pretty helpless, so we all said a little prayer or took on extra chores to show we cared.

The girls I felt the most sorry for were the girls who never got letters. It was understandable when you didn't get letters from friends or even the baby's father. Our whereabouts were supposed to be a national secret, like we were a bunch of undercover spies. When I was in eighth grade, my dad was sent somewhere out in the middle of the Pacific. We didn't know where he was or what he was doing. We couldn't mail him any letters the whole six months he was gone. He never sent any to us, either, which made those six months harder on my mom than the eighteen months he spent in Vietnam. I couldn't imagine what it would be like to never have any contact from anyone back home.

Glenda's package was on the table to the left. As soon as Mrs. York finished handing out the mail—no letters for Jo or me—we grabbed the package and headed for the rec room.

A hungry flock gathered. Out of habit we usually sat around the television set that time of day to watch "Dark Shadows," but they cancelled it in April, so we had to make do with "General Hospital" and "The Dating Game." After a few weeks of watching soap operas, the characters were becoming as real to me as they were to Georgie. I couldn't believe that Jessie and Dr. Hardy hadn't managed to get it together. They seemed so right for each other.

I placed the box on the card table. Before the box was even opened, the dark, rich smell of chocolate made the hair in our noses stand up and take notice. Glenda always sent plenty to share, and within seconds outstretched hands surrounded the table. We were all so desperate for something good, something homemade, and Glenda did not disappoint.

Three-dozen cookies filled the box, arranged in six neat layers. Glenda had experimented with some of the recipes she baked while at Sellers, and she sent a mix of all the best cookies possible—chocolate chip, snickerdoodle, peanut butter, and oatmeal.

I passed around the cookies, and soon a Gospel chorus of yummy noises filled the room. Munching my own heavenly morsel, I searched the box for a letter. "Let's hear how Glenda's doing," I announced, peanut butter still clinging to the roof of my mouth.

I unfolded pink stationery printed with robins and roses, and smelled the spicy scent of Tabu, a fragrance that always seemed out of place with Glenda's good girl image. "Let's see. *'Hi Lani! What's new? Things here are about the same. I got a letter from Betty last week. She sure sounded glad to be home!'*"

"Who's Betty?" Anita interrupted.

"She was my temporary roommate, before I moved in with this bunch of thugs." I smiled at Jo and Renee, both chewing a second cookie. "Betty left here in April, but her folks wanted it to seem like she was away at college, so she had to go stay with relatives until school let out."

"That sucks. I'm gonna go straight home and see my pig."

Jo interrupted. "Enough with the pig, Anita. Lani, finish the letter."

> "Who's running the kitchen now? Is Mary still down there? Please tell her I said "Hi!" I can imagine what a mess everything is. Is the food just as bad? Don't worry—you won't starve. I still need to lose five pounds. I just can't seem to get rid of it. And it's all in my tail. If I don't get rid of it soon, I'll just get an ax and chop it off."

Anita reached for her third cookie. "Well, I'm gonna have five pounds in my tail if she keeps sending cookies like these."

Jo rolled her eyes, her patience running thin. "Anita, no one is forcing you to eat the cookies. That's your third one, but who's counting. And if you keep interrupting, we'll never finish the letter. Lani, please continue."

> "Guess what I did last night—went on a date. I couldn't believe it when I got asked. We went to eat steak at the Bonanza Steak House with mom and dad. Then we went to see a show and my folks went to see some relatives. We saw "Pretty Maids All in a Row." Lani, I've never been so embarrassed in my whole life! That's the type of movie that you have to see to believe! After we saw the movie we rode over to some friend's house."

"Who's she dating? She's not seeing Dale again, is she?" Renee piped up, her face pinched, eyes narrowed.

"I don't think so. It must be someone new. She woulda said if it was Dale."

"Good, 'cuz he sounded like one huge asshole."

I shrugged. I had heard Glenda's stories about Dale, and he definitely sounded like a jerk, but I also knew that the heart goes where it goes. Lots of the girls went back to the baby's father. I was one of them. Of course, I believed Randall was different, but then we all said that. Sometimes it just came down to making the wrong choices over and over again. But isn't it the optimist who keeps doing the same thing expecting different results?

I continued reading.

> "I got home about 11:45 and Mom & Dad were just as nice as ever. Actually, I was surprised! I was so afraid they'd think something—you know? But I didn't do anything. We didn't even go parking! For some odd reason I wasn't in the mood! Ha! Bruce doesn't know

> *anything and I'm glad. I'd kinda be afraid of him if he did!"*

"So, do you think if guys know we've been pregnant, they'll be expecting us to put out?" Georgie stared out the rec room door. She was worried about her weight, and she barely touched her cookie. The courtyard, shaded by afternoon sun, looked as cool as a polar bear's cage at the zoo, but it was merely a trick of the eyes, and heat rose from the concrete slab along with Georgie's anxiety.

"Sweetie, no one is going to know unless you tell them. OK?" I tried my most comforting voice, the one I used with the babies in the nursery. The one I heard my mother use a thousand times when one of us kids came running to her with a scraped knee or elbow. "Now, back to Glenda."

> *"This morning I went to see the doctor. I'm still bleeding. Honestly, I've never seen one doctor so much in my whole life! I've seen him three times since I've been home! And I've got to go once more. But at least it doesn't hurt anymore."*

"I wonder why it hurts," Anita queried. "I thought they're supposed to knock us out. They better. I don't want to know nothin' about it."

No one, not the nurses or the social workers or the doctors, ever explained to us what it would be like to experience labor. No one explained what it would be like to actually deliver a baby. I knew from movies that it was a scary prospect and that it hurt like hell. In *Gone with the Wind*, Scarlett told Melanie that she didn't need to be brave. She could yell all she wanted to because there was no one to hear. Would we be knocked out? Would it hurt? And, if so, how much?

"It's probably nothing. It just takes a while to heal. I heard something like six weeks." Jo grabbed her third cookie and looked over at me. "This is it. I'm stopping here."

"Well I should hope so. Especially since you could go into labor any second now." I looked down at Glenda's beautiful handwriting, searching for my place.

> *"I got a letter saying summer school starts Monday. I can't wait! This place is so boring. Everyone has changed. I still haven't seen Dale anywhere. One of these days I'm going to ride by his house just for meanness. It'll be my*

luck his mom will see me and then I'd die. She's been so nice and sweet about the whole deal.

Tomorrow is Father's Day. It took me a long time to decide what to get him. I finally ended up with an orange striped shirt and a beautiful tie and some Old Spice aftershave lotion. I started to make him a tie and then decided not to. Have you ever made that tie yet? How's your sewing coming along?"

Anita piped up. "I love Old Spice. I even put it on Susie once, when I took her to the fair."

Brenda, one of the new girls and due in the middle of October, broke into the conversation. "Who's Susie?"

"Anita's pig. Just ignore her. Anita, no one wants to hear about your pig." Jo's pancake-thin patience had worn thinner than Glenda's stationery, and her face was just about the same shade of pink. I couldn't tell if it was because she was mad about always hearing about the pig, or maybe now something might be happening with her body and her baby.

Before Anita has a chance to answer, I returned to the letter. The next few paragraphs seemed too personal to read aloud—Glenda complaining that Mrs. York hadn't written and bemoaning that fact that Miss Popwell was so nice and still unmarried—so I skipped a few lines.

"Has Mrs. York gone on her vacation yet? Bless her heart. I think she's so sweet. Glad we got a new nurse, and I hope Miss Popwell's dad will soon be better so she can come back to work. There's not much more news. I'll close for now. Take care of yourself and be good. Write me sometime real soon. Love ya! Glenda"

Jo looked up with a cookie still stuffed in her mouth. "Nice letter. Ummm, these are so good." She brushed the crumbs off her generous chest. The white peasant blouse rode up and exposed more than half the stretch panel of her red linen shorts. Her nipples were leaking, but Miss Popwell said they couldn't give her anything to dry up her milk until after the baby came. I hoped for Jo's sake she wouldn't have to wait much longer.

Temporarily satisfied, the hungry horde dissipated, and Jo and I were left with an empty box of cookies. "Oh, shoot. I didn't save any cookies for Candy."

Candy had only been at Sellers for a few days, but her mother had already come down from their home in Mississippi for a visit. She planned on spending every Saturday with Candy until her delivery.

I was envious of Candy's relationship with her mother. They almost seemed like best friends, not mother and daughter. I knew my mom loved me, but Candy's mom was there for her every step of the way. Candy talked to her mom on the phone a few times a week. They spent every Saturday together. My mom came to visit once. After the first couple of months she never called, and she hardly ever wrote. I felt like laundry that had been hung out to dry and then forgotten. I was faded almost to nothing by the sun, and so whipped by the wind that I was nothing but tatters. I knew my mom was busy with work and church and my dad. I knew taking care of him was almost another full-time job for her. And of course, there was Kathy, Carla, Janet, and Billy, but I needed desperately to know that I still mattered to her. I missed her so much. I had disappointed her grievously, but I couldn't change that any more than I could change the direction the earth circles the sun. I had been such a good daughter—straight A student, hard worker, involved at church and extracurricular activities at school—I wondered if she would ever feel proud of me again.

Jo interrupted my rumination. "Well, Lani, doesn't your Memaw always say, when you snooze, you lose?"

"What? Oh, right, Candy's loss is our gain. Whadya think, Jo? A glass of cold milk would taste mighty good right now. Want some?"

We gathered up the empty box and headed to the kitchen.

With school out, I could feel the creep of something coming in—maybe it was boredom. If I were back home, even stocking shelves at Steven's Pharmacy would beat my day-to-day life at Sellers. At home, I had choices that felt so luxurious compared to what I was doing in New Orleans: What do I bring to the July 4th barbeque? Do I want to go to Falls Creek Camp this summer? Do I want to bake cookies today? Do I want to go with Randall to a movie on Saturday?

Back in Moore, my friends were hanging out and doing something, or maybe they were doing nothing at all. But they were doing it together. They were sharing experiences—good, bad, it didn't matter—because they were creating a story, and I was just plain written out of it.

I wanted to go back to that. A life of choices. A life of creating new stories with my friends. I wondered if, when I got back to Moore, I would make a grand entrance—return to being a star of the show—or would I hang out in the background with no lines to say, just an extra with no name.

Gin Rummy

"You call that shuffling? You'll never break them in that way." Candy reached for the deck of Bicycle playing cards. "Give 'em to me."

I bought the deck the previous day at the St. Charles Woolworth's just on the off-chance Candy might like card games. We played cards a lot in my family—after all the turkey was eaten and we had washed up the Thanksgiving dishes, Grandma and Aunt Erma played Rook while they were eating their last bite of pecan pie. But I got turned off Rook during those vacations alongside Indian Creek when I was forced to partner with my dad. The summer I spent at Sellers, I was partial to Rummy, or Gin Rummy, if there were only two, and I would play Queens or Spades when I could get together a table of four.

Usually I could tell a lot about a girl by the way she shuffled cards. The way she dealt the cards. Did I have a competitor on my hands, or someone needing to kill time? If I were the dealer, I watched to see if my opponent waited to look at them all at once or if she picked up each card as it was laid down. Was she impulsive or deliberate? Take Candy for instance. She exuded confidence. She took my brand-new deck, bent it almost in half, and started shuffling like a professional card shark. The cards arched like a church window and fell gently, alternating, one after the other.

Me, I didn't get the art of the shuffle. When a deck was new, the cards dropped in clumps, so I stood half the deck on its side and wiggled the rest of the cards down from the top. Or I just spread the deck out on the table and moved the cards back and forth under my hands. Certainly not the proper way to shuffle, as Candy pointed out. I knew it wouldn't be long before she figured out my confidence was fake too.

"So, what do you want to play, Lani?" Candy held the deck in her hand, ready to deal. "A hand of Gin Rummy?"

Sitting cross-legged on top of Candy's bed in the pink roses room, our bellies grazed the ribbed surface of the matching pink chenille bedspread. "Sure, sounds good."

Candy dealt each of us ten cards, and a three of diamonds started the discard pile. "You go first, Lani."

Card playing was a good way to get acquainted. I could ask personal questions without seeming too obnoxious. I drew a six of hearts and discarded the five of diamonds. "Are you still seeing your baby's father?" Sitting near Candy had me all flustered. I felt flickers of happiness, like I'd taken the first bite of a summer strawberry after a whole winter of mealy apples.

"Heavens, no. You?" Candy discarded an eight of clubs.

"Yeah. His name's Randall. We've been going together for more than a year. He calls every week—Thursday night, 8:15 on the dot. And he's paying some of the money for me to stay here." I drew a six of clubs. "He's pretty much promised we'll get married after we graduate."

Candy examined my face instead of her cards. "I don't understand. If you're gonna get married anyway, why don't you do it now so you can keep your baby? Don't you want to keep your baby?"

Without thinking I laid down one of my aces by mistake. "Randall won't turn seventeen until October. His folks say we're too young, and a baby will screw up everything."

"What do you think, Lani? Would a baby screw up everything?" Candy discarded a ten of clubs, and the briefest hint of a smile crossed her face. At least one of us was focused on the game.

I drew a three of diamonds and discarded it. "It's hard to imagine getting through high school with a baby, let alone college. You wanna go to college?"

"Not sure. I think I'll go to Vo-tech for cosmetology." Candy discarded a nine of clubs.

I didn't get Candy's strategy. She had discarded an eight, nine and ten of clubs. Maybe I was making her a little flustered, too. I picked up my second jack, a diamond. "You like to cut hair? I've been thinking about getting my hair cut before I go home."

"I could do that. We could have a beauty shop night." Candy ran her fingers through her curls, wild and tangled like weeds. I wanted to touch it. I'd never seen a blond with such natural, thick curls. I laid down the four of clubs.

"Did you notice Georgie's hair?"

"Yeah, she told me she hasn't even had a trim for five years." Candy discarded a two of spades.

I picked up the ace of clubs. "I would think in this heat she'd hate it that long. I know it would drive me crazy. Is your hair natural? It's such a pretty color." I wasn't sure what to do since I had discarded that other ace, but I decided to hold on to this one and discarded the nine of diamonds.

"Thanks. Yeah, it's mine. No bottle. I could do something with yours if you want."

"So, I don't look like such a mouse, you mean."

"Naw, don't take it like that. Your hair's fine. I was just thinking when we cut it, we could frost it or something." Candy laid an eight of diamonds on the discard pile. I picked up a six of diamonds.

"OK. Randall might like that. Though I'm not sure he'll like it too short. He keeps his as long as he can get away with." This time I decide to place the ace of spades on the discard pile. Candy picked it up and discarded an eight of hearts. "Hot, huh?"

"I'll say. I'm here, aren't I? What about you?" I picked up Candy's eight and discarded the other ace in my hand.

"Well, Ray, my baby's father, we started going out when I was a freshman. He was a junior. My mom was OK with it 'cause he was a good friend of my brother's." Candy laid down the four of diamonds.

"They played basketball together. I held him off for about six months, but when he was a senior, and a BMOC, well, the pressure was on. Not that I didn't like the attention. Then this year he went off to Southern Miss, about two hours away, and we got together every time he came back on a weekend." She looked down at her belly. "This is probably the result of homecoming."

"What'd he say when you told him you were pregnant?" I picked up a king of diamonds. I had another run worth 30 points. I threw the eight of hearts back on the discard pile.

Candy examined her cards and picked the eight back up. I couldn't figure out what she was doing. First, she didn't want it and then she did.

"He didn't say much. Except to wonder if the baby's his. Asshole. Sorry, excuse my French. Like he didn't know he was my first and only." She discarded a five of clubs.

"Hey, I'm sorry." I picked up a queen of diamonds and quickly laid it back on the pile.

Candy picked up the queen with a straight face. Like I didn't know she was probably holding two others. "It's OK. Connor, that's my brother, he coulda killed him when he found out. They'd been best friends since fifth grade. But it's all over now, baby blue." She discarded a four of hearts.

"Because we're stuck inside New Orleans with the Memphis blues again?" I picked up a four of spades and laid it on top of the other four.

"Because we've been listening to 'Lay Lady Lay' one time too many." Candy picked up the four of spades and discarded a three of hearts. "Gin." She exposed her hand—three queens, the eight, nine and ten of hearts, the ace, two, three and four of spades. A total of sixty-seven points.

"Candy, you're just like a woman, and a Dylan fan to boot. I've got forty-eight points. Wanna play another hand?"

"No, I want a Butterfinger. Let's walk to Woolworth's."

A Month of Sundays Summer

The summer dragged on.

Miss Popwell's dad seemed to be getting better, so she came back to work, only to have him die within days of her return to Sellers. Miss Popwell was devastated beyond words. Even though she must have been in her forties, she still referred to herself as "daddy's little girl." She told the story to anyone who would listen about how two men saved her life. The first was Jesus, of course, since he died for our sins and all. The second was her dad because about ten years back he gave her one of his kidneys when both of hers failed and she went on dialysis. Miss Popwell hated dialysis. She said she hated the time it took—the waiting, the weakness. The doctors said the quickest way to find a match was through a family member, but she didn't want her dad to do it—give her his kidney—since it was such major surgery and he was getting on in years. Eventually her dad convinced her it would be okay, and so the doctors took one of his kidneys out and put it inside her. She had been fine ever since—never felt better, she said. Her dad? Not so much. His recent illness didn't have anything to do with the surgery or from having only one kidney—he had brain cancer—but Miss Popwell had blamed herself ever since his last bout in the hospital. I was afraid she would hate herself forever when he died without her by his side.

I wanted to make her feel better, but there wasn't much I could do except care for Tigger while she was away. Ornery cat. She should have gotten him fixed to keep him from running away every night, but Miss Popwell said that she wanted to keep him the way God made him. For such a smart person, that was one of the stupidest things I had ever heard. As my Memaw would have said, "That idea is dumber than a box of rocks." It was always my way of thinking that God made plenty of things that needed fixin'. Rivers needed bridges and farms needed wind breaks and streptococcus germs needed penicillin. And unless we wanted our alleyways to be overrun with unwanted litters of kittens, outdoor cats needed to be fixed. Regardless, Tigger at times was a good cat, and I liked the way he rubbed against my legs, purring like he had hidden a tiny motor in his chest.

Baptists sing, *"my life flows on in endless song,"* but our days flowed on in endless boredom and our desired and dreaded expectations about going home. Almost everyone I knew and loved was gone. First, Cheryl, then Glenda, finally Jo and Georgie. All delivered from the lion's den, our prison or insane asylum depending on the day. Only Anita and Renee remained of my original group of roommates and friends. I was so thankful that Candy showed up when she did.

The summer of 1971 did have a soundtrack—*Tapestry* by Carole King. After the album was released earlier in the spring, I went to a record store near Tulane University to buy it. Every track rang true for one of us (except for maybe "Slapwater Jack"). "It's Too Late" for those moving on from the no-good boyfriends who couldn't keep promises. "(You Make Me Feel Like) A Natural Woman" for the desperate longing for love and acceptance that sent many of us into the arms of men for validation, only to wind up pregnant and in our current predicament. "Will You Still Love Me Tomorrow" was for those who were abandoned or rejected when the answer from our lovers was a resounding, "No." "So Far Away" was the song that cried us to sleep. "You've Got A Friend" was what we believed about each other.

Letters from Sellers' friends provided insight into what life might be like when I returned home. Nothing seemed like it would be easy. First, explaining away our disappearance and picking up where we left off with friends and family, all the while worrying about our baby and suppressing shame and guilt. I had been away from home for four months, and I still had two more to go. How could I ever pretend to be the same person I was when I left?

June 27, 1971

Hi Lani,

How are things in the nursery? Now that I'm home, I'm so happy I have a friend working there.

I just got back from church. Man, it feels great to be singing in the choir. I really did miss that! Our Youth Choir is going to Callaway Gardens in a few weeks. Boy, I can't wait. It really should be fun—especially since the boys will be going.

You'll have to write me and let me know about my baby and when he gets adopted. Please look at his eyes and let me know what color they are. When y'all weigh babies, let me know how much he weighs now. Thanks.

How's Miss Popwell doing? Is she getting any happier? I wrote her a note yesterday. Did she say anything to you about those clothes I made for her? Bless her heart—she's really had it rough.

No one has said anything to me about being gone except for June. She tried to find me while I was away, and she called last Thursday night. She was so nosey. Said she wanted me to know she understood everything! I'm never going to admit to anyone I was pregnant—never! So, if she thinks she's getting something out of me, she's crazy.

Well, I guess I'd better go. Take good care of yourself and don't get too fat!

Love, Glenda

July 1, 1971

Dear Glenda,

I'm heading to bed, but I want to give you a quick update about Charlie. He's doing fine. He's everyone's favorite and we give him plenty of love and attention. He's also beautiful, with eyes as blue as his mama's. Maybe they'll stay that way. He's a good eater, too, with no spitting up. Bethany is about the only one that really spits up much. But I won't tell Cheryl that—I wouldn't want her to worry.

Miss Popwell is away for a couple of weeks in Williamsburg. When she comes back, she's bringing her mom to live with her in the yellow house. I'm watching

Tigger. Big, fat, happy cat. Last night he was on the prowl. Seven of us spent hours looking for him. Hooped and hollered up and down the street, just to have him come walking across the fences like one of our no-good boyfriends after a late-night drinking binge.

A new girl came in the beginning of June from Mississippi. Real sweet. A senior like me, and our due dates are the same. Unfortunately for her, she ended up working in the kitchen. It's a mess—every week there's a different person in charge—at least she will only have to do it until the end of July.

I'm sorry you've got a little gnat being a nosy parker. Just ignore her and all the rest of the busybodies. You don't owe anyone any explanation.

It's been a long day, so I'll close. I'm trying my best not to get fat, and it's certainly easier since you left. No one can bake the way you can. Write soon.

As always,

Lani

 The administrative staff was in and out on vacation, and some days it felt like we were fending for ourselves. Good thing most of us were resourceful, responsible and obedient. Beds got made, food was cooked and eaten, laundry was washed, folded and put away, and the babies in the nursery always had Freddie and Shirleen. I wondered when they ever spent time with their own families; they were the one constant in our lives.

 I was getting bigger by the day, and I worried about our care. Ever since Miss Popwell's dad died, she had been away for weeks leaving an older, easily distracted part-time nurse in charge. The doctor situation was iffy for most of the summer. One was supposed to come every week, especially for the girls expecting within the month, but we were lucky if a doctor showed up every other week.

 I believed from the start that I was having a boy. Freddie said it must be so since I was already carrying low and I craved savory foods instead of sweet. I really needed my baby to be a boy. I didn't think I could bear to give up a daughter.

The Fourth of July fell on a Sunday. There were no fireworks, not even sparklers, but after church we had a barbecue with a hibachi that Mrs. Stafford brought from home. Hamburgers and hot dogs. Potato salad and baked beans. Deviled eggs. It was just the kind of Independence Day supper I had a hankering for and would have had back home in Moore. I baked an apple pie, and the Powers-that-Be bought us ice cream so we could have our pie à la mode. For once, they let us eat outside in the courtyard.

Jason was adopted the second week of July. We didn't get any advance notice. I came into the nursery to take Jason out for his afternoon walk, and he was gone. I thought my heart would break into a thousand pieces. I hung my arms around Freddie's neck and cried and cried. I had worried about him for more than four months, praying every night that his forever family was out there somewhere. But without his laugh and sweet baby talk, we had a Great Blue Hole in the nursery where his crib used to be.

July 10, 1971

Dear L,

How is life at Sellers? Just like always, probably. I'm doing great. I can walk like I use to. My clothes are all too small, except some shorts that were too big before. Almost all of my stomach is gone. Boy, I'm glad of that.

My girlfriends came to see me yesterday. I saw Darrell too, but I didn't speak. I was scared to. I saw Eldon and Harper today and they were nice to me. Everybody got married while I was gone. Even my cousin ran away and got married.

How's Catherine? Did they have to change her name? I hope not. I wish I didn't have to give her up. But it's too late now. Take care of her.

L, tell everyone hi for me and tell Candy and Renee I'll write as soon as I get a chance. I got to go. Write soon and be sure to write Claudia on the envelope.

Love ya, Georgie

P.S. Has anybody got my bed yet? I hope it's not Susan. Boy, I pity you if it is.

July 17, 1971

L,

I just got your letter. I couldn't believe it. I figured it would be a couple of years before you wrote. I wanted to start taking the pill, but Danny said he didn't want me to use it because they're bad for you, but I don't think they are. Anyway, I'm using contraceptive foam. I miss Sellers. Everybody at least understood everyone else. I bet you miss me bossing you around. Ha. My puppy said hello—he's so cute, he's 6 mths old. Summer school started last week, and one colored girl asked me if I'd had a boy or girl. I told her politely but in no uncertain terms that she was crazy. You know what I did? I wrote Stacy a letter and told her about me & Danny and all about what happened when she was born and a lot of stuff. I'm going to continue it too, because she'll wonder about it (& herself). She'll get it when I die or either when she's 15 & almost 16. I miss Sellers so much that I want to work there when I graduate. Just think this is your last year of school. Danny is playing tonight and I'm just sitting home. All those people who are mean make me sick. The people here are nice but they're not sure I was P.G. My stretch marks are fading out pretty good. I need to lose 4 lbs to be normal and I'm doing exercises every day. My hips are still big, but I can wear my clothes. Danny swears my legs got skinnier and every time I wear a dress, he makes fun of them. His hair reaches his shoulders. I wish he'd get it cut. Maybe you and Georgie can come stay with me next summer. I've got to take a bath now. No More Showers! But write and tell me what's going on. Oh, I forgot to tell you I have an infection on the bottom of my womb. The Dr. said it's common after childbirth. He gave me some sulphur tablets to 'insert' and he painted the bottom of my womb with Silver Nitrate. I have to go back in 3 weeks—I'm sick of going. Write me soon.

Love, Jo

I couldn't fathom why Jo thought Stacy would ever receive the letters she was writing to her. Not a single person at Sellers had ever given us a single reason to hope that we might be able to communicate with our babies in the future. Adoption records were closed. Even if our children wanted to find us, they would have no information to go on. Each of the girls at Sellers had a small 3" x 5" notecard with non-identifying information. Mine said that I was a member of Future Teachers of America and that my dad was in the military. Certainly not enough information to find someone, even if you wanted to. And I knew I would never really know what happened to my baby. He was something I was supposed to forget, a secret to carry to my grave. I was unfit to be his mother and I needed to remember that.

July 28, 1971

Hi Lani!

I was so glad to hear from you. I'm so, so, so glad you've only got one more month! Remember that day I walked to the library? Well, you keep walking down there and it'll all be over! Then you can breathe again—and everything else!

L, once you get home everything will be great. You'll soon forget about S.B.H. And everything bad about it. But you'll miss it. L, there have been so many times I have longed for that place. It's really weird. When you're there, you have security. You don't have to face anyone you don't want to. And you're on a regular schedule. Once you get home, you'll probably do just like I did. Sleep 2 hours a night and eat the rest of the time.

Guess what? Today is my birthday! I'm nineteen years old and feeling great! The main thing that makes me happy is the fact I'm dating Bruce. He's so sweet. He's taking me out to eat and giving me a party.

I had this humagus (sp?) test in math today. It lasted an hour and I still wasn't through.

Did I tell you Cheryl called me the other night? She's so happy. I think she's going to get married soon. She also told me some sad news—Betty's pregnant again.

I got a letter from Mrs. Stafford yesterday. I had a feeling Charlie hadn't been adopted, but she says he will be soon.

I've seen Dale 3 or 4 times. He never looks at me or anything. I don't know if he hates me or is ashamed. Once he was playing tennis and I walked by the court. I was scared to death.

Bruce, the boy I'm dating, knows all about Sellers. It seems Dale told him I was pregnant. Bruce told me he'd love me no matter what, so I broke down and told him the truth. If Dale's parents knew he'd ever, ever talked about it, he'd really be in for it!

I'm so glad Jason got adopted. Do you know how much Charlie weighs? Does he have any more hair yet? Bless his heart, I hope so. If it's not too much trouble, please write me back and tell me all about him. If by any chance at all you see the people who adopt him, please let me know – what they look like and all.

The other night I finally saw "Love Story." L, I cried like a baby. That was the saddest movie I've ever seen. Even Bruce cried!

L—you keep the faith, say your prayers, and things will work out great. It's so important for you to deliver early. That way you can start school on time.

> Well, I'll quit boring you for a while. Please write me again real soon and let me know how you're doing. Be good and please take good care of yourself.
>
> Love ya! Glenda
>
> P.S. How much weight have you gained? How much do you measure? Excuse my sloppiness—I was kinda in a hurry.
>
> I'm praying for you!

Candy wanted to get some hair-cutting practice in before she delivered, so we set up a beauty shop in the shared bathroom between my blue forget-me-not bedroom and Candy's bedroom papered with pink roses. Alice, one of the newer, less pregnant girls, brought up a chair from the dining room, and we placed it on a towel in front of the mirror.

I had gone to Woolworth's the previous day and bought a box of frosting. Not frosting for a chocolate cake or sugar cookies—no, this frosting was for my hair, and the plan was to have platinum or silver strands mixed in amongst my dish-water blonde. By this time my hair fell below my shoulders; I had added at least three inches since coming to Sellers. Candy showed me pictures of what was all the rage—a shag haircut, kind of like Jane Fonda in *Klute*.

Randall took Dayna to see *Klute* when it was released at the end of June. Of course, I didn't hear about it from her. I left Moore at the end of February, and since then I hadn't heard hide nor hair from her. Randall just dropped their date casually into one of our phone conversations. Just friends, he said, but I had the first flickers of distrust. I pouted that I wanted him to wait and see it with me when I got home, but he was afraid it would leave the theaters before he got a chance to see it, especially since it starred Jane Fonda. Lots of people hated her for her anti-war, "Free the Army" shenanigans. My dad, service man to the core, thought she was a traitor and a half, and should have been hung up by her thumbs to dry. Funny, it was the same sentiment I was starting to have about Dayna.

The only takers of a free haircut beside myself were Anita and Peg. Alice hung out to provide the requisite "oohs" and "aahs" at the moment the finished product was finally revealed. Anita was a dishwater blonde like me, and her hair was long, but not as long as Georgie's, and thin, shapeless, with stringy ends. Peg had dark, medium-length hair, and she wanted it cut as short as Jo's before going to the hospital.

Candy started trimming Anita's hair to just above her shoulders.

"That looks good," Anita said. "Can you cut me some bangs?"

"Sure. I can go shorter all around, too, if you like. Sort of like a bob. It would frame your face."

"You think so? I ain't never had my hair cut short in forever. Been growing it out ever since I was ten. When I was little, I wouldn't let my mom brush the rats out in the morning. So, one day she just took a pair of kitchen shears to it and cut it off right here." Anita pointed to the base of her neck. "She nicked my chin, too. Boy, I cried and cried. Didn't want to go to school; I felt so bald."

"Anita, bless your heart," Candy pooh-poohed. "You are letting yourself get upset over nothing. First off, if I cut it short, it won't be with kitchen shears. I'll be giving it shape. It'll highlight your cheekbones, draw attention to your eyes."

"You really think so?" Anita brightened. "They're my best feature."

Anita had a large round face with small features—thin lips, snub nose. Her eyes were tiny pig eyes, much like the ones I imagined on the face of her precious Susie. Actually, in thinking about it, going only on looks, Anita and I could have been related. We both had the Okie/Arkie too-close-together eyes and lips as thin as reeds.

My mother never cut my hair with kitchen shears, but one Easter she decided that my three sisters and I would have curly hair to go along with our new shiny black patent leather shoes. We set up our beauty shop in my Aunt Veda's kitchen. Aunt Veda, my grandfather's sister, still lived on land my great-grandfather settled after the Run of 1889, and unlike the tiny kitchen in our tract-house, Aunt Veda's farmhouse kitchen stretched out for an acre, holding my mom and me and all three of my sisters in it with room to spare. We placed a tall three-legged stool in front of the gleaming porcelain sink, and, in turn, we each squirmed while our mom tortured us with a Toni Home Permanent. Through the window above the sink, we gazed out on cottonwood trees running along the creek and then out beyond to black & white milk cows that grazed in the pasture. The ammonia-like smell knocked us off our feet, and the pain of having our fine hair yanked around soft foam curlers brought tears to our eyes. The chemicals burned and the solution was too strong, and when it came time to take out the curlers half of our hair was gone.

Candy stopped trimming Anita's hair and handed her a mirror.

Tears welled up in Anita's eyes and trickled down her cheeks. "Ahh, I'm bald, I'm bald."

"No, no, it looks great." Peg, Alice and I all rushed in to comfort Anita and reassure her that everything was okay. Anita no longer had stringy, lifeless hair that fell to the middle of her back. Instead she had a bob that fell just below her chin, and it had both shape and swing. "Candy was right. It does set off your eyes. And even if it is a little short, it will grow back soon."

Anita wasn't convinced, but she seemed to feel better when almost all of Peg's dark mane was scattered on the bathroom floor.

Now it was my turn. To give my hair a frosted effect, Candy applied a bleaching mixture that smelled similar to the solution used for my childhood permanent. I could only hope that this time my hair would stay on my head.

I caught Candy's gaze in the mirror.

When I was younger and my Memaw visited from California, I loved her going-to-bed rituals. Sitting at her vanity table, she removed the dozens of tiny tortoise shell clips that kept her hair in check throughout the day one by one, until a silver waterfall flowed down her back. Then she would let me brush it. One hundred strokes a day, she said, and I would count each one carefully—one, two, three and on to a hundred. Memaw would gaze into the vanity table mirror until she caught my eye in the reflection. I was always spooked looking back at someone in a mirror. Like when I sat in the backseat of our Rambler, and all I could see was the back of my mother's head. I thought her gaze was fixed straight ahead on the road and the traffic around her, but then I would catch her looking at me in the rearview mirror. At the moment our eyes met, I felt looked at in a way I never did when we were face to face. Was it judgment or consideration? Face to face, we rarely made eye contact. I looked over her left shoulder or down at my feet. If I took a chance to glance at her face, she was staring above my head.

Holding eye contact was hard, even with someone I loved like Candy or Randall. I felt like I was opening up some place so soft and fragile that even a hint of displeasure could make me bleed. This time though, Candy smiled as she held my gaze, and I was happy. The frosting chemicals did not cause my hair to fall out, and after my haircut, I felt remarkably free and unencumbered—almost like a different person. Anita only had a short while to worry about her haircut; she went into labor the next day.

Postmarked August 5, 1971

To Susan, Candy, Lani, and anybody else.

Well, I got home allright. And there were so many different things that changed.

Well, what about you guys has anybody went to the hospital. Or has there been any changes in the kichen or anything like that. Ha ha. Martha I'm still hopen that they will take you out of the kichen.

Lani. How are you doing. I hope find. I'm sure your find because they woant let you get sick and go into laber. Well what aboet Candy. Has she had her baby? And how about Renee tell her I had so good meats when I got home. I have four baby pussy cats and they are little brutes. And Susie is twice a big before.

Wed. I went to church and it sure was a lot better than going to church there. And Susie is going to have babys. Anybody want one. Ha ha.

What new there? Besides nothing. Tell Marcia, Renee to write and not Lydia. Please Don't tell her I even write O.K. Because I didn't sign her book. I'm the first to get out of it. And that's the truth.

Boy, I can't get into my people pants. And now my sister, this week in is goning to go and buy me so pants. Well, it's Friday night and there not a thing to do. I'm not going to go anywhere. But it sure is good to be home.

Take care and write when you get a change. Because I know how buss you guys are. Tell all the cool people I said hello and to write.

Love,

Anita

One evening in early August, Dr. Rutledge, Sellers' psychologist, took Candy and me to the French Quarter for dinner at The Court of Two Sisters. We certainly got lots of stares from the other diners—two about-to-burst pregnant teenagers with one really old man. Dr. Rutledge must have been at least thirty since he had just finished his doctoral dissertation. I didn't know if I should be flattered or mad that some university somewhere thought that unwed mothers were a proper subject of study. But the Powers-that-Be certainly let us know all the time that there was something wrong with us. Of course, it had to be that we were flawed somehow. We sinned and we sinned willingly. I was sorry for all the pain and distress I had caused my mother and the rest of the family, but I had no remorse about making love with Randall, predicament aside. If given half a chance, I would have willingly crawled into the back of his Impala and sinned again and again. I was sure that made me triply crazy.

Dinner was lovely. Cloth napkins and gleaming white tablecloths, flowers on every table. I had hoped we could have grownup conversations like I had with friends back home. At Sellers I felt so isolated from the outside world. We never watched the news, and we didn't get a daily newspaper. What was happening with the war? Were students still demonstrating in Washington? What was happening with the efforts to desegregate schools and enforce bussing? Instead, we stuck to safe topics, like our favorite subjects in school and whether or not we wanted to go to college.

After dinner, Candy and I waited while Dr. Rutledge paid the bill. I really needed to pee, but I was too nervous to go in the restaurant. I carried the baby so low it was hard for me to get up and down from the toilet. Candy better not make me laugh, I thought, or I would be in a world of hurt and not fit to sit in Dr. Rutledge's car. A few minutes later he joined us in the in the courtyard, where the air was fragrant with the sticky sweet smell of jasmine. Standing between us, he rubbed his slightly moist hands up and down our backs. This gesture seemed inappropriate, and I felt unsettled not knowing his intentions. Candy must have felt the same way. We shuddered in unison.

"Let's take a walk in the Quarter," Dr. Rutledge suggested. The restaurant was located on Royal Street just a block to the east of Bourbon Street, renowned for all of its bars with frozen daiquiris and Hurricanes in their signature glasses. We didn't understand why he wanted to stroll amongst the raucous crowds and take in the sights, because in 1971, besides bars, Bourbon Street was also the destination for strips shows. Women—some not much older than me and some old enough to be my mother—stood on the upper balconies calling out to the men below. A couple of windows held swings and scantily clad women soared back and forth over our heads, daring men to look up for a glimpse of their singular delights.

Candy and I had never witnessed anything like that—tits of all sizes and shapes with only glittery stars covering the nipples. Hot, sultry jazz, thick as molasses, poured out of the first-floor bars and into the street, and the women's butts with only a slim string caught between their cheeks jiggled to the steamy beat. I felt a familiar tingle in my own personal place of singular delights, and I had to force away the desire to touch another naked body, especially Candy's body, out of my mind.

Postmarked August 7, 1971

Dear L,

I spent last week with my Daddy. Boy, you talk about some good-looking boys. They all around where my Daddy lives. He took me and my stepmother bowling Sat. nite. I saw a lot of boys there that I knew.

Has anybody delivered yet? How about Martha? Has she? I sure hope so.

I've saw Darrell two or three times, but I've not talked to him. I was talking to Mom yesterday about it and she said that she could never hate him. Buster has asked my cousin about me so maybe he don't know. I'll see him Sat. nite at the rodeo. We have to help my Uncle and my cousins move Sat. morning.

Has Catherine been adopted yet? I hope she gets adopted soon. She'll be six weeks old tomorrow. I'm getting my pictures of her developed tomorrow. They said they might not be able to. If I don't get a picture of her, I'll just die. Every time I think about her, I cry.

I've just about quit bleeding. Boy I'll be glad. I'm getting a lot of new clothes, but since school won't start for a while I'm going to make some more. They consolidated the schools and now nobody going to send their kids to school.

I guess I better close for now. Take care of my baby and write me when she gets adopted.

Love ya,

Georgie

One afternoon the kiln in the back of Miss Popwell's yellow house caught fire. We didn't want the house to burn down, but the days had been so long and the heat so oppressive, we welcomed the least bit of excitement. As my Memaw would say, we were as happy as dead pigs in sunshine for the much-needed distraction. We flocked together on the sidewalk, shuffled our feet, giggled and vied for the best viewing position when firemen showed up to put it out. Fortunately, little damage was done, so it wasn't long before we were back to making ashtrays and candy dishes, along with decoupaged wooden wall hangings, and cross-stitched tea towels.

Postmarked August 20, 1971

Hi L,

I'm beginning to wonder if you were going to write me or not. Boy, I sure was glad to here from you.

I'm going to school. The subjects are, Life Science & Hem E II. English, World History, P.E, Math. You know I will have to start study a lot hard if I don't make good grades.

I still have all my pussy cats. The nine of them, the matter of fact. Well, I had puppies too. There are about two week old. There eyes ann't open yeat. I have six and they are so ugle. But I want to keep of them. But I don't think the'll let me keep all of them. But, I sure do want too.

My pig is doing fine. And she is getting pretty every day. And a little fatter to.

Well, I got a new boyfriend his name is Buddy. He so sweet. He cute to. He's got Broun, blond hair and brown eyes. He go's to church with me. And he's seventeen. He don't know how to drive. But he's learning. He's from Chicolo. The 18th of September we are going on a Church Hay Ride. Boy I can't wait. I've never kiss him yeat. But I'm wanting. You know all my girl friends like him. As crazy as I am I got him I don't see how.

I got some good news none of my friends new I was P.G. And I'm so glad.

Well, my hair growing out. And it looks pretty good. But I'm still balled. Ha ha.

I sure do miss you. I wished that some day that we can get it together and talk about the good times we had.

Anita

One night in late August, well after midnight when everyone had gone to bed, the doorbell's incessant ring sounded like a siren. I headed into the hallway. What was going on? No one should have been calling at that time of night. Sinners at the gate of heaven, the big bad wolf at the door, all were pounding, "Let me in, let me in, let me in." A few other girls began to stir. The doorbell rang again. I headed down the hall to Mrs. York's apartment, and began my own frantic pounding. "Mrs. York, Mrs. York, wake up. There's someone at the front door."

The sound of feet shuffling in slippers slid under the door, and within seconds Mrs. York opened it a crack. "My goodness, Lani, what's all this fuss about?" Mrs. York hadn't taken the time to put on her glasses, and her eyes, which usually looked so enormous behind her thick lenses, were no more than tiny pin pricks in a soft, saggy curtain. Her words slurred like she'd been drinking, but I realized she didn't have her dentures in, and without her teeth it was impossible for her to form clearly enunciated consonants.

"Someone's ringing the doorbell, Mrs. York."

"What? At this time of night? My word, give me a minute."

More girls gathered in the landing at the top of the stairs, peering into the darkness below. Soon Mrs. York appeared, still in her terrycloth bathrobe but with her familiar owl eyes and a mouthful of teeth. She lit up the stairs with a flick of a switch and made her way to the front door. A tearful "due-any-day" young woman stood on the porch holding only a brown paper bag. With jagged breath she begged to come in.

Mrs. York called up the stairs, "Girls, get back to bed now. I'm handling this."

The young woman and her pregnant belly were gone in the morning. The whispers on the grapevine gave the reason as Sellers didn't want to take responsibility for a girl so close to her due date. I also heard that she didn't have any money, and she wasn't Southern Baptist.

August 24, 1971

Dear Lani,

Boy, I have been worried about you! I thought maybe something happen to you. I've written Jo three times and haven't got a letter from her. I've been having dreams that are driving me crazy. I dream about Catherine every night. I cry a lot too. You remember the pictures I took of Catherine? None of them come out any good.

Would you believe I haven't started school yet? Most parents boycotted the school because of bussing and consolidation. Would you believe on top of that they had bomb threats and then last Wednesday morning about 2:15 a.m. the school burned down. They had several thousand dollars worth of equipment burn. It was suppose to go to the new school they was suppose to build. It started back today, but mom said wait till Monday to start. I've gotten a lot of new clothes. Tomorrow I going to town and get me some pant suits. I'm in the 10th grade, too. I made a 13.8 on my achievement test.

You better not get pregnant again. Unless your married hear. I miss talking to you, too. I get lonesome and I just start crying. I started my first period yesterday. I have the cramps today. Jo asked me to come stay with her awhile next summer. I might but I not sure.

I've got to run, but be sure to answer my letter. I miss you a lot. If you have any extra pictures of yourself send me one. Excuse my writing. Write soon and take care of yourself.

Love ya,

Georgie

P.S. I'm going to keep trying to get Darrell. Tell Randall hi for me.

I was tired of being pregnant. I wanted this, whatever "this" was, to be over soon.

I don't know how many times I had heard, even from myself, that the journey was better than the destination. Waiting was hard, putting one foot in front of the other was hard, the platitude "take one day at a time" was hard, and doing nothing sometimes required greater strength than I thought possible. The last few weeks of my pregnancy seemed to drag on forever. My patience had worn thin. New girls came and went, and I was loath to form any attachments. Why bother when there was less than a month until my due date? I was desperate to go home and resume my life in the real world. I began to wonder if it was ever going to be possible, because, as unbelievable as it seemed, most everyone who wrote to me missed Sellers like the dickens.

Baby Booties

August in New Orleans was oppressive. Candy and I walked south along Peniston, and heavy air draped our shoulders like diapers left soaking in a bucket of bleach. The air had a wet diaper stench, too. Sharp and sour and slightly sweet.

Woolworth's on Canal Street was my shopping destination, but I wasn't sure we were up for the trolley ride. Every day it was harder and harder to get out, even though I promised myself I would find time to walk until the end. The baby was just so big. Each and every step was excruciating. My pubic bone felt pulled apart by a giant pair of pliers, and I worried about getting caught too far from a bathroom and wetting my pants. The slightest thing—a cough, a sneeze, a giggle—could make me pee, and the jostling of the St. Charles trolley was much worse than laughing.

Yes, it was far easier to stay at Sellers and behave like a slug. No one expected us to do anything in the last days of our pregnancy except get dressed and make our beds, but I wanted to get my baby something special to wear home from the hospital. Mrs. Stafford said that would be OK.

If I were back in Moore and having my baby the conventional way, with a husband, I would have been given a baby shower. At First Baptist every new mom received a baby shower, courtesy of the Ladies Auxiliary. I had been to my share of them; the first one I remember was for my mom when she was pregnant with my brother Billy. Baby showers always unfolded the same way. In the days before sonograms, we played a few silly games to try and figure out the baby's sex and weight and eye color. Whether the baby was bald or had a thick head of hair. Then the gifts were unwrapped carefully, so the paper and ribbon could be reused. In my family, "waste not want not" was right up there with the Ten Commandments.

Each gift—the pastel onesie, the teddy bear with button eyes, the hand knitted receiving blanket—was passed around the circle of adoring woman and greeted with a Greek chorus of "oohs" and "aahs." "Oh my, how cute." "Isn't that just the sweetest thing?" Even the practical gifts—pacifiers, burping cloths, Johnson & Johnson baby shampoo—were fawned over.

"Now that will come in mighty handy." "You can never have too many of those."

At the end of the shower, after the chorus of "oohs and aahs" subsided and the "thank yous" said again and again, we got to eat cake. This was my favorite part as a kid, and usually worth waiting through all the other grown-up silliness. A white sheet cake, half the length of the table, decorated with butter cream frosting in the shape of a yellow duck or alphabet blocks. Of course, we'd have punch, and, if we were really lucky, it would be spiked with orange sherbet.

Most of the time the gifts were small—things homemade or costing just a few dollars. But sometimes a group of friends would pool their meager savings and come prepared with a surprise—a highchair, a playpen—once someone even got a crib.

But I wasn't home with the Ladies Auxiliary at First Baptist. At Sellers, no one would give me anything for my baby. I liked to believe that his adopted mom would get a baby shower, and I was sure my baby would have everything he needed. On my own I wouldn't be able to give him much in the way of worldly goods.

Yet I wanted to give him something tangible. Even if he could only wear it for a few hours. When we came back to Sellers from the hospital, his clothes would be supplied by the Home, but I could give him some booties or a tiny knit cap. He couldn't keep them, of course—he couldn't keep anything from me—so I knew I would need to leave them in the nursery or take them back to Oklahoma.

I was torn about what to do. Maybe it would be nice to keep some small thing he wore, something he touched, something that kept his feet or head warm, but then again, maybe I wouldn't want a reminder of him at all.

Everyone was different. Anita seemed to understand she was pregnant, but she never seemed to connect the pregnancy with a real, warm blooded, breathing baby. In her letters Georgie said all she could think about was little Cathy. She cried all the time, dreamt about her every night. Since the photos she took didn't come out, she had nothing left to remind her of the life she carried for nine months.

The air weighed Candy and me down, and we seemed to be moving in slow motion. An eternity passed before we reached the little-bit-of-everything store only a block south of Sellers. Three girls loitered on the red brick sidewalk, smoking cigarettes. They pressed their glistening brown and copper bodies against the peeling aquamarine paint of the store's clapboard siding as they sought the tiny bit of shade created by the roof's overhang. Three black, distinctly non-pregnant high school girls stared at the two of us, white and humongous. I took Candy's hand and guided her to the other side of the street.

"They're still staring at us," Candy whimpered.

"So, let them stare. Want me to stick my tongue out at them? Shoot them the bird?"

"Lani, you wouldn't dare." Candy laughed. "And cut it out. You know the rules. No laughing."

"Yes, ma'am." I leaned over and pretended to go for the tiny bit of rib cage still tucked between her enormous belly and her enormous boobs. "So tickling is completely out of the question?"

Candy pulled away and slapped at my hand, still laughing.

"OK, OK, I'll leave you alone. But don't worry what anyone else thinks. I thought you'd be used to the stares by now."

"I don't know if I'll ever get used to it. The staring, I mean. But we haven't got much longer now."

I was right that we'd never make it to Canal Street. We were so tired by the time we reached St. Charles; I was sure the trolley ride would do us in. Instead of the adventure of going downtown, we headed over to the local Woolworth's, which was just another couple of blocks away. Maybe they had something I liked.

"Do you think we'll miss this place?" Candy asked as we made our way from the front of the store to the half aisle devoted to baby items.

My eyes scanned all things practical—baby bottles, nipples and rings, hard plastic rattlers, plastic bibs, tiny white t-shirts with snaps in the crotch to make diapering easier. "Of course. We don't have a Woolworth's in Moore."

"Silly, you know what I mean."

"Of course, I do. You're asking if I'll miss Sellers. I know I'll miss you, but yeah, there are probably lots of things we'll miss. Glenda says she misses the freedom we have."

"Freedom?" Candy looked incredulous. She picked up a yellow onesie, the color of baby chicks left in springtime baskets by the Easter bunny. "We're anything but free."

"Yeah, we're not free to completely come and go as we please—we have rules to follow, chores to do. I would give anything in the world to keep my baby, and we both know that's not going to happen. But somehow here we're free to be ourselves. You know, free from game playing."

Candy exchanged the yellow onesie for one the green of Granny Smith apples. "I get it. Like in high school. Everyone takes on a different role. The jocks, the popular girls, the nerdy band kids. Everyone plays their part, whether they like it or not. And half the time the part you play isn't of your own choosing. It's thrust on you."

I gently fingered a soft pink receiving blanket. "It's different here. We're more authentic somehow. Maybe because we're all in the same boat. Maybe because we can't pretend to be something we're not. Maybe because we're vulnerable. All I know is that for the first time in my life I'm honest with myself about who I am."

Candy placed the green onesie back on the shelf and turned to stare deep into my eyes. "And who are you, Lani?"

"I'm a girl who likes sex."

Candy laughed.

"I'm a girl confused about God. A girl who feels out of control. A girl who feels scared. And even though I love you to death and I don't know what I'd do without you in my life right now, I'm a girl who sometimes feels very alone."

Candy started singing, "*You gotta walk this lonesome valley.*"

I gave her a big hug. "See, you know exactly how I feel." We broke into harmony on the old gospel song, "*Ain't nobody else gonna walk it for you. You gotta walk it by yourself.*"

I examined the items on the baby aisle. "Looks like slim pickin's here. But my Memaw always told me that if wishes were horses, then beggars would ride. It was her way of saying you can't always get what you want. I might have to bite the bullet and head downtown after all."

"What about this?" Candy handed me a clear plastic box containing two white knit booties. A white ribbon laced through the top of each could be gently pulled and tied to make sure the booties didn't fall off the tiny newborn feet.

"Oh, Candy, they're perfect." I exclaimed. "And they'll work for either sex, even though I'm sure I'm having a boy."

Candy nodded. "We both are. At least I hope so. I think it would be next to impossible to give up a daughter. Georgie sure struggles with it."

"I know. Poor thing. In her letters the ink is always smudged like every word contains a teardrop. I'll take these. They're so sweet. It's amazing how tiny their feet are."

At that moment the baby tried to stretch out in the tight enclosure of my womb, and my ribs ached with the pressure. "His feet don't feel tiny from the inside. Maybe he's got Randall's size tens."

Candy and I headed up the aisle to the cash register. "I'm glad we found these. He can wear them back from the hospital, and then when I go home, I'll take them with me."

I placed the booties on the counter and fumbled in the pocket of my shorts for a five. We were getting the stare again. The cashier couldn't—or wouldn't—take her eyes off our bellies, each as big and round as a full moon. I ignored her. "You know, Candy, I wasn't sure I wanted any reminders of him, but now I know I do. I'll take whatever I can get and keep it for the rest of my life. Maybe even take them to my grave."

I pocketed the change, took the bag and Candy's arm as we left the store.

"Lani, I can picture that," Candy said. "Everyone will wonder what deep, dark secret you've been keeping when you, in your coffin, clutch an ancient pair of white baby booties in gnarled, arthritic hands."

Past Due

At the Home they were worried about our mortal souls, and they preached Jesus three times a week. They worried about our state of mind, so we saw a psychologist. But our bodies were another matter entirely. We didn't hear much about the mutation that happened when a girl's lean, compact body transformed into a gargantuan, drooping, oozing mess.

As my due date came and went, I felt like an experiment gone awry, like the scientist in *The Fly*. I couldn't breathe, a roadmap of scars covered my belly, walking seemed nigh unto impossible with ankles the size of soup cans. Even sitting was agonizing. The baby's head pushed apart my pelvic bones, and I couldn't keep my legs together. I wondered if labor and delivery would bring relief. I wish I could ask someone what it really felt like to have a baby. The girls who had already delivered were required to stay downstairs away from the rest of us like they were lepers. We knew them, we felt sorry for them, but we were kept apart except for meals. Sometimes they joined us at the table, but under watchful eyes we were unable to have frank conversations. We were fed the illusion that this would all be over in no time. This pregnancy was a slight aberration—a blip on the radar. We were led to believe that we could live in this world as if nothing had ever happened, but I had my doubts.

From the first of August, it seemed like girls were going to the hospital almost every other day. Every crib in the nursery was full. Sellers had a limited medical staff, and a doctor had been in short supply for Home visits. In the last few months of my pregnancy, I had only seen a doctor four times. Of course, we didn't have an experienced family doctor like Dr. Dycus. Just a bunch of rotating interns, nameless strangers doing their residency at Southern Baptist Hospital, who came and went depending on their shifts. We weren't supposed to form an attachment to any one particular doctor; when it came time to deliver, we weren't even sure we would get someone we had met before.

"Honey chile, you seen the doc today?"

Freddie threw Charlie, Glenda's baby, over her left shoulder. As she gently patted his back, "Shush, shush," she looked over at me, concern filling eyes the color of filberts. She had reason to worry. I was officially a week overdue, and the Powers-that-Be never let any girl go this long beyond her due date.

I finally saw a doctor that morning, one day after Candy went into labor, and the doctor said if I hadn't gone into labor by Friday, I would be dropped off at the hospital to be induced. They were going to make my baby come out whether he liked it or not. If everything went well, I would be a mother by dinnertime. But aside from this limited information and being told to "pack a bag and bring a gown," I had no idea about what to expect when I got to the hospital. None.

I slumped in the rocking chair, swollen feet stretched out on a small, padded stool, my hand resting on top of a mastodon belly. "Yeah, he came by this morning. He says if I haven't delivered by tomorrow, they'll induce me on Friday."

"Good. That baby's sure been takin' his sweet time." Freddie laid Charlie face down in his crib and picked up Catherine. She was almost nine weeks old now and starting to smile. There was no mistaking her for Georgie's little girl. She looked just like her mother, as perfect as Snow White, with fair skin, dark eyes and thick, black hair.

Freddie cradled Catherine in the crook of her arm. "You talk to Candy yet?"

"No, not yet. She should be coming home on Friday."

After sharing the same due date and both going late, Candy went into labor on Monday. Miss Popwell posted her card on the bulletin board in the rec room. Candy had a boy, seven pounds, eight ounces, and for now he was named Johnny, after her younger brother.

"I did get letters from Jo and Georgie last week."

"Oh, yeah, what'd they have to say for theirselves?"

"Not much. School, boys, you know, the usual."

I stretched out open arms. "Mind if I hold Cathy awhile?"

Because I was in my ninth month, I no longer had any formal chores. I quit working in the nursery in early August, but I still came in every day to shoot the breeze with Freddie and Shirlene. I also wanted to see the faces of my friends in their babies.

"Did your children come natural, Freddie?" I rocked Catherine back and forth, and she tightened her tiny fist around my index finger.

"All four of 'em came in on a wing and a prayer. Don't worry, hon, you'll be fine. No way through it, but to do it."

I nodded my head, then leaned over to kiss Catherine on the top of her head. Nothing smelled as sweet as a newborn baby. Not even cotton candy at the Oklahoma State Fair.

I wanted my mom so bad. I wanted to talk to her, ask her all my questions, and most of all, I wanted her to hold my hand. But instead of my mom, Miss Popwell promised to take me to the hospital. Going on Friday meant that I would miss saying goodbye to Candy. As soon as she got out of the hospital, she was going to leave for Mississippi. As early as Sunday. Even in a best-case scenario, I wouldn't be back to Sellers until Monday at the earliest. But I understood her urgency to get back home. Her high school, like mine, had already been in session for more than a week, and it would be hard to explain what was making us so late to show up for classes. Aside from our overdue babies.

I thought maybe we could say we had mono. We both had a bad case of mono. But mono is the kissing disease, and kisses had been in short supply, except in my imagination.

Ever since Candy arrived in June, we had been inseparable—everyone called us the Bobbsey Twins. I never had a friend like her. I would have gone insane a few times if it weren't for her. I couldn't fathom the idea of never seeing her again.

No, we'll write, I told myself. We had to find a way to stay connected. Mississippi wasn't that far from Oklahoma.

On Thursday I started having real contractions. Every ten minutes my belly was as hard as a cast iron skillet. I almost skipped into Miss Popwell's office.

"OK, kiddo, let's have a look at what's happening down there."

For once I was actually happy to take off my clothes and put on the scratchy hospital gown. When I arrived at Sellers the first of March, I could wrap it around me twice, but now it stretched with nary a wrinkle across an upside-down washtub and it gaped open in the back. Yup, that was my butt back there. I was fully exposed. Betty told me that first night I would have to get over my modesty and she was right. In those gowns we strutted around like Michelangelo's nudes, except those nudes were young men with nice tight asses, and we were young women with great, albeit leaky, tits and saggy bottoms.

After five minutes of maneuvering, I was in position on the table with my bare feet in the stirrups. Another five minutes and one contraction later,

Miss Popwell came in to check on me. She lubed up two gloved fingers and inserted them into my vagina. The way she dug around, you might have thought she was searching for oil.

"You're about two centimeters dilated, but no effacement. Sorry, Lani, you're not going anywhere today."

The disappointment must have been written all over my face. Miss Popwell took off the latex glove and helped me sit up.

"Don't worry about it. You're being induced tomorrow. What's one more day?"

What's one more day? She had to be kidding. At that point I had been at Sellers one hundred and eighty-six days; I hadn't seen Randall in one hundred and eighty-eight. What's one more day?

When I was young, each time I heard the news that my dad was coming home from overseas, I would go to school and say, "My daddy's coming home next week;" then, "My daddy's coming home tomorrow;" then, "My daddy's coming home today." After months of patiently waiting, I still remember the sensation of not being able to wait even a second longer. We would clean the house until it gleamed, and, when the big day finally arrived, my mother would prepare all of my dad's favorite foods—pot roast, potatoes and gravy, biscuits, peach cobbler. Then she would dress us all in our Sunday best, and we would drive to the base and wait on the tarmac for my dad's plane to land. When the plane touched down, the engines were so loud we couldn't hear ourselves talk. My sisters and I would jostle each other for the best view of the stairs, and as soon as we saw him descend from the plane, we would run and hang on my dad's legs while he tried to lean over us and kiss my mother.

What's one more day? It was another twenty-four hours of waiting. Another twenty-four hours of living in a pregnant pause.

That morning I had prayed for patience. And then I prayed for all the other virtues that can flow from that. I knew that when I was not patient, I was not present, and when I was not present, I could be thoughtless and unkind. I gave a half-smile. "You're right, Miss Popwell, tomorrow is a fine day for having this baby."

I trudged back to my room and began packing for the hospital. I didn't have an overnight bag, so I put a few things in a paper bag—the white baby booties for my son to wear home from the hospital, a nightgown, hairbrush, toothbrush, toothpaste, my trusty blue slippers, two pair of socks, six pairs of clean underwear, which I hoped would be enough since I knew I would be bleeding, a bra, my wallet, and a flannel bathrobe I borrowed from the communal clothes closet. I didn't need real people clothes. All the girls came back to Sellers dressed in nightgowns and spent most of their time in bed until they were able to leave. Miss Popwell was right. What's one more day? If I came back to Sellers on Monday, then I might be able to fly back to Oklahoma on Thursday or Friday—that was only one week away.

Home again, home again, jiggety-jig.

After long months of waiting and longing, I found it hard to imagine that in a little more than a week, I wouldn't have my belly, I wouldn't have my baby, but Randall would finally hold me in his arms again.

He called at his usual time. Eight o'clock on the dot.

"I started having contractions today."

"They hurt?"

"No, they don't hurt so bad. But they're not too close together. That's why they're gonna induce labor tomorrow."

"So, you're going to the hospital?"

"No, Randall, the women's prison. One step up from Sellers. Of course, silly, the hospital. I'm gonna have the baby tomorrow. September 3rd. Exactly one month before your birthday."

The silence on the line weighed as much as a pink elephant in the corner of the room. I rambled on to fill the emptiness.

"Candy had her baby last Tuesday. A boy. Seven pounds, five ounces. His name is Johnny. She's coming home tomorrow. I won't get to see her before she leaves."

"Do you have her address?"

"Yeah, I have her address. I'm sure we'll write."

I waited for some response, then blurted out, "If truth be told, Randall, I'm scared."

More silence. The elephant started lifting a 100-pound dumb bell with its trunk, while I feigned good cheer.

"I'll get to see the baby in the hospital."

"Do you really think that's a good idea?"

"Maybe, maybe not. Doesn't matter. I want to see him."

"Still think it's a boy?"

"Yeah, everyone thinks so. Freddie told me just the other day, 'Lawd, chile, you carrying so low. That some big boy you got there.'" I laughed.

Randall usually enjoyed hearing about Freddie and Shirlene, but tonight my Freddie impression fell on deaf ears. His response was terse. "Well, I guess you'll know tomorrow."

"Yeah, tomorrow." Since Randall wasn't talking, my voice trailed off into the silence. "Well, I better get off the phone. Tomorrow's gonna come early."

More silence. An entire circus existed in the space between us. The strong man stood on the elephant with the 100-pound dumb bell, and then he lifted a fifty-pound weight in each hand. If I didn't get off the phone soon, Randall and I were going to have all of The Flying Wallendas balancing on the telephone wire between New Orleans and Moore.

"I best skedaddle. Like I said, tomorrow's gonna come early. I'll be at Southern Baptist Hospital on Napoleon Street. Will you let everyone know? Well, not everyone, but, well, you know what I mean."

"OK."

I was willing myself not to cry. Randall hated for me to cry. Most men seem to find women's tears repellant, but tears have a mind of their own and mine trickled down into the crack of my tight, needy voice.

"Randall, I love you."

How hard could it be for him to remember that I was the girl with hands smaller than rain? Couldn't he remember that I was the girl he wrote about on the banks of Wake Forest? Wasn't I still his one, true love?

"Love you, too. Go get some sleep."

I felt relieved. Good, he said it back. Randall said them, those three little words. But I didn't feel reassured. When it came to the baby, Randall was not in my corner with the elephant or the strong man and the master of ceremonies. It was just me, alone with the clowns.

Randall never wanted to talk about the baby. He didn't care about how much the baby might weigh. He didn't want to know the baby's eye color or his hair color or that he had ten perfect toes on two beautiful feet. I knew that if I was going to get through this ordeal, I needed to be like Jesus' mother, Mary. After the angels appeared to the shepherds, they went all over town telling everyone about what they had seen and heard. But Mary—Mary stayed quiet, treasuring the truths that she knew and pondering them in her heart.

The phone rang again. My heart skipped a beat, hoping that Randall realized he was an ass and was calling back to apologize.

"Hello, you've reached 596-9625."

"Lani, is that you?"

Candy's voice spilled into the booth, a voice as pure and true as the Gospel. But I no longer believed that the Gospel was true anymore. Her voice rang as true as the friendship we shared. And without another word, we both sobbed.

Out to Lunch

Friday morning, I was downstairs by seven o'clock, paper bag in hand, only to discover Mrs. Simpson was the charge nurse for the day. When I saw Miss Popwell on Thursday, why didn't she tell me that she wouldn't be on duty? I had always believed that she would be the one to take me to the hospital.

I waited by the back door. The smell of frying bacon filled the dining room and kitchen. As my Memaw always said, "I'm so hungry I could just about swaller my tongue." I would have loved some bacon (not crispy—I love to chew the fat) with eggs over easy, but I wasn't allowed to eat anything. Nothing but water until after the baby came.

I stood around salivating for fifteen minutes.

Where is Mrs. Simpson?

I was supposed to be at the hospital by eight. I looked around the room. Girls I barely knew carried bins of dirty dishes into the kitchen and started running the dishwasher and scrubbing pots and pans just like I had done when I arrived at Sellers in March. They looked at me in awe. For almost a month I had been the oldest resident at Sellers. Not in physical age, but in time spent inside those red brick walls. I had been the sentry on duty as all of my friends had their babies and left. And finally, it was my turn. It was September 3, 1971, and I was going to the hospital to have my baby.

Donna spied me waiting by the door. "I persuaded Mrs. York to let me take over your job in the nursery."

I smiled. "Donna, that's great. You'll have a blast." I had hoped she would get the job, and I was thankful there would be someone I knew and trusted who could watch over my baby just like I watched over Glenda's and Cheryl's and Jo's and Georgie's.

Just then Mrs. Simpson arrived all in a fluster. She was always in a fluster, a squawking chicken running in circles in the yard with feathers flying everywhere. She was certainly not the most calm or reassuring presence even in the best of times. What could Miss Popwell possibly be doing that was more important than taking me to the hospital?

"I'm sorry," Mrs. Simpson gulped. "My daughter called and Trey, my grandson, is running a fever."

Donna turned to face me and rolled her luminous brown eyes. She leaned in to hug me, but we bumped bellies, laughed, and sidled up, side to side. "You'll be fine, Lani. See you when you get back."

Mrs. Simpson headed out the kitchen door, and I waddled behind her, a baby duckling following its mother, to the green Dodge Dart parked in the back driveway. It was in need of a good washing, both inside and out.

"Just throw that stuff in the back, shug," Mrs. Simpson pointed to the trash at my feet. But it was impossible for me to bend over and pick anything up, so I dropped my paper bag on the floor amongst coke cups and burger wrappers.

We headed down Peniston to St. Charles Avenue. Mrs. Simpson started jabbering on about her family. "Trey's toddling now. I worry so. Karen, that's my daughter, she got divorced even before Trey was born. Her ex was a no-good son of a gun."

I wasn't paying attention, but I made tiny mewing sounds of agreement. Thoughts swirled around inside my head like a tropical storm off the gulf coast. If I wasn't careful, I was sure my brain would soon blow away in the gale.

I was excited and depressed. Yesterday's contractions dwindled down to nothing. Walking—I should have gone walking in the afternoon instead of worrying about what I was going to tell Randall when he called. My mother always said walking was the best thing to bring on contractions. It certainly worked for Glenda. I wished they would let me walk to the hospital. It wasn't too far away. Just five blocks west to Napoleon, then north seven blocks to Magnolia.

Candy and I walked this neighborhood a zillion times early in the summer, before it became physically impossible. We imagined we were the ones sipping mint juleps behind the columns or making love beyond the wrought iron balconies. I couldn't believe she called last night. She said Johnny was beautiful. She said she was feeling good, up and around, and she walked the halls down to the nursery to stare through the glass at Johnny in his little crib. She said you got to hold your baby three or four times a day for the feeding, just like the other mothers. I was happy she decided to see her baby. She wasn't sure at first. Johnny had blue eyes like hers, she said. I wondered if my baby might have hazel eyes like mine.

I hoped I could see Candy in the hospital before she was discharged, but she said she had to get home for school, and she was going to insist on going home on Saturday. Her mom was coming down to get her. Even though we joked about it, Sellers wasn't a prison. They couldn't keep anyone there against her will. I wondered when she would sign her papers.

It was strange riding in a car. I hadn't ridden in a car for months. The last time was the end of May when my folks came to visit. Back then I had a medium-sized bump, easily hidden. Now my belly was so big it touched the dashboard.

Mrs. Simpson dropped me off at the hospital. "Wait right here, Lani. I'll be round soon as I get the car parked."

Not being in labor meant I entered through the front door instead of the emergency room. I climbed the short flight of steps, clutching my paper bag against my chest. Inside the lobby, leather chairs were grouped in twos and threes. Men in suits paced around the perimeter, smoking cigarettes. Women huddled with heads close together, clutching handkerchiefs, dabbing heavily made-up eyes.

I shuffled my feet, first placing my weight on the left, then on the right, conscious of a dozen pair of eyes staring at me, aware that I must look young, too young to be having a baby. "Yes," I wanted to shout at them, "I'm pregnant, and I'm a teenager. Just get over it, why don't you?"

Within minutes Mrs. Simpson was by my side. She took me by my right arm and led me over to registration. Behind the desk a thin, older woman typed on an IBM Selectric, much like the one I used in my typing class the previous year. Her nameplate read Mavis Herbert, and her sleeveless dress, covered in red and white polka dots, looked straight out of the 1950s. Its plunging neckline seemed more suited to someone twenty years younger, and out of place in a hospital setting.

"Why, hi there, Virginia. Got another one of your girls, I see." Obviously, she and Mrs. Simpson knew each other, but the woman was way too cheerful for her position, which I felt required solemnity, deference. After all, she *was* dealing with people like me, sick people, people needing surgery, people who were dying. Although I should have been there for the happiest of all reasons, as far as I was concerned, there was little to smile about.

"Yes, this is Lani Lassiter. She's getting induced this morning. Lani, show Mrs. Hebert your driving license."

I reached into the paper bag for my wallet and pulled out the Oklahoma State driver's license I had been issued the previous summer. Mrs. Simpson finished the rest of the paperwork while Mrs. Hebert typed it up. In minutes it was done.

"Hon, hold out your arm," Mrs. Hebert told me. I stretched my right arm across the desk, but she shook her head. "Not that one—your left arm." She placed a plastic identity bracelet on my wrist, and I glanced down to read it. "Mrs. Lani J. Lassiter," "1021536," "Ward D-D." Obviously, "miss" wasn't appropriate or acceptable for a new mother.

Like Cinderella's Fairy Godmother waving a magic wand, Mrs. Hebert picked up a phone, and an orderly appeared with my coach, a well-used wheelchair. I let out a huge sigh and climbed in, the paper bag of meager belongings on my lap. Mrs. Simpson stayed by my side while the orderly pushed me to the elevator and up to the sixth floor. After going past three sets of heavy double doors, and at least one nurses' station, the orderly ushered me into a labor room with walls the same putrid shade of green as my grade school cafeteria.

Although there were no windows, the room buzzed with a dizzying bright light. On the right side there were several cupboards, with a sink in the center of the counter. In the middle of the room a bed, its metal stirrups plainly visible, was covered in stiff white sheets; it was surrounded on one side by what looked like a tall metal coat rack, and on the other by a large ominous monitor covered with knobs. I wondered if I could pretend it was a receiver/amplifier for Randall's stereo system. Now all I needed was some speakers and a turntable, and I would be all set to listen to Derek and the Dominos.

The orderly left the room and Mrs. Simpson handed me a thin, hospital gown. "Put this on, shug, open in the back."

I undressed and stuffed my clothes into the paper bag. I hoped that would be the last time in a long time that I needed to wear pants with a big stretchy panel.

Mrs. Simpson fiddled with some levers at the foot of the bed. "I'm going to lower this for you. We've got some things to do before we get started. Do you need help climbing up?"

"No, I can manage," I lied. I stared at the bed for a moment, realizing my big belly would make the manuever a Herculean task. The bed was adjusted with the head raised. I sat on the side of the bed, leaned back against a scratchy pillow, and pulled up one leg at a time. Mission accomplished with a heave-ho.

"Can I keep my glasses on?"

"No, it's better if I take them." Mrs. Simpson held out her hand and it quickly swallowed my cool John Lennon wire frame specs. I should have thought to bring my glass case. "It's OK," Mrs. Simpson said in an effort to assure me, "they'll be waiting by your bed when you wake up."

I nodded in her direction, but since I was as blind as a bat I could no longer distinguish her facial features. Talk about living on blind faith.

Mrs. Simpson placed her hand on my arm. "Lani, I've got to run back for a little bit. You know how shorthanded we are these days."

Someone from the Home was supposed to stay with us, but there wasn't much use in protesting. Besides, I always knew this day would come. One way or another the baby was coming out, and I was the only one who could make that happen. A swarm of butterflies darted about in my stomach, taking the place of my baby's tiny leg kicks.

Mrs. Simpson patted my shoulder. "They'll take good care of you, Lani. I'll be back before noon."

The light hurt my eyes, and it felt like Rodin was chiseling the Burghers of Calais right behind my eyes.

In a few minutes, the door opened, and a hospital nurse came into the room. "How you doing, hon? Any contractions yet?"

"I had some yesterday, but they stopped last night."

"That's OK, we'll fix you right up. Now, first things first. I need to shave your private area, and then I'll give you an enema. Ever had one of those before?"

"No, ma'am."

I wondered what Randall would think when and if he saw my "privates" again. Having pubic hair made me feel powerful, womanly and 100% sexy. Without it I would look like a pre-pubescent girl.

"OK, just lift up and I'll put this pad under you to keep from getting the bed all wet. That's right. Now spread your legs."

The nurse wiped my vagina with a warm washrag and then I felt the sharp tug of a razor against my skin. I closed my eyes. I was sure the nurse had seen a million vaginas, but I was embarrassed to have a total stranger so intimately acquainted with me.

She made one last swipe with warm water. "There, that's all done. We have to make you as sterile as possible, and this makes it easier for the doctor to see what he's doing when he gives you an episiotomy. Now time for your enema. You said you never had one, right?"

"Yes, ma'am, I mean, no ma'am, I mean, I've never had one."

"That's all right. It doesn't hurt; it's just a little uncomfortable."

The nurse reached into a cupboard and took out what looked like a big red water bottle, the kind my grandmother used at night to keep her feet warm. It was attached to a long hose with a clip at the end. The nurse turned on the tap water and tested the temperature with her hand.

"That's about right. Don't want to get it too warm."

When the bottle was full, she turned off the water. "Now, just lay on your right side facing away from me. Can you pull your legs up a little?" She parted the back of my gown until my rear was exposed and started to insert the nozzle into my rectum. My body and my bottom began to tense. "Listen, hon, you've got to relax." The nurse fiddled with the nozzle again, until it was fully inserted. "Now, the water is going to flow into you, and then you have to hold it for ten minutes. Got it?"

"Yes, ma'am." I heard a small banging sound as she hung the water bag from the stand. Then a small click, and I felt warm water rushing into my body. It was a strange sensation. At first it was almost calming, but as the water kept flowing into my body, I had the strongest urge to take a shit.

Finally, another click and the valve closed. The nurse removed the nozzle from my bottom. "How you doing, hon? Now, you just hold that for ten minutes and then you can go to the bathroom. Oh, wait, I forgot to show you where the bathroom is. But that's OK, I'll help you get down there. It's just on the other side of the nurses' desk."

She pulled my gown together in the back, so I felt somewhat less exposed. My face must have conveyed the pain of holding back my tears along with massive amounts of water and poo.

"Hang in there. Just a few more minutes."

"I don't know how much longer I can wait."

"You can wait longer than you think you can. We need to do this because it's easier to keep everything sterile. You don't want to have a bowel movement in the delivery room, do you?"

"No ma'am."

I needed to think about something else. A record player. Derek and the Dominos. Listening to "Layla" in Randall's room. Balling during the guitar solo.

"OK, see that wasn't so bad. Let me help you get up."

Back in the labor room, I climbed back in bed with empty bowels. The nurse put my feet in the stirrups and checked the veins in my right arm. After a hit and a miss, I was attached to an IV.

"Hon, you're doing great. Just wait here; the doctor will be in to see you soon. We're gonna give you some medicine to get those contractions started, and something to help you relax."

Wait? Like I was going anywhere with those tubes in my arms.

And relax? Was she kidding? It was impossible to relax; I was so uncomfortable. All I wanted to do was turn on my side. Did I really have to lie flat on my back with my feet in the air?

Within minutes the contractions started in earnest. The door opened again, and I could make out the figure of a man in a white coat. Was it the doctor? He didn't introduce himself. He looked at my chart, and then felt around inside me. How could something that usually felt so good when Randall did it feel so demeaning? Maybe it was the gloves.

The doctor stared up from between my legs. At least I thought he was looking in my direction, but I couldn't tell without my glasses. Finally, he spoke to me. "I'm going to break your water, and you'll be out of here in no time."

I couldn't see what he was doing but I felt a huge rush of warm water like there had been a break in the Hoover Damn. The doctor left, and a different nurse came in to mop it up with a towel.

I was so cold I started to tremble. "Can I have a blanket, please?"

"Hon, you just take it easy. This'll be over in no time."

The nurse left the room, and I was on my own once again. I thought of Sean alone in the dark, cold ground. I tried to imagine him in heaven with light perpetual shining on him as promised in the prayer said at his gravesite. Light. Rest. Peace. But I couldn't find the image in my mind. The contractions were harder now. The features of Sean's face were fading from my memory. When would the meds kick in? Was Mrs. Simpson ever coming back?

I wanted to lie on my side. I felt out of control, disoriented, dizzy. I tugged and tugged at the IV until I pulled it out. Blood streamed down my arm. I took my feet out of the stirrups and rolled over on my side into a fetal position.

It seemed like hours passed, but it was probably only a few minutes before the first nurse came back to check on me. When she saw the IV dangling at the side of the bed and the blood pooling in the crook of my arm, she yelled out the door, "Orderly, I need you in here quick."

No more Mrs. Nice Guy—she turned on me. "Look what you've done, young lady." The orderly arrived within seconds. They replaced the IV, stuck my legs back in the stirrups, and I struggled to get away from them.

"We'll have none of that," the nurse said, slapping at my hands. She and the orderly pulled up rails on either side of the bed and strapped both my arms and legs to them. "That should keep you."

I was alone again—scared and in pain.

I felt like my brain was out to lunch. The meds weren't doing anything for the pain—they just shut me up. I tried to speak, but I couldn't make a sound.

Then I was floating. I could see my body on the table, and I floated above it. Then I was back in my body and I was in line at a bank, or maybe it was a library. It was in a large city. Was it New Orleans? Oklahoma City? I didn't know, but I could hear the noise of a thousand people—friends talking, children laughing, lovers arguing, feet rushing to unknown destinations. I heard the sound of traffic—tires squealing, horns honking, motorcycles revving their engines while they waited at stop lights.

The building I was in was old, with cold marble floors and more than a dozen grey granite columns holding up a massive dome. I was in line waiting, but I was lying on a mattress on the cold floor. The mattress was covered in a sheet, threadbare, blue, and one corner kept coming up, exposing stains of urine and blood. The mattress was thin, no more than two inches, like one from a hide-a-bed. I could feel the coolness of the marble under my legs and my back. I was lying on my right side, and my arm made a V, my head held in my hand. I kept looking behind me. I was waiting for someone.

Now I was at the front of the line. Behind me, on another mattress sat a young man in his early to mid-thirties. He was handsome with dark hair and dark eyes. He was aloof, distant, haughty, and dressed in a three-piece suit. He held a gold pocket watch in his right hand, and he kept glancing down at it. "It's your turn," he said. "Please go in front of me," I told him. I kept waiting.

Suddenly there was a flurry of activity. My party, a group of people I did not know, arrived. I got up off the mattress and went to the desk in front of me. It was massive, carved out of oak, and taller than I was by several feet. I stretched my neck, but I couldn't see the person talking to me. Then Randall was there; he came up and stood next to me. He was holding a record player in his hands. He was wearing the same three-piece suit as the imperious young man standing in line. I said to Randall, "I like your music," but he was talking to someone behind him and he ignored me.

The person behind the desk leaned over and began handing me baby bottles, clothes, cans of formula and then a baby, a little boy about the same age as Jason. I was holding him with my left arm on my hip and I was trying to cradle all of the other things in the crook of my right arm. I kept wondering, "Why isn't there a bag for all of this stuff?" I turned and followed a young woman who was headed outside. It was Candy. She walked in front of a line of six or eight children. They were girls about the age of four. They all wore smart wool coats in navy or red, with French berets the same color as their coats. Candy stopped to talk to someone who had rushed up to her. I continued walking towards the door. Then someone, the first young man in the three-piece suit, said, "Here, let me help you," and he took all of the things I was carrying.

I repositioned the baby in front of me. I tried to place his tiny arms around my neck.

I went outside into a blinding white light. I was squinting from the glare, standing on a narrow granite ledge. Looking out across a wide chasm, I could tell from a building directly across from me that I was ten or eleven stories above the ground. I looked down at my feet. I was wearing black leather boots. I moved forward but there were no steps.

The side of the building was cut with tiny grooves. It was possible to climb down, but I needed to use both my hands, which were holding the baby. I tried to move my foot down to the first groove, but I slipped and started falling. I looked up at the man holding all of the baby's things and I wondered if I could possibly throw the baby to him but decided that I didn't have the strength. I would just be hurtling the baby into the abyss. I continued falling, and I looked down to see the sidewalk coming up to greet me. I tried to curl my body around the child. I felt the air rushing past my face. I heard a scream—it did not come from my mouth—and I closed my eyes and waited for the impact.

One-Mississippi, Two-Mississippi

I woke up alone and groggy from the anesthetic in a private room. How long had I been out? Noxious chemicals coursed through my body. I was nauseous; bruises from the straps and IV covered my forearms. My abdomen was swollen and tender. I felt like Joe Frazier had been using it as a punching bag. My vagina was on fire. I tried desperately to remember giving birth, but the anesthetic made my mind a blank slate. Where were my glasses? I tugged at the high table next to my bed. It was on wheels, but I had trouble moving it. I felt so dizzy every time I moved. Blindly, I patted the top of the table until I located my glasses. Mrs. Simpson had put them there at some point. I wondered if she stayed with me for a while. I put the wire rims over my ears and pushed the glasses up on my nose. I glanced around the room. The clock on the wall said it was four o'clock. When did I deliver? I looked down at my wrist. I was wearing a second identity bracelet that was pre-printed with the word "Mother," and the number 8171. OK, so I was a mother, but I didn't know if I had a boy or a girl.

I pressed the call button, and a nurse came within a few minutes, but the wait felt like three weeks. "You had a boy," she answered to my unspoken question.

"Can I see him? Is he all right?"

"No, I'm sorry, you'll have to wait to see him."

She handed me a pill and a plastic bottle with a thick straw. "Here, take this. It will stop your breasts from leaking."

When she left the room, I burst into tears. I didn't understand why I couldn't see my son.

I had no idea I would feel such anguish about not being allowed to breastfeed. My mother nursed all four of my siblings and me. I remember watching her feed my sisters and my brother from her breast, and when I played with dolls, I didn't feed them with a bottle. When my breasts began to leak in my 7th month, I felt a thrill knowing my body could produce a substance capable of nourishing and sustaining life. I wanted to nurse my baby so much, and I was heartbroken that I would never know his sweet and painful hungry tug.

My friends at Sellers knew the gender of my baby before I did. A card was always posted on the bulletin board at Sellers on the day any baby was born. Normally this type of card was placed on the newborn's crib in the nursery. But since our babies were the unfortunate offspring of unwed mothers, their cribs in the hospital nursery stayed unadorned. In my son's case, the card was blue and white and decorated with a giraffe, a teddy bear, balloons, a building block, a rabbit, a rattler, and a ball. It announced to the world "IT'S A BOY!"

Name:	Lassiter, Emerson Townsend
Mother:	Lani
Date of Birth:	Sept 3, 1971
Time:	12:10 PM
Birth Weight:	8 lbs., 8 oz.
Length:	20 ½ inches
Obstetrician:	Dr. Ward
Attending Pediatrician:	Dr. Charlstrom
Head:	13 ½ inches
Chest:	13 inches
Abdomen:	13 ½ inches

Bo was my son's nickname. If we chose to, we were allowed to name our babies—something to go on the original birth certificate. For those who couldn't bear the thought of naming their sons and daughters, the birth certificates simply listed last names: "Baby Boy Jones" or "Baby Girl Smith."

I thought a long time about my son's name, even though I knew he would only keep it until his adoption. Candy and I talked about the names for hours on end. I knew if she had a boy, she was going to name him after her brother, Johnny. I final decided upon Emerson Townsend for the birth certificate. But Emerson Townsend was much too big of a name for such a little boy, so I gave him the nickname, "Bo."

I liked the name Emerson Townsend though. I thought it sounded rather British and literary. Emerson was Randall's middle name, and also my Memaw's maiden name. Townsend came from Pete Townsend of The Who, and last summer, when Randall and I made love anywhere, everywhere, without a care given to any moment but the present, The Who's version of "Summertime Blues" was our soundtrack. And given my current predicament, a reminder that the blues had no cure seemed fitting.

I fell asleep again, and when I woke up it was six o'clock, and an orderly was bringing my dinner. "Can I see my baby now? Is my baby all right?"

The orderly checked my chart. "No, I'm sorry, you can't see him yet."

Pictures from the covers of national tabloids flashed in my imagination. "Baby Born with Two Heads!" "Infant Lives with Heart Outside of Body!" I was sure something terrible must have happened during the delivery. I was terrified at the thought that my baby might have been dead, and they were waiting until someone from Sellers could come and tell me.

"Please may I see my baby?" I begged the nurse who came by around eight.

"We'll bring him to your room for a nine o'clock feeding."

Again, I didn't understand why they were making me wait to see my baby. I wanted to see him right then. I didn't want to wait another second. I wanted to count his fingers and toes, trace my fingers along the crook of his neck and elbow. I wanted to press my lips against the top of his head. I had so many unanswered questions, like "Does he have much hair? Are his eyes blue?"

There was no television in my room, and I forgot to pack a book or magazine to read. I passed the next hour counting each second. "One-Mississippi, two-Mississippi." If I had read the New Mother's pamphlet on the side table next to the hospital bed, I might have known that the babies weren't brought to their mothers until a full twelve hours after birth. I waited for what seemed like an eternity with ever increasing anxiety until at last I heard the rumble of a cart in the hallway outside my room.

The door opened without a sound and a nurse stood framed in the doorway holding a tightly wrapped bundle. It looked like an ice cream cone with a cherry on top, but the cherry was not red, it was blue.

I reached for the button that controlled the bed, and I moved the head up until I was in a sitting position. With my heart in my throat, I stretched out shaking arms, anxious to hold him.

"You do know how to hold a newborn?" she asked. "You have to protect his neck; don't let his head drop back. And don't touch the soft spot on top."

"I know what I'm doing," I said with a snake's hiss. "Please give him to me now." I wanted to get up and smack her up the side of her head—take my baby by force if necessary—but I knew that wouldn't do any good; she would have called security and I would never have gotten to see him. I tried to still my emotions, until he was safely in my arms, and I could unwrap the thin blue blanket that covered his face and body.

The nurse set a warm bottle of water on the tray table next to the bed.

"Feed him this. It's sugar water. You have ten minutes."

I couldn't take my eyes off of his beautiful face.

"But, what….? Shouldn't he be getting some formula?" I worried that he might get hungry and my breasts were already feeling the effects of the medication to dry up my milk.

She shook her head. "Didn't you read the pamphlet?"

"What pamphlet?"

She picked up a small brochure from the table. How did I not see that? My mind was over-occupied with visions of two-headed babies.

"Everything is explained in here." She laid the pamphlet back down on the table. "He's fed sugar water for the first 24-hours. If he cries, I'll come back to get him. Make sure you read the pamphlet after the feeding."

Finally, I was alone with my son, and I unwrapped the precious bundle. He was so red and wrinkled, it looked like he had been soaking in a pan of dirty dishwater for hours, but I didn't care. He had ten fingers and ten toes, with fine, brown hair that stood up on end, and two eyes so deep and blue I was afraid they would sear into my soul, yet that is what I wanted, too. To have that moment imprinted on my memory long enough to last a lifetime.

He lay in my arms quiet of voice and limb and since I didn't hear his first cries, I wondered what his voice sounded like. I cooed like I did with the babies in the nursery at Sellers. I hummed "My Little Buckaroo," and I had no idea how it came to me, when or where I had learned it. I stared at his square little head; I gazed into his eyes. I looked for me, I looked for Randall, but all I could see was Bo.

Bo was wearing a teeny-tiny identity bracelet, much like mine. They were fastened to our wrists when he was born, and in a way, they bound him and me together. His bracelet also bore the pre-printed number 8171, but the attending nurse added my name, "L. J. Lassiter," the date, "9-3-71," and his sex, "boy."

I gave him his bottle of water, but he didn't seem to like it much. He had only drunk less than half the bottle when the nurse came back to get him. When she took him from my arms, an ache spread across my chest and down each limb.

Still without anything to take my mind off of my son and his absence, I decided to read the all-important pamphlet that had been left on the table beside my bed. It said we wouldn't receive our baby until it was twelve hours old. It said we would only receive our baby four times a day for its feeding. It said, "Enjoy Your Baby!"

I wanted to enjoy my baby. To see him only four times a day for his feeding wasn't enough. I didn't care if they got me up in the middle of the night. I had a private room; I wouldn't disturb anyone else. I was supposed to go home on Monday, but I hoped and prayed they would let me stay at the hospital until Tuesday. I wasn't ready to let go of him.

Saturday morning, two bouquets of flowers arrived from Frank J. Reyes & Company on Canal Street. With the first there was no preprinted message, and the blank card simply said, "Mrs. LaPrairie."

The second card said, "Thinking of You," and I examined the handwritten message that read, "We love you, Uncle Carl & Aunt Ann."

Friends closer than family, Aunt Ann had known my mother all of her life. Both families had been in Moore ever since that part of the state had been opened to white settlers during the Oklahoma Land Run of 1889. They went to the same school, attended the same church, and when winter weather made it impossible for Ann to travel from her family's farm for after-school activities, she lived with my grandmother in town. My sister, Kathy Ann, is named after her.

My father, John, met Uncle Carl soon after joining the Air Force. They quickly became the best of friends, and right after my mother and father were married, they played matchmakers for Carl and Ann. My father and Carl also made a pact to name their first sons after each other; Carl's oldest is John Michael. When my parent's third and thought to be last child was born a girl, she was named Carla. When child number five was thankfully born a boy, he was named William Carl.

I didn't know how Carl and Ann were able to break away from the unwritten code of silence that surrounded my pregnancy and Bo's birth. I never asked them why they could reach out to me at this time and say that they loved me. There were no cards or flowers sent by my parents, or Randall, or Dayna. There was nothing to remind me that the people who mattered the most to me loved and thought about me during that hard and lonely time.

Tiny Blue Bundle

My time in the hospital felt uncertain, out of focus. On Monday, three days after Bo was born, it was time for me to go back to Sellers, but oh, what a difference those three days made. All told it was less than 72 hours, but in that short amount of time I had become Bo's mother. I was blessed with three days to caress his face and kiss his toes. Three days to tell him how much I loved him. Three days to cover him in a blanket of love that I hoped would protect him until he drew his last breath.

Every time the nurse brought Bo to me, I gazed into his eyes, trying to glimpse the man he might become. I imagined him a toddler, an eight-year old playing Little League baseball, a freshman trying out for junior varsity football. I imagined him placing ten-year old fingers on a piano or backing friends in a rock & roll band while they practiced in his parents' garage. I imagined his graduation from college. Would he be a professional? Maybe he would become a doctor, a lawyer, an engineer or an architect. Maybe he would inherit my own love of words and become a writer or a successful journalist. He would marry, of course, the most beautiful and kind woman in the world, and I imagined him tucking his own children into bed and helping them say their prayers.

I knew my days of mothering my son would end when I left the hospital. As I readied myself to leave, I faced the reality that by the end of the week, I would be returning to Oklahoma. Back to my old life. But what kind of life could it be without Bo? From the first time I laid eyes on him, he burst open my heart like a raging river bursts a damn. He was so tiny, just a little more than eight pounds, but when I held him in my arms, I felt like I was holding the universe. This earth. The moon and sun. All the planets. All the stars.

Next to Bo I felt puny and insignificant. Humbled. Any belief that I had even the smallest semblance of control in my life was just an illusion.

Shimmering light streamed through the open window and enhanced the otherworldliness of my life. Light so clean and bright, with no dust mites hanging in the air, it seemed God or an army of angels could ride down the beams like a child on a metal slide. Laughing. Full-throated. I didn't know why I felt so happy.

I heard a quick knock on the door and Mrs. Simpson stepped into the room with a wheelchair. She was the first person I had seen from Sellers since she left me in the labor room last Friday.

"You 'bout ready to go, Lani?"

"Yes, ma'am. But I can walk. Every few hours I walk down to the nursery to see Bo. Have you seen him yet, Mrs. Simpson? He's so beautiful."

"No, haven't seen him yet." She moved the wheelchair close to my bed and locked the wheels in place. "But we're fixin' to get him now. Hop in. Hospital rules."

A pillow shaped like a doughnut was in the center of the seat. When I sat down, I struggled to pull my bathrobe down over my knees. My nightgown felt all bunched up in back. The bulky sanitary pad between my legs chafed my butt crack. It was attached to maternity underwear with two safety pins. I hoped I didn't have to use pads for too long. I was thankful I didn't need to wear real people clothes for a few more days. My belly was puffy and soft like bread dough rising. I smelled slightly yeasty, too, almost as if I was putting off that sweet new baby smell.

Earlier that morning I placed my few belongs in the grocery sack I brought to the hospital on Friday. It contained the clothes I was wearing at the time, a few pair of soiled panties, and the things I received in the hospital—the pills to dry up my milk and the instructional pamphlet about how to care for a baby.

"What about the flowers, Mrs. Simpson? Should I bring them with me?"

"Sure, Lani. An aide can bring them down to the car with the rest of your things. We'll put the flowers in the dining room so everyone can enjoy them. Now let's go get that baby of yours."

I laid my son's booties in my lap. Mrs. Simpson unlocked the wheels and pushed me through the door. It was the first time I was sitting upright since giving birth, and the stitches from the episiotomy pulled. I flinched. What if they came out?

"So, did anyone else go to the hospital? Have you heard from Candy? I sure wish I coulda seen her before she left. She had to get going though. Her school's already started. My school started, too. Three weeks ago. But I'm sure I can make up the work."

After three days of solitary confinement, I found myself talking a mile a minute, grateful for the chance to converse with someone who would talk back. Bo didn't talk to me. He just mewed like a kitten and gazed at me with deep knowing looks. He seemed to understand everything I said to him. He seemed to have the answers to all the mysteries of the universe.

"Lani, slow down. Sometimes you talk so fast a person can't think."

We stopped at the door to the nursery and she locked the wheels in place.

"Don't want you going anywhere."

Inside the nursery, Mrs. Simpson walked between the rows of tiny cribs. Babies of all sizes and colors were wrapped tightly in pink and blue blankets. A hospital nurse handed her a tiny blue bundle, and Bo let out a wail. A pain surged in both breasts. I still had some milk. I wanted desperately to breastfeed him.

Mrs. Simpson began to chat with the nurse in the starched white uniform and cap. I was impatient. Bo was still crying. I couldn't hear what they were saying. I didn't care what they were saying. I wanted to hold my son. Mrs. Simpson must have been reading my mind. Within a few seconds she placed Bo in my arms. His cry subsided.

Coming around behind me, Mrs. Simpson reached down to unlock the wheels.

"Wait, Mrs. Simpson. I need to put his booties on him."

"OK, Lani, but hurry up. I've got to get back."

Bo was almost invisible, wrapped up like a little mummy. I unpacked the bundle, until I unearthed my precious boy. On his head he wore a soft blue cap. A cotton gown with a drawstring drawn tight beneath his feet enveloped his body. I positioned Bo firmly in the crook of my left arm. His arms and legs began to move in rhythm to a melody only he could hear. Like a marionette dancing before a crowd of delighted children, the puppet master was hidden. Another illusion. My right hand shook as I untied the drawstring and exposed his tiny feet.

Right foot, left foot, Bo wore the white booties I bought for him. They would come off in less than an hour, and they would be mine to keep, but for a little while, at least, he was wearing my only gift. Other than his life.

It's So Hard

September 5, Sun.

Dearest Lani,

Hi! I hope this letter gets to you before you leave. I was going to write sooner but it is trying to get settled at home and all.

I start school tomorrow. I think I'm gonna die, I'm so scared. It all seems so strange. And I bet I've got so much make-up work to do! Also, all the kids at school won't believe the fact that Ray & I are broken-up. They got used to seeing us together after 2 years.

Lani, it's so hard. My mom & Connor don't want me to have anything to do with Ray, but Lani, he's making it so hard on me. I've only been home two days, but he keeps calling. He keeps throwing it up to me about giving Johnny up. He just will not leave me alone about it. It hurts bad enuff without all of Ray's sarcastic comments. I guess he's just trying to hurt me as if I haven't been hurt enough by him already. And, the sad thing about it is that Ray knows he's hurting me, and it just doesn't matter to him. I guess he's just got a guilty conscience and is releasing his tensions the best way he knows how to. Oh!! I needed to talk to someone about it so bad. I thought I was gonna bust before I was able to write & tell you. Also, he keeps asking me to marry him. He said he would never give up on me for as long as he lives. What does a person do?

My cramps are so bad. I should have stayed at Sellers a while longer, but I was worried if I started school too late everyone would be talking. I wrote Miss Popwell & told her about how NONE of my clothes fit me. I'll bet she'll say, "I told you so!" I say give it a week or two.

Ya' know despite it all I miss being pregnant. I felt all empty inside being away from Miss Popwell & Sellers. Like you said, "I miss the security." Well, I really do more than I ever thought I would.

I miss Johnny so bad! I miss holding him, feeding him, and kissing him & all those gentle things mothers always do. Lani, I didn't realize it would be so awful. I want my baby so bad. I'll be glad when I have more children, but I'll always love Johnny more. He will be and is the most special thing that ever happened to me in my whole life. God knows, I love that baby.

You asked if I took pictures. No! I knew better.

Would you believe I measure 37 in the bust? I have gotten so much bigger. I used to be 34. My mother laughs at me all the time. Clarence calls me "boo-boo!" He's so crazy.

Lani, I miss you so much too. You'll just never know what your friendship has meant & will always mean to me! Write soon.

Love always,

Candy

Don't Look Back

After six months, one week and three days at Sellers Baptist Home, in the City of New Orleans, I was going home, but not as the same person. My bag was packed. My records, my marble egg. An envelope filled with letters. My empty stationery box filled with Bo's keepsakes. I gave most of my maternity clothes to Renee and left the rest in the clothes closet. I packed the "real people" clothes I brought with me. The pink polyester pantsuit. A pair of jeans now completely unzippable. My waist was at least eleven inches wider than it was when I left home in March.

My mom sent me a new dress as a going-away outfit. A red polyester A-line shift, with enough give in the front to hide my still bulging belly. But she made it without any measurements, and she had no idea that my boobs were so much larger. The dress was tight across the shoulders, but it was a vast improvement over the pink polyester pantsuit I wore when I arrived at Sellers in that long-ago other lifetime.

It had been one week since I left for the hospital, and I sat down to my last meal at Sellers. Grits. Of course, it had to be grits. I should have been happy that I would never look a pot of grits in the face again, but I wasn't happy in any way. I would have given anything to still be pregnant with Bo safe inside me. Still mine, all mine.

The dining room was noisy. A bowl of fruit sitting on the sideboard was distracting. A pineapple in amongst the apples, oranges, and bananas. Pineapples don't grow in Moore, Oklahoma, and I had never seen one in the flesh. Only pictures on Del Monte cans. Its exterior was prickly and uninviting, and I couldn't imagine how they expected us to eat it.

Right at 8:30, Mrs. Stafford stepped in and motioned me back to her office. I gathered my dishes and placed them in the bin next to the kitchen. I leaned over and whispered to Donna as I made my way out of the dining room.

"I've got to go sign my papers now."

Donna's face looked pained. "Be strong, girl. Will you come back and say goodbye?"

"Sure. My plane doesn't leave until 1. I'll see you later and let you know how it goes."

I followed Mrs. Stafford down the hallway to her office. I had been down that hallway a hundred times before. They were the same green walls, the same bulletin board with Christmas cards and school pictures of Sellers adoptees, the same picture of praying hands, but nothing in the hallway looked familiar.

Mrs. Stafford quickened her pace. I realized I was dragging my feet, wanting and waiting for time to stop.

"Lani, you're slower than molasses in January."

"Mrs. Stafford, can I see Bo one last time?"

She turned and gave me a sharp look. "Lani, it's best if you don't see him again."

Never again? I wasn't ever going to see him again? Why didn't they tell me that yesterday?

If I had known that the previous day was going to be the last time I would see him, I would have talked to him a little longer, held him a little closer. There was so much left unsaid. I didn't tell him about the good life I wanted him to have. I didn't count his fingers and toes one last time.

This little piggy went to market,
This little piggy stayed home…

I didn't tell him how beautiful he was. He had moved beyond the tomato red face he had on the day he was born. In fact, his square little face was perfectly adorable in every way.

I needed more time. I didn't burn into my memory the little kitten mewing sound he made when I cradled him in my arms. I didn't imprint on my soul his deep knowing look. I couldn't close my eyes and smell his sweet new baby smell.

Against the rules, in my last visit with my sweet boy, Miss Popwell took two pictures of him with her Polaroid. In the photo a white hospital gown covers my clothes. I'm holding Bo in the crook of my left arm. He's wearing a pale blue seersucker onesie that snapped under his diaper; his white crocheted booties on his feet.

These Polaroid photos were a sorry substitute for my Bo. In only a week he looked different, smelled different, sounded different. I knew that one day he would be a toddler, a boy, a teenager, a man, and I would never share more than this tiny moment of his life.

Mrs. Stafford's office was crowded. Mrs. LaPrairie and Thomas Barr III sat across from Mrs. Stafford's desk with an empty chair between them. Thomas Barr III was Mrs. LaPrairie's son-in-law and he handled all the adoptions. Mrs. Stafford sat behind a stack of papers on her desk. Since there was nowhere else to sit, I slouched in the empty folding chair, which had been brought in from the chapel. I was at least a foot lower than the others, and I felt overwhelmed and intimidated.

I glanced at the papers on Mrs. Stafford's desk. The first one had the word relinquishment across the top of it. Mrs. Stafford pushed it toward of me. "OK, Lani, sign here."

I hesitated. "Shouldn't I read these first?"

Thomas Barr III piped up immediately. His voice was harsh and gravelly. "You've gone over this before with Mrs. Stafford. There's nothing new here."

Mrs. Stafford nodded. "You're doing the right thing, Lani. Bo is better off without you. Go ahead and sign the paper."

Her voice held a sternness I hadn't heard before.

Mrs. LaPrairie chimed in. "Your son will go to a good home. We will make sure of it. You must understand you are unfit to be his mother."

Thomas Barr III looked sullen. Without another word, his long, boney finger pointed to the place on the page where I was expected to sign. The pen felt heavy in my hand. On the first page I scribbled my name fast just to get it over with. It was hardly legible.

Mrs. Stafford leaned across the desk and shuffled the stack of paper. "Slow down. You're not going to a fire."

First, I was moving too slow, then I was moving too fast. Once again I had the sinking feeling that nothing I did would ever be okay.

Thomas Barr III stretched out his boney finger once again and pointed to the next spot for my signature.

The pen felt heavier. This time I wrote in slow motion. The initial "L" in my name came out as two big loops. I didn't want to pull a "John Hancock" on the paper—covering like he did half of the page of the Declaration of Independence with his signature. Ashamed, I scratched out the "L."

An audible sigh escaped Mrs. Stafford's lips.

"Lani, get on with it. Sign the paper."

My chest was tight. I thought I might be having a heart attack. My heart was surely breaking. I couldn't think; I couldn't breathe. My ears filled with the sound of crashing waves.

One more page to sign. Thomas Barr's finger belonged to the Ghost of Christmas Future, and it pointed to my tombstone. I put pen to paper.

Lani Jo Lassiter.

Mrs. LaPrairie looked satisfied.

"Lani, put this all behind you; I cannot stress this enough. This is a secret you must take to your grave. Bo will go to a wonderful family." She repeated her earlier admonition, "At your age, you are unfit to be a mother. He is better off without you."

Thomas Barr III gathered the papers from the desk and dropped them in the open black brief case next to his chair. He and Mrs. LaPrairie stood to leave. She turned in the doorway to face me.

"Have a good trip home, Lani."

"Wait, will you let me know when Bo's adopted? Please, you've got to let me know."

Mrs. LaPrairie's high heels click-clacked down the hallway. Mrs. Stafford stood up from behind her desk.

"We've got your bag by the front door, Lani. There's a taxi waiting to take you to the airport."

"Can't I say goodbye to Renee and Donna? Bonnie is waiting for me in the kitchen. I didn't say goodbye to Mrs. York or Miss Popwell."

She shook her head and escorted me out of her office. "We don't want you to be late for your plane. You can write when you get home."

Mrs. Stafford walked me as far as the front door. My suitcase sat on the floor next to my shoulder bag and pea coat. I picked up my purse, unzipped the outside compartment and checked for my one-way ticket to Oklahoma City.

Mrs. Stafford opened the door. "All set?"

I nodded, grabbed my purse and coat, and picked up my suitcase. I stepped out into my last sticky New Orleans morning, and strode down the sidewalk to the waiting cab.

"Lani, don't you ever look back," I told myself. "Don't you ever look back."

Part Three:
Roll On, Columbia

There is another world and it is in this one.

~Paul Éluard

Adjusting

My mother picked me up at the airport. Alone.

She stood outside the gate wearing the same dress and scuffed pumps she had worn for her visit to Sellers. There was no "welcome home" banner and cheering throngs.

My mother didn't have much to say to me outside of, "Did you have a good flight?" In the little keepsake box that had once held stationery, I kept the two Polaroid photos of Bo that Miss Popwell had taken the day before I left Sellers. I ached to share the photos with her, but my mother didn't want to see them. And if she didn't want to see the photos, I knew I couldn't share any of my experiences with her. I didn't press the issue. My mother seemed determined to act as if nothing had happened. Even my sisters didn't ask any questions. Everyone behaved as if I had only been out to buy a tube of lipstick or a pair of underwear, not six months away in a strange, far-away city for a life-altering event. That was pretty typical of our family dynamic. We didn't know how to talk with each other about anything that mattered.

Dayna called me up the day I flew home and told me that she was oh, so terribly sorry, but her reputation would be ill served if she hung out with me. After all, she was the editor of the *Lion's Roar*. She was in the National Honor Society. After being best friends forever and inseparable since seventh grade, poof, Dayna was gone and out of my life. After not hearing a peep from her for six months, I kinda figured something like that was going to happen, but I didn't realize how much it was going to hurt.

There was an opening at the day care center at First Baptist, and I wanted to apply for it—I had plenty of experience from working in the nursery at Sellers. But my bad girl reputation meant I wasn't a suitable candidate. Pastor Bodine told my father that I needn't bother with an application.

Two days after I returned, the pastor's wife, Mrs. Bodine, prayed for me by name in Sunday school, calling me the returning prodigal daughter, and hoped I would find comfort and solace at the feet of my Lord and Savior, Jesus. Although she surely had the purest intentions, I never went to Sunday school at First Baptist again. I was no longer looking for salvation, and my good girl reputation was shot. In fact, when I confronted my next-door neighbor, Andy, about why he wasn't speaking to me, he said that the word on the grapevine was that I had taken most of the football team out to Draper Lake and fucked them all.

Because I showed up three weeks after school started, and I hadn't been at Moore High the previous spring, I was passed over for any position on the school newspaper. With Dayna as editor, I wasn't even welcome on the staff. I wasn't allowed to audition for the Select Mixed Chorus. In fact, I wasn't even welcome to join the non-auditioned Girls Chorus, and the Future Teachers of American didn't want me as a member, either.

Randall, true to his word, stuck by me even though it meant he was also ostracized at school by the "in crowd." Unlike me, he could still participate in any extra-curricular activities that he liked, but instead he threw himself into work and started saving money for college. I got hired at the local five & dime store, and within a month I was manager of the dry goods department. I started wearing Randall's "drop" again. Over the summer, our friend Kip had moved to Lubbock, Texas, so when we weren't working, Randall and I hung out with our long-time friend David, Dr. Dycus's son, who had admitted to us that he was gay. We were all outcasts—too smart for our own good, and desperate to leave.

My friends from Sellers commiserated with my situation; some had it better and some had it worse on their return to real life. The fall of '71 was a time of tremendous adjustment for most of us, but we had to move on with the business of living as if nothing had happened. Our days were filled with high school and college football games, family funerals and weddings. Georgie turned fifteen in December and started driving. Renee had a new boyfriend. Candy secured a job at Miss Priss Beauty Salon. Anita's latest pig was growing along with her hair. Jo sounded like she drank until drunk every weekend. Candy had a medical scare.

> *"...a week from Monday, I have to go to the hospital in Jackson and have an operation on my uterus. ...I will*

probably be in the hospital about a week. I dread it but suppose it will be all for the best..."

Friendships I knew at home, even the friendship I thought I shared with Dayna, never compared to the ones I formed and nurtured at Sellers. Our early letters to each other reinforced our belief that we were different with each other there—more authentic and transparent. Less competitive. More giving of spirit.

However, the love I felt for my friends—especially Candy, Jo, Georgie, and Glenda—never eased the debilitating pain I felt every time I thought of my son and struggled with the knowledge that I had given him up and would never see him again.

All of us needed to know how our babies were faring while they remained at Sellers, and we wanted news that our babies were adopted. More than anything we wanted to believe that we had been able to give them a happily-ever-after.

In late October, I received a legal-sized envelope with an eight-cent stamp bearing a drawing of the White House superimposed by a large United States flag. The typewritten return address was Box 15276-Station B, New Orleans, and it was addressed to Miss Lani Lassiter.

The letter inside was dated October 26, 1971—fifty-three days after I gave birth to my son.

Dear Lani:

I was so glad to hear from you and relieved to hear that you are doing fine. I knew you were having problems with your friends. You are really fortunate that Randall has been such a help.

I know you have been anxious about Bo. He is the "baby" in a family with two older children and doing great. The couple was so thrilled with him and felt like he belonged in the family. Although the father is a very successful professional in business, he has always made sure he had plenty of time to spend with his family. That is important especially for a little boy. Bo will be spoiled by all of the attention. Lani, I hope his happiness can give you peace of mind.

> *You have already gone through the toughest part of adjusting. It will get better because you are willing to work for it. Take care of yourself. We think about you often.*
>
> *Sincerely yours,*
>
> *(Mrs.) Allegra LaPrairie, ACSW*
> *Director, Sellers Baptist Home*

Randall and I were making plans to get married the following summer after graduation. For the most part, my friends' relationships with the young men in their lives were complicated. I especially felt sad about Candy's situation.

> *Lani, Ray has caused nothing but one big "problem" since I got home. …he will simply <u>not</u> let me forget about having to give Johnny up. He throws it up to me <u>all</u> <u>the</u> <u>time</u>! Sometimes I get <u>so</u> hurt. I just wanna die sometimes! He actually slapped me the other nite, and this hurt me mentally as well as physically. He slapped me because I told him I don't love him like I used to.*

Jo was still going out with Danny, but also sleeping with her best friend's boyfriend whenever his parents were out of town. Georgie started dating a new guy who was in college. In March she wrote that she might be pregnant again.

"Such a time as we shared," Beverly said in her last letter to me. And such a time it was. I experienced genuine love and acceptance from my friends at Sellers. But the memories were too fresh and too raw. Mrs. LaPrairie, Miss Popwell, Mrs. York, Mrs. Stafford only had one piece of advice, "Forget about it and move on." I knew that forgetting would be impossible if I continued to have contact with my friends. I withdrew into a shell. I was a coward and unable to live with any reminders of Sellers, my baby and the pain of having given him up, even if meant losing the dearest friends I had ever known. Candy sent a description of what it meant to be a friend, and sadly I wasn't that person.

What Is A Friend?

One who multiplies joys, divides griefs, and where honesty is inviolable.

One who understands our silence.
A volume of sympathy bound in cloth.
A watch which beats true for all time, and never runs down.
A friend is the one who comes in when the whole world has gone out.
Am I united with my friend in heart?
What matters if our place be wide apart?

By June, I had stopped corresponding with everyone I knew from Sellers, and I had no close friendships in Moore. I held tight to the belief that if Randall and I could just get married, it would legitimize all that I had gone through. Getting married would prove to the world that my relationship with Randall hadn't just been about sex. I gave our baby up for adoption so that Bo, Randall and I would all have better lives, lives filled with love and possibilities.

By October of '71 I was on the pill, and Randall and I resumed having sex. It remained enjoyable, but seemed to lack some of the urgency we felt in the early days of our sexual exploration. We didn't need to go parking on any Lover's Lane, either. Randall's parents pretty much just turned a blind eye to whatever we were doing in his bedroom.

I applied for and received a journalism scholarship to the University of Oklahoma, and Randall was a National Merit scholar. We were going to college after all, and our first home together would be in student housing.

Randall was still too young to get married in Oklahoma, so with both our parents' permission, at the end of August we went to Wichita Falls for the license and the legal contract. The wedding took place the following day at First Baptist, and my three sisters served as bridesmaids. David was Randall's best man. My mom made all of our dresses out of dotted Swiss fabric. I didn't care what anyone thought; I wore white, and my sisters' dresses were each a different color of the rainbow—yellow for Kathy, pink for Carla, blue for Janet. We each wore a floppy wide-brimmed garden hat with a grosgrain ribbon around the crown in the color that matched our dresses. One of the few girls at school who still spoke to me, Shirley, sang "*Love*" from the John Lennon/Plastic Ono Band album.

I needed to be loved, but I had my doubts about whether or not love was real.

The previous January, after my first visit to Dr. Dycus, I sat in the car fantasizing about our wedding and our marriage. I remembered the wishes

I left at the grave of Madame Marie Laveau. Everything I had imagined was coming true—except that when it came to the wedding, David, Randall's best man, drank too much the night before and starting puking right before he was supposed to give Randall my ring. And of course, Dayna wasn't there.

A little more than a year after Bo's birth, I received one more letter, this one from The University of Oklahoma Medical Center, and addressed to Mr. & Mrs. Randall Wallace.

September 27, 1972

Dear Mr. & Mrs. Wallace:

We wish to thank you for your recent donation in the amount of $10 in token of your son's first birthday. What a nice way to remember a birthday – by helping other children that desperately need our help. Your donation will be used for a birthday celebration of a hospitalized child.

Thank you for your contribution and your interest in our hospital and our patients.

Sincerely,

Sandra Nathan, Director
Volunteer Services

I sent the money without Randall's knowledge. At the time I thought I would commemorate Bo's birthday every year by sending money to a children's organization in his name. I thought that eventually Randall would understand what we had and what we lost. I thought that he would soon join me in celebrating Bo's life and commiserating his loss. But by the next year, our marriage was already in trouble, and we divorced in 1975.

Finding a Keeper

In the eleven years after my divorce from Randall I went through a string of relationships and plenty of one-night stands. I was able to admit I was sexually attracted to women and, while a student at SUNY Binghamton, I even acted on those feelings. Most of the time, however, I gravitated toward men who were either jerks or assholes, men who were emotionally cruel and mean like my father. You could have placed me in a room with twenty equally attractive, intelligent men and I would use my keen spidey-sense to choose the one who would abuse me, ridicule me, reject me. I picked some doozies—several guys who were alcoholics, a couple who were married and cheating on their wives, one who was a pathological liar, one who wet the bed, one guy who could only get it up when he fantasized about raping his old girlfriend, one 40-year old who still lived with his mother.

One bad relationship had a wonderful outcome, however. I started going out with Neil in the fall of 1978, and by December, we had already broken-up when I learned that I was pregnant. After sharing the news with Neil, we decided to give our relationship a shot, and we married in January. With this pregnancy I was determined to have a "good birth." We didn't have practicing midwives in Oklahoma, and after my experience with Bo, I refused to use an OB/GYN. Instead I went to our long-time family practitioner, Dr. Dycus, David's father, for my care. I had heard of Lamaze childbirth education, but couldn't find an active group in Norman, where we lived and attended Oklahoma University. What I found was "Gentle Birth," a local group that provided guidance, support, and compassion to expectant mothers, along with classes that taught breathing exercises to use during labor. More than anything I learned to adamantly say, "NO!"

No, I do not want an IV. No, I do not want equipment hooked up to monitor me or my baby. No, I do not want any pain medication. No, I do not want an epidural. No, I do not want an episiotomy. No, I will not stay in the hospital after I give birth.

Dr. Dycus respected my position on every request. I went into labor on the evening of September 8, 1978, almost seven years after I gave birth to Bo. I went to the hospital, but this time I had someone with me. Neil and I played cards for most of the night, taking breaks during contractions. I wasn't placed in stirrups, and I wasn't strapped down. Whenever I needed, I could get up and penguin shuffle down the hall outside the labor room—back and forth, back and forth—stopping and leaning on my partner's arm when the pain became too intense to stand. Fortunately, my water didn't break until close to 5am when my daughter was crowning. This made the pain more bearable and I could breathe or pant right through it. Without an episiotomy, I did tear, but Dr. Dycus sewed me up without using anesthetic. Fern was born covered in the white coating, vernix caseosa, and I used my Gentle Birth training to emphatically state, "No, you cannot wash her." The nurse handed Fern to me even before I had expelled the placenta, and I placed her on my breast immediately. She latched on and didn't let go for three years.

Getting married and having a baby together was not a panacea for the difficult issues Neil and I faced in our relationship, but for some reason I believed that if we just had another baby, we could magically become the ideal American family. Mom, dad and two kids. I got pregnant again the following year, and Dustin was born in February 1980. Once again, Dr. Dycus delivered my baby at Moore Hospital, but this time I barely got there in time. I started having contractions early in the evening and I went to the emergency room to get checked out, but when the nurse told me I was only dilated four centimeters, I decided to labor in the comfort of my own home. I fell asleep only to wake after midnight with the baby on its way. I never made it to the delivery room, and Dustin slipped out while I was in the hall waiting to be wheeled in. Just like I had with Fern, I left the hospital before noon. And since I was in my last semester of my senior year in college, I took Dustin to class with me the next day.

Of course, we were still not the perfect American family. A second baby only exacerbated all the reasons Neil and I couldn't stay together. We separated before the year was out.

I know I wasn't a bad mother. But sometimes I felt like the experience of having and losing Bo held me back from fully enjoying my children. I was in a constantly anxious state. What if something happened to them? I didn't think I could recover from losing another child.

After a while I started dating again, but I continued to pick jerks and assholes. It's not to say that I didn't meet and even love a few men who were generous and kind. But it scared me to care about them, and I drove them away.

Roger was different. We met at work. I had just started a new job at a downtown Los Angeles financial services firm; he had been working there for almost a year. On my first day at work, Chris, the office manager, walked me around to introduce me to everyone in the office. Although LA was already the land of perpetual casual Friday, the firm's headquarters were in New York, the land of strangled neckties, and the standard office attire was definitely Wall Street formal. Before taking the job, I bought several smart looking suits in non-scratchy summer wool, and some great fuck-me pumps. I was in costume for the thrilling role of Executive Assistant to the brilliant star financial analyst. Everyone there dressed for success. Everyone, that is, except Roger.

On the tour, Chris took me to Roger's office, which was one of the largest on the floor and had great views of downtown. He was the head of the graphics department and needed lots of light and space for his cool toys (or so he had convinced the management). When we met the first time, Roger's dark, curly hair hung down past his collar, his thick beard and mustache surrounded full, red and gleaming lips, and, instead of wearing a tie, his shirt was unbuttoned to the middle of his chest. He looked like an Italian Mafioso, except he didn't wear any gold chains. And he was hairy— the hairiest man I had ever seen. Hair sprouted, blossomed, flowered on the broad expanse of chest exposed by the four unbuttoned buttons. When we were introduced, he repeated my name with a smile. He told me later that with a first and last name both beginning with "L" I could have been one of Superman's girlfriends.

About a week later, on his 24th birthday, we talked for the first time over drinks in the bar downstairs where we had gone with a few other people from the office. He was almost nine years younger than me—a puppy with unbridled enthusiasm and big teeth that filled his face with a beam that could have lit up Dodger Stadium. We started going out for lunch every day, and I told him everything about me. He heard the entire litany of losers. He heard about how much I liked sex, but hated men. I confessed my favorite sexual positions and fantasies. I titillated him with stories of my escapades, and, not surprisingly, within a few weeks we went from lunch partners to "fuck buddies." Good friends who just happened to like screwing each other's brains out, whenever and wherever.

Sometimes we extended our lunch hour and drove out to his apartment in Hollywood for a quickie. When we didn't have that time to spare, we did it on the hillside park north of downtown and west of Dodger Stadium. Once we even tried to do it in a paddleboat on Echo Lake. Most nights I waited until my children were fast asleep in their beds, and then, leaving them in the care of my roommate, Debbie, I drove the 18 miles from our house in Pasadena to Roger's apartment in Hollywood. I arrived around ten and we made love again and again, then we fell asleep around two, after setting the alarm for five so I could get back home before my children began to yawn and stir.

The movement to him and away from him became like breathing or the gentle in and out of his body on mine.

Eventually I introduced Roger to my children, then eight and six. In November, we went camping up in the redwoods about four or five hours north of Los Angeles. We hiked for several hours, gawking at the enormity of the trees. For dinner, Roger fed our hunger with spaghetti and garlic bread cooked over an open flame, and I learned that he was an Eagle Scout, another surprise. We put Fern and Dustin to bed in a tent he had pitched, and then we sat around the campfire drinking Old Bushmills and listening to John Prine and Bob Dylan. We told stories, shared visions and dreams, and I got extremely drunk. Roger kept trying to keep me quiet. "Shhhhhh, you'll wake the kids," but I sang to the heavens about getting stoned and going home as I boogied my way around the circle of flames. I laughed and kept intoning, "eleven years, eleven years." Aside from song lyrics, all other words escaped me. I wanted to explain to him that I hadn't felt the way I felt that night in eleven long and lonely years, since my early twenties, when hope was fresh and true love still seemed like a possibility, but words failed me. I kissed him instead.

That night we made love under the stars and in the back of my cramped '86 Dodge Colt. I felt loved in a way that was new and unknown. And I woke up in the morning hung over and scared.

All right, now I'm feeling vulnerable again. When is the other shoe going to drop? When is the pain going to start? When will he abuse me, ridicule me, reject me?

So, I started doing what I had always done with the one or two nice guys who came my way. I started slicing into Roger with my nasty tongue. I tried to burn him alive; I tried to drive him away.

"You're a baby. You don't know how to love me. I was fucking guys when you were still in diapers. You don't have what it takes to be with me." It went on and on.

Roger listened quietly, and then he told me to stop it. That was it. He didn't hit me, he didn't try to argue with me, and he didn't leave. He just stood his ground.

"Listen, I like you and I want to keep seeing you, but you can't make me hurt you. I'm not going to play this game. So, if you want us to stay friends, you better stop this right now."

Stop it? I could stop it? But weren't my problems with men their fault?

I became conscious of my own culpability and intensely aware that I could control what happened to me. I realized that in previous relationships, I had been the hand inside the glove. But I could make different choices. I could both love and be loved.

Something new was created that weekend. Together we gave birth to an "us." We are separate and complete individuals, yet together we are something more. We created a relationship that is like another being. This relationship, this us, has grown and developed much like a child. When new, it squealed for attention. It threw tantrums, and was, at times, petty and jealous.

It wasn't always easy. We had a few rough patches. In the twelfth year of our marriage something got lost. We fought, and cruel, ugly words spilled out on both sides. My psyche felt like it had stayed out in the sun too long, defaced by blistered, oozing sores. Our bed, once an island oasis, was now as wide as the Gulf of Mexico, and each night I slept fitfully, robed in grey flannel. We moved through our days in studied politeness. Emotionally abandoned and betrayed, for the first time I danced with the specter of divorce.

We were in a period of transition—in limbo between selling our business and figuring out what to do with the rest of our lives. For years we had denied ourselves vacations because of family and work obligations, and now we planned to travel for most of a year. Our emotional estrangement came when we'd already rented a small, studio apartment in Paris for the month of March. I hoped that the blossoming chestnuts and the charm of spring could rekindle the connection and the fire.

Our first few days were awful, trapped in a foreign city in a fourth-floor walk-up with a man I felt I no longer knew. We decided to get out of the city and head to the small village of Bayeux to surround ourselves with tapestry and gravestones. Despite our fascination with the story of William the Conqueror and the horror at seeing pretty English roses hiding rows upon rows of D-Day dead, we stayed caught in our personal pain, our conversations stilted and unnatural, like members of two alien species who don't know how to coexist.

On the two-and-a-half-hour train ride back to Paris, we sat across from each other, at first barely talking, crossing and uncrossing arms and knees, avoiding gazes. Then a brief glance, a brush of thigh against thigh, and a reach across the void to entwine hesitant fingers. We spoke, tentatively at first, dipping one toe at a time into the vast, cold ocean of our mistrust. We tried to remember some self-help psychology. Stick with "I" statements: "I hurt," "I'm sorry," "I love you."

Outside the train window, fields and villages rushed by. Inside our small compartment, we waded in, waist-deep, then up to our chests, until in fading daylight we began swimming out over our heads in familiar water as warm as the womb.

Once in Paris, we caught the Number 4 line of the Metro to the Odeon station, and walked the few blocks to the apartment on rue Dauphine. We passed the same le marché, la pâtisserie, la boucherie, la pharmacie that we passed in that life before Bayeux, but when Roger took my hand in that foreign city, this time I knew I was walking home.

This May Be a Miracle

I don't believe in miracles,
yet here we are years later
still fucking like newlyweds.
Highly improbable to say the least,
if not downright miraculous.
Sometimes I wonder how we
manage to kiss without breaking our teeth.

Stuck between the Age of Reason and the
Age of Enlightenment, Hume tiptoes around
blasphemy, avoiding a hanging like Aikenhead.

*But a gauntlet hits the ground when it
comes to miracles.*

*They germinate in barbarous nations,
he says, in barbarous times, and that certainly explains
serpentine queues outside temples in Calcutta,
where idols of the god Ganesh lap offerings of milk
(and gods are nothing if not finicky and sip only from
silver spoons).*

*There's no image of Allah or of his prophet Muhammad,
so
he's partial to writing his name in vegetables.
In London Mrs. Patel slices an eggplant and the seeds
spell out the Shahada.*

*Here in the US, we've got a grilled cheese sandwich that
looks like the Virgin Mary selling on eBay for
twenty-eight thousand dollars. A miracle indeed.
Jesus' face on a tortilla in Lake Arthur, New Mexico, was
a
roadside attraction for almost thirty years until Mrs.
Rubio's
granddaughter took it to school for Show and Tell, and
well,
I've got a ten-year old grandson myself, so I understand
completely the need to close the backyard shrine.*

*Hume says we want to look for miracles.
The imagined proximity to the divine fuels our
passions; sets our hearts to racing with wonder and
surprise.
Maybe that's why I have no need for them.
Under our covers we've got passion enough to
power the energy needs of the entire west coast,
hell, maybe all the way east to the Mississippi.
Everything about our love is a miracle,
and I've still got all my teeth.*

It's taken constant feeding, love, and thoughtful consideration, but now married more than thirty years, Roger and I are friends, partners, companions, lovers, and, lucky for me, still fuck buddies.

Chanel No. 5

We have a family myth about the perfect wonderfulness of my mother. Myths contain elements of truth—our mother was wonderful—she gave and gave far beyond the point of having anything to give herself. She gave even when the price was her own health. But deep down, I still felt betrayed by what happened when I was seventeen. I didn't believe my mother was there for me. I was left alone without family or friends. Maybe her heart was breaking, too. My sister Kathy thinks so. She told me that while I was away in New Orleans, mom grew visibly older, and that she cried most evenings. But when I returned, we never shared our similar feelings of loss.

We muddled through by always acting like nothing was wrong, although there was a constant undercurrent of resentment on my part and disappointment on my mother's.

At thirty, I had a job as an administrative assistant for The Salvation Army—a respectable job—nice people, easy work, but not much of a salary. In 1983 the economy was tough—according to my favorite evening news broadcaster, Dan Rather, we were in a recession. Reagan had been in office more than two years, but the tax cuts hadn't trickled down to where I was living. After college I had a good job as communications consultant at a training center for developmentally disabled adults until Reagan cut its Title XX funds, putting me out of work for almost six months. So, this administrative job was at least gainful employment, and I was happy I could afford to pay my own rent.

I was living in a small shotgun duplex off NW 23rd Street in Oklahoma City, and I didn't own a washer and dryer. The summer of 1984 was hot as blue blazes with temperatures constantly hovering in the high 90's. With two kids under five, washing clothes at the Laundromat was not only a chore, it was a CHORE, so I hightailed it to my parents' house and the free washer and dryer every chance I could. It was a pretty sweet deal. My mom fixed my favorite foods, and while she watched the kids, I could talk on the phone in the comfort of her air conditioning.

One evening, I sat at the well-worn oak dining table, drank ice-cold sweet tea, and listened for the buzz of the clothes dryer. Instead, my mom's voice traveled down the short hallway from her bedroom to the living room and took a sharp left turn into the kitchen. "Lani, have you seen my bottle of perfume?"

Oh, shit, she's found me out.

Again, I heard her voice coming from the bedroom.

"Lani, didn't you hear me? I'm sure I had it right here in the medicine chest."

Should I fess up? The last time I was at my parent's home, Dustin's boo-boo needed more than just a kiss to make it better, so I scrounged around my parents' bathroom looking for a Band-Aid. Pulling open the overflowing medicine cabinet, I spied a small black and gold jewel surrounded by bottles of Calamine lotion, Milk of Magnesia, and baby aspirin. Without thinking, I slipped a tiny, mostly empty bottle of Chanel No. 5 into the front pocket of my Gloria Vanderbilt jeans.

This was a chance to say I borrowed it. "Oh, yeah, Ma, remember? You loaned it to me the night I had my big date with Dennis. He was taking me to Sizzler's."

The bottle was in my purse. I could slip it back into the medicine cabinet next to Doan's Superior Treatment for Back Pain, Carter's Little Liver pills or one of my mother's myriad heart medications.

Feign a headache; go off in search of Excedrin. "Look, Ma, here's that perfume you were looking for. If it'd been a snake, it woulda bit you."

But I didn't say I borrowed it. I didn't put it back.

"No, ma. I haven't seen it."

And she never asked after it again.

I had an undercurrent of anger at my mother that I refused to acknowledge. But I had no reason to treat her so shamefully. Her generosity knew no bounds. I always left with more than just clean laundry; she put together weekly care packages—a Strawberry Shortcake shorts set for Fern, a Scooby-Doo t-shirt for Dustin. Packages of pinto beans, boxes of macaroni and cheese, cans of Spam. Sometimes I found hamburger or a chuck roast from her meat freezer; or home canned green beans, beets and apple butter from her pantry. And she always slipped me a five-dollar bill when my father wasn't looking. My mother deserved better. Maybe she felt she was in some ways responsible for the mess I had made of my life after giving up my son.

Maybe she was trying to make up for it by how she supported me, cared for me, worried about me, sacrificed for me.

How could I possibly justify the theft and the lie? Well, I had champagne taste on a beer budget, and my mother simply had no business owning a bottle of Chanel No. 5.

Chanel No. 5 is one of the most recognizable and expensive perfumes in the world. A timeless classic, Marilyn Monroe's signature scent. Wearing it is like wearing expensive lingerie or slipping between silk sheets with your lover. And this wasn't just a bottle of eau de toilette hiding in the medicine cabinet. No, this was the real stuff—parfum, as the French say—thicker than water, oily like baptismal chrism; its flowery scent lingered on the skin for hours. Standing in my mother's cramped half-bath, the pink sink clearly showing the twenty plus years of wear and tear, I took one sniff, breathed in luxurious aromas of roses and jasmine, sandalwood, cedar and musk, and I coveted that treasure.

No. 5 is mysterious, sensual, sophisticated, sexy. No. 5 was not my mother.

Overweight by more than sixty pounds, my mother lived a life of extreme exertion, but no exercise. Chores like cooking and cleaning every day. Ironing on Wednesdays, Tuesdays for sewing. On weekends, baking, gardening, canning. And there was always mending and scrubbing to be done.

She cooked plenty, mostly typical Oklahoma fare. At breakfast, our plates were piled high with biscuits and gravy thickened with sausage drippings, eggs fried over easy. At dinner, the table groaned with overcooked greens seasoned liberally with bacon grease, chicken fried steak or country fried chicken, slow cooked pinto beans with a left-over ham hock from Sunday dinner, followed with peach cobbler or pecan pie. Everything cooked with lots of butter, lots of sugar, lots of salt.

With a military husband away on overseas assignments at least six months of every year, my mom raised five children almost single-handedly. When it came to spending money, she kept her needs at the unreachable bottom of the list, behind band uniforms and school supplies and church camp. Her everyday clothes of polyester and cotton were threadbare and ill fitting, and although she could make a silk purse out of a sow's ear, her face remained creased with permanent worry lines. My mom wore her heart on her sleeve, cried at the drop of a hat, and always, always when the situation warranted, laughed like a loon.

It was easy to justify keeping the Chanel in my purse. I was the one going on dates. I was the one with the chance to be mysterious, sophisticated, sexy. If anyone wore No. 5, it should be me, and not my mother.

Two days after the theft of the perfume, I had another date with Dennis. I left Dustin and Fern with my mother overnight in case there was an opportunity to get frisky. Just dinner and a movie, no need to change out of jeans and a t-shirt, but I rummaged in my purse for the small bottle of perfume. I opened the glass stopper, hoping to inhale the promise of sex.

That wasn't what escaped the bottle. Instead I was five, sitting at the foot of my parent's bed. My sisters, Kathy and Carla, played in their bedroom down the hall; the new baby, Janet, slept in the nursery next door.

We were living in England, in the small village of Abbotsley, not far from Cambridge. My mom and dad entertained other service families at our home, and they meandered to the local pub with friends. They went to the theater in London and came back to regale us with tales of the handsome Rex Harrison and the nightingale Julie Andrews, both stars in the West End production of *My Fair Lady*.

From my vantage point at the foot of my parent's bed, I watched my mother in a state of reverie. She was more beautiful than any movie star. I loved her going-to-the-theater dress—deeper than midnight and splattered with large, crimson roses. The wide red belt had a big gold buckle, and the scoop neck with red piping showed just the tiniest bit of cleavage when she bent over to pick us up.

My mom always told me to mind Maria, our housekeeper. "No fussing at bedtime. And help take care of your sisters." Before leaving the house, she said, "Come give me some sugar"—her way of asking for a kiss. I would wrap my arms around her neck and nestle my face next to hers. Then she would kiss my cheek and I could smell her smell—*that smell*—roses and jasmine, sandalwood, cedar, musk. The smell of No. 5.

Who was I kidding? I couldn't wear that damn perfume.

I marched through my small duplex, past Dustin's crib, Fern's tricycle, past my empty, unmade bed, the small bottle clutched in a damp fist. The screen door of the utility porch complained like a hungry cat when I pushed it open.

What do I care about a silly bottle of perfume?

I hurled the bottle into the alleyway behind my house and went back inside to wait for Dennis.

A few hours later, after mediocre pizza, the seven o'clock showing of *Flashdance*, and some insincere kisses, Dennis and I returned to my empty apartment. But I wasn't interested in sex without love that night, so I feigned a headache and sent him on his way. I sat alone at the kitchen table, sick to my stomach at the thought of the discarded and squandered bottle.

I grabbed a flashlight and headed out to the alley to hunt for it. Crawling on hands and knees, I searched under an abandoned car. With bent back I ransacked boxes of stuff left over from a neighbor's yard sale. I scoured relentlessly in the dirt behind the hydrangea bush. But the bottle was nowhere to be found.

Back in the house, the wooden kitchen chair was cold and hard against my backside. I was ashamed, tired of lying to myself. I thought I would never have what my mom and dad had. I wasn't in love; I probably would never fall in love. I would grow old, alone and lonely. I wanted to replace the bottle, but I couldn't afford to buy a new one. I wanted to fess up, but I was too much of a coward.

Time passed, and the overwhelming sense of guilt subsided. But a tiny, scrap of conscience hung on a nail in the back of my mind.

Mother's Day 1987. I forgot to send a card. I was busy with Fern and Dustin, first at church and then a picnic at the park. Roger and I picked up hummus and pita bread from Trader Joe's, along with a big stack of Sunday newspapers, and so I sat basking in the Pasadena sunshine, forgetting about the time difference. I called my mother as she was getting ready for bed. With everyone out of the house she was finally getting more rest, and at 56 she needed it. She still worked at Buchanan's Grocery Store, but they moved her from the meat department when her arthritis and pain in her back kept her from lifting the big slabs of beef. Now she worked at the checkout counter, where she knew everyone's name.

Our call was short. Long enough to say, "I love you," long enough to share our excitement about my upcoming trip to Oklahoma with Roger. I think she understood that he was someone special, and she looked forward to meeting him.

Out of nowhere and in the most awful and frightful and exhilarating way, Roger and I were moving to a far deeper level of commitment than either of us had ever imagined. So, on the first of June, I boxed up all of my belongings—the furniture, the knickknacks, the photographs, my children's toys—and stored them in a nondescript shed that we rented for $25 a month. I crammed a small suitcase full of clothes, hugged my best friend and housemate, Debbie, said goodbye to Pasadena, and moved to Hollywood. In the small Shari Vine apartment that Roger shared with his friend Frank, we were going to explore our growing relationship. "Yes," we told everyone who asked, "We are getting serious."

Roger and I were going to spend the summer enjoying our time alone without the constant care of my two children, who were with their father in Austin, Texas. Weeknights we were going to drink with our friends at The Cat & Fiddle, the Firefly, Bordner's or the Frolic Room. Weekends we were going to play with friends in the Lucky Lager jug band at street fairs or an occasional "real" gig.

We were going to have fun. We were going camping, maybe back to Sequoia National Park, the birthplace of our relationship. Or maybe to Death Valley and Joshua Tree. We could drive up the coast and watch the sun set over the Pacific from the balcony of the wonderful B&B that our friend Mike constantly raved about.

We had also planned the obligatory parent-introduction trip. First, a non-stop drive out to Oklahoma to spend a few days with my parents. From there, fly to New York to meet Roger's parents and a few of his college buddies. Then back to Oklahoma for another couple of days. For the return trip to LA, we had no set itinerary—just one week, the open road, and a long wish list of sites to see—Santa Fe and the Grand Canyon, the Acoma Indian Pueblo and Canyon de Cheilly, the Petrified Forest and Carlsbad Caverns.

We were going to find pleasure at every turn. We were going to make love in 41 exciting new positions. We were going to look for a place to live in LA—a new place for the four of us and a new start when the kids returned for school.

That summer had such promise, but we hadn't gotten to any of it yet. On June 4th, Roger and I had just returned home from work after stopping at Ralphs for some groceries. I had been having a "la la day" in "LA LA land." Everything was perfect, and my heart skipped inside my chest like a three-year-old. Unabashedly innocent and with my guard down, the world was a wonderful, safe and happy place. We had splurged on oysters on the half shell, and we were looking forward to an evening filled with more amazing, wild, sexual abandonment after a few hours of dinner and drinking. Roger was concocting his own version of cocktail sauce with ketchup, Tabasco, lemon juice, a touch of cilantro, and lots of horseradish. When the phone rang, Frank answered it.

"Lani, it's for you."

My sister Kathy's voice, words I couldn't understand, and then my breath was knocked out by an invisible hand. A left hook jarred the receiver and it struck the kitchen's tile floor. Jacob's angel came at me from behind and forced me to my knees. And God or the devil thrust its fist down my throat and pulled from my heart a sound I had never heard before or since.

My mother had suffered a fatal heart attack.

I don't know how long I lay on the floor keening. From far away, I could hear Roger talking on the phone. At some point he gently led me back to our bedroom and I curled up in ball, my arms behind my head, my elbows over my face, and my knees tucked under my chin. Roger sat by my side, tenderly stroking my hair, and breathing into my ear the comforting sounds a mother gives her colicky baby, "Shush, shush, it's ok, shush, shush, I'm so sorry, shush, shush, I love you, shush, shush." Late in the night, I turned to him and we made love—tears streaming from our eyes and down our pale cheeks.

We needed to get back to Oklahoma right away; Roger made all the arrangements for the trip back for my mother's funeral. I was of little help; I couldn't even pack a suitcase. First, we flew to Austin to pick up Fern and Dustin. They had only just arrived there to spend the summer with their dad, and still hadn't settled in. They were both devasted; Fern was inconsolable. We rented a car for the nearly four-hundred-mile trip to Moore, my hometown. We drove for hours without talking, all of us too numb. We arrived late Friday night, and the next few days were a blur of trips to the funeral home, answering calls, seeing visitors, talking with Mom's pastor, comforting my dad, comforting my children, comforting my sisters. Going through the necessary motions of every day—socks on, shoes, walk, speak, respond, eat food that tastes like sawdust. Repeat.

We managed to survive those few days in Oklahoma. On Tuesday, we drove back to Austin, and returned to LA on Wednesday. But nothing seemed right. The world was no longer a wonderful, safe and happy place. There were times when I wouldn't let Roger close to me, times I couldn't bear to have him leave my side. Didn't he understand? My mother was dead. She was my blueprint, my road map. How could I know who I was anymore? Now I would never be able to talk with her about my baby and how I felt about being sent away.

Roger and I still took our parent-introduction trip just weeks after my mother's funeral, but nothing was as we had planned. Roger never heard my mother's laugh or tasted her cooking. Everyone in Oklahoma was still shell-shocked. I helped my sisters sort through her clothes and papers. In

New York, I was cold and barely polite to Roger's mom, Barbara. She was sweet and understanding, but the fact that she was still alive and breathing seemed like an affront. Why was she alive when my mother was dead? Roger's parents had planned a wonderful trip to an Amish country fair in Pennsylvania, but everything there reminded me of my mother, who loved antiques and quilts and sausages and canned jams. At every craft stand or food booth I burst into tears.

When we got back to LA, I went for weeks without working. I couldn't sleep. When it came to Roger, I had two personalities. Sometimes I couldn't make love. Sometimes I wanted him so desperately inside me, I suffocated him with my neediness. I rented old movies to watch on TV. I ate bag after bag of potato chips. By the time Fern and Dustin returned from Texas, I had pulled myself together, but while the pain eases up at times, like ocean waves licking the shore, it is always there. Sometimes it's tolerable, almost gentle, and I can bask in sweet memories. But sometimes the pain is a tsunami and it's all I can do to keep from drowning.

For Melissa: Welcome to the Club

I heard today you were inducted into a club
not a single woman is anxious to join.
Most of us would put it off as long as possible
although some have been members since birth.

I'll give you some clues into this sisterhood:
First, there are no perks—
no water bottles or grocery bags with colorful logos,
No committees to join, no meetings to attend, but
membership is a lifelong commitment and
we pay for it daily with haunting
reminders of why we belong.
Maybe it's a voice in our dreams,
our mouths without warning forming the words
"Close the door we don't live in a barn."

For me it is familiar handwriting on a recipe card,
white swans, yellow roses, clowns,
my reflection in a mirror.

*I see a hand reaching out from a sweater sleeve
with the shocked realization that the hand is mine
and yet, it is not.*

*In this club, holidays are hard,
joyful occasions like weddings and births
are tinged in sadness.*

*I wish I could ply you with platitudes and cheap liquor;
tell you it gets easier but that's not true.
I was inducted many years ago
on a late Thursday afternoon and each day since
has been colored in rosy shades of loss.*

*Being a member myself I wish I could say I know
or understand what you're going through.*

That too is false.

*Your relationship was unique, your loss is unique,
and my heart calls out to you
one motherless daughter to another.*

In 2009 my dad turned eighty, and to celebrate this milestone, Roger and I made the trip back to Oklahoma from our home in Portland, Oregon.

After the party, in the home my father shared with his wife, Eunice, he opened one of the family photo albums. He told with zest the story of how he and my mom met.

"See, here is your mom in high school. The Neals had a farm not too far from ours, and I knew your mother in passing."

My parents had grown up in similar circumstances, both families trying to scratch out a living from the hard, red dirt of central Oklahoma.

"So, when I got sent on my first tour of duty, your Memaw asked your grandma, Velma, if Mary Ann would like to write to me. By this time, she was working as a secretary in Oklahoma City. Back then we had us a trolley that run all the way up from Norman."

My mother always wanted to go to college and study to be a Home Economics teacher. But when her dad died on her eighteenth birthday of a massive heart attack, my mom put aside her dreams of college and stayed at home to help take care of her younger brother.

"Anyway, your mom said that she would write to me, and she did—at least once a week. Not like when I was in Vietnam when she wrote every single day. I was coming home on furlough, and I'm thinking I should go pay her a call—you know, as a courtesy for all the letters. I hadn't seen her in person in several years, and I guess I still thought of her more as a kid. But, believe me, when I saw her, she was no kid. I took one look at her and positives and negatives started flying all over the place."

They married in less than a month. In the photo, my mother is stunning even in a borrowed wedding dress. Within six months they were stationed in Hawaii.

My dad pointed to another black-and-white photo. In it he's wearing a white jacket and bow tie. My mom is in a fancy mu-mu. They're both wearing leis. They seem oblivious to the photographer. They're not looking at the camera, they only have eyes for each other. My mom couldn't have been more than twenty-four.

"This is on the campus of the Kamehameha School where your mom worked," my dad continued. "She was there for most of a year before she found out she was pregnant. That little belly pooch is you."

That night after crawling into bed with Roger, I started thinking about my own keepsakes box at home, which contained a near empty perfume bottle—a Valentine's Day gift from Roger. It's not Chanel. My favorite scent is Estée, and a single whiff makes me feel mysterious, sophisticated, and sexy. It's a constant reminder that when Roger and I met there were positives and negatives all over the place.

I was thunderstruck with the realization that my mother must have kept her bottle of No. 5 to remind her of those times when life was easier, when love flowed in and through our home like a river of light. A gift from my father, that bottle signified that she was and would always be his special lady, his wife and his lover, and despite the passage of time and the gaining of pounds, whenever he gazed into her hazel eyes, she still looked like a million bucks.

The day after my dad's birthday party, I asked two of my sisters to join me on a mission.

Late April is the beginning of tornado season, and it was less than five years out from one of the biggest local tornadoes on record. It ripped through our part of the state and killed more than thirty people. On this day the wind wasn't too bad, though it did look like rain. We stopped at Crossroads Mall on the southeast side of Oklahoma City, and headed in to Dillard's Department Store.

We looked around for the cosmetics section. Chanel had a huge display case, and lots of perfume offerings – Coco, No. 19, Allure. I asked the sales clerk for No. 5. The small ¼ ounce bottle of parfum cost more than $100. But at that point, I would have paid anything to try and clear my conscience.

Carla, Kathy and I took I-35 to Moore. We got off at the 12th Street exit and drove past Buchanan's, the grocery store where my mom used to work. The town seemed emptier than I remembered. Lots of the small, downtown businesses closed after Wal-Mart built their big superstore by the interstate. We passed KOMA, the local country and western radio station, and then turned up the gravel road leading into the cemetery and my mother's final resting place. I was determined to give her back her perfume.

I had just turned 55; my mother was 56 when she died. Although I said it would never happen, I was overweight by about sixty pounds. My face was already creased with some worry lines, but mostly lots of laugh lines. And in all the living I'd done since my mother died, I learned that age and circumstances and appearances don't ever change who we really are. I learned that yes, Chanel No. 5 *was* my mother.

My mother is buried next to lots of family—parents, grandparents, aunts, uncles, cousins. We've probably got four or five generations of family planted in that hard dirt. My dad had his own name engraved on the tombstone above my mother's grave. On my mom's side it says, "Loving wife and mother." There are two interlocking wedding bands in the center of the stone with 36 years carved beneath them.

I wanted to leave the entire bottle of perfume on the tombstone, but Carla and Kathy were appalled.

"Lani, it cost $100, and it will just get stolen or ruined."

"Just tell mom how you feel, and then pour a little bit on the grave. A little bit—not the whole bottle."

I knelt in front of the tombstone, not yet ready start my apology.

"Ma, you probably never thought it would happen, but I'm doing pretty good now. Roger and I moved to Portland, Oregon, and we really like living there. You would love it, too, Ma. You should see all of the roses. I love being a grandma. I guess that's something I learned from you. I was always so sad that you never got to meet Roger. You would have liked him, though he would have teased you to no end."

I opened my purse and pulled out the small white box with black and gold accents.

"Ma, I'm here to apologize. Years ago, I stole your perfume and then I lied about it. I threw away the bottle. But that wasn't the worse part. You know, I'm almost the same age you were when you died. I look down at my hands and I see your hands. I look in the mirror and I see your face. When you were alive, you were simply "mother" to me. I never looked beyond that. I never saw how beautiful and sexy and young you really were. And for that I'm sorry."

I opened the brand-new box of Chanel No. 5 and poured a little bit of the perfume on her grave.

"Mom, I'm going to keep the rest and whenever I wear it, I'll be thinking of you. I love you, Ma."

With shaky knees, I stood up from wet, cold ground. Kathy, Carla and I daubed No. 5 on our wrists; wiped away tears with musky fingers. Two days later back in Portland, I placed the bottle of No. 5 on a shelf in my medicine cabinet.

I still can't bear to wear the perfume. But from time to time, I open the bottle and inhale the roses and jasmine, the cedar, sandalwood and musk. I am five and I am thirty. I see my mother, beautiful in her going-to-theater dress, and in her threadbare polyester. I see her auburn hair and her grey-streaked tresses. I see her thin as a rail and overweight by 100 pounds. And in every remembrance, she is the epitome of No. 5—lovely and loved.

Welcome to the Circle

Growing up Southern Baptist, church was everything. I belonged there with my friends and family. I sang out my longing to be whole, to be healed, to be loved.

Just as I am, poor, wretched, blind;
Sight, riches, healing of the mind,
Yea, all I need, in thee to find,
O Lamb of God, I come.

I had a lifetime of Bible study. Every Sunday night at church, for as long as I could remember, we had sword drills, a system used by Youth Leaders everywhere to increase Bible study and memorization. With commands like "sheathe swords," and "draw swords," and "charge," we raced with military precision to look up book, chapter and verse. If you didn't know the order of all the books in both the Old and New Testaments inside and out, you were a loser. I was a master at sword drills.

I loved singing hymns, and church music filled every sad, empty void in my life, both real and imagined.

Are we weak and heavy laden,
cumbered with a load of care?
Precious Savior, still our refuge;
take it to the Lord in prayer.
In his arms he'll take and shield thee;
thou wilt find a solace there.

But even as a young child, there was something tenuous about my relationship with God. For all the assurances of unconditional love, I felt it was pretty easy to piss him off. I had to watch everything I said and did, because God was always watching, always stalking. I was terrified of losing his favor; his moods changed faster than the Oklahoma weather.

As the years passed, I grew more and more uncomfortable with the feeling that I couldn't be fully myself in my faith. I was a dog begging for a bone, desperate for approval, and I knew I could never measure up.

Something was missing. I tried to pray about it, and the answers I found in the church's teaching or in the Bible were "just because," or "my ways are not your ways," or "you'll understand it in the sweet bye-and-bye." Why couldn't God be more like Paul Harvey and fill me in on "the rest of the story" in the here and now? Did I really have to die before I could get some answers to life's deepest mysteries?

When Sean committed suicide, I could never accept the idea that he went to hell. Baptist teaching didn't condemn Sean because of the suicide (I guess God could overlook that), but because Sean was Roman Catholic and not "born again." I kept trying to believe, but throughout my time at Sellers, I found it harder and harder to pray. My senior year, even though I lived at home and often heard "Not while you're living under my roof, young lady," I stopped going to First Baptist and my parents never argued with me about that decision.

My disdain for God and religion lasted about nine years. At 27, I was divorced with two children and dead broke. On a humid July Sunday, a new boyfriend took me to St. Michael's Episcopal church in Norman, just south of Highway 9, near the banks of the South Canadian River. The sanctuary was modern with a soaring wooden ceiling that reminded me of the bottom of a boat. The clear glass window behind the altar stretched from floor to ceiling, and only a large wooden cross interrupted the view of the river. Everything was foreign to me, so unlike the Baptist churches I attended as a child. Much like St. Andrew's, the Catholic church where Sean's funeral was held, St. Michael's had an altar and incense, candles and icons. During Holy Communion, an usher stood at the end of my pew. With a smile, she beckoned me to come forward. Communion here was open to everyone. I got up off my knees and filed behind the other parishioners to the front of the church. Someone was strumming a guitar and softly singing, "I am the bread of life, he who comes to me shall not hunger, he who believes in me shall not thirst."

A short metal rail separated the altar from a line of red embroidered cushions. I knelt on one covered with a sword and remembered St. Paul's admonition from Ephesians about putting on the whole armor of God.

> *Stand firm then, with the belt of truth buckled around your waist, with the breastplate of righteousness in place, and with your feet fitted with the readiness that comes from the gospel of peace. In addition to all this, take up*

the shield of faith, with which you can extinguish all the flaming arrows of the evil one. Take the helmet of salvation and the sword of the Spirit, which is the word of God.

When the priest came by with whispered words, my tears started to flow. I ingested the small bite of bread placed in my outstretched hands and I took a sip of wine only to find that I was unable to stand. I stayed there until an usher gently led me back to my pew.

I felt as if I had been Lawrence Oates, headed for sure death in an Antarctic blizzard, when God invited me to come in out of the cold. The sensation was akin to being wrapped in a heavy woolen blanket and given a steaming cup of hot cocoa. I felt enveloped by love for the first time in many, many years. My head kept saying, "this is crazy, you've gone insane and you're headed over to the dark side," but my heart was home. In the dim stillness, in the bread and the wine, in the quiet presence of the community I believed I could see and taste God. And I kept coming back—week after week—to be filled.

As a child, after being saved, I thought that God was calling me to a life of service. I would grow up and be a missionary in China like Lottie Moon. Like her I would labor tirelessly to bring the good news of Jesus to the world. In 1984 I once again believed I was being called by God for a life in ministry, so I applied for and was accepted to Fuller Theological Seminary in Pasadena, California. While Fern and Dustin stayed with my parents for a few weeks, I made the first trip there alone, my 1974 Dodge Dart stuffed to the gills with all my belongings. Before I left Church of the Resurrection in Oklahoma City, Father Reardon, the parish priest, sent letters to churches along the way requesting a free place for a night's stay as I journeyed west. I was on the third day of the road trip from Oklahoma to California, when I made my way to an Episcopal monastery tucked deep in the heart of the Sangre de Christo Mountains.

Since I arrived in mid-afternoon, I decided to take a walk to the grotto, its path half-hidden by tall pines. Bennett, the Abbot of the monastery, momentarily broke his vow of silence when he pressed a flashlight into my hand.

"Take this. You'll need it."

The path to the grotto was covered in gravel, and I heard a delightful scrunching sound under my feet. Without warning, my heart took flight and a laugh, uninvited, escaped from my throat.

The surrounding pines were closely packed together, and my entire being became engulfed by their woodsy scent. I gulped it in with each breath, like some golden retriever lapping water at a river's edge. I couldn't see the sky from this footpath on the forest floor, and I was surprised once I reached the clearing that dark storm clouds had gathered overhead, and lightning strikes were visible on an adjacent mountain.

Rain began to fall in earnest, and I had no time to contemplate the beauty of the clearing. I ducked into the cave. Years ago, this might have been home to a mother bear and her cubs, snuggled up against each other in the twilight sleep of winter. Maybe trappers, too, once sought shelter from the rain beneath this rocky bough. Now the simple cavern was a safe house, where pretenses fell away and my truest identity could be revealed.

There were no artificial lights in the grotto, except for the one I carried. Although it was only four o'clock in the afternoon at the height of summer, storm clouds, like a flock of swirling crows, blocked the sun. I said a quick and silent "thank you" to Bennett as I turned on the flashlight and adjusted its beam.

The cave was small, no more than twelve feet in diameter. A statue of Our Lady stood in the center. Mary appeared to Bennett in a dream many years ago. "Come away from the world," she said. "Come away and create a place where prayers can be said for peace and the reconciliation of humanity."

At the time, Bennett taught philosophy at a small liberal arts college in southern California and lived the comfortable life of a tenured professor. When he broached friends, family and colleagues with the idea of starting a monastery, they all thought he was losing his mind. Bennett also questioned his sanity. But night after night, his sleep was troubled. The Blessed Virgin continued to appear, repeating the request, "Come away and pray for peace," until Bennett felt he had no choice but to obey.

Carved from a single piece of walnut, the statue of Mary was a tangible, material representation of the likeness Bennett saw in his dreams. She was the Queen of Heaven; a halo of stars surrounded her face. Her feet were firmly planted on the moon, though it was not the crescent sliver fancied by the Virgin of Guadeloupe. This moon was full, ripe with promise and expectation.

In the cavern wall, small niches held votive candles. A thoughtful pilgrim left behind a box of kitchen matches. I picked up the box and circled the cavern, lighting candles one by one. Light flared from three or four before flames licked my fingers. When dozens were lit, their flickering shadows danced the samba on ashen walls.

The flashlight became unnecessary. I turned it off. In the glow of candlelight, I studied the face of Our Lady. Her eyes were those of a doe—gentle, benevolent, accepting. With arms stretched wide, she seemed ready to embrace the world. The folds of her robe fell like waves breaking on a shore and lapped at her bare feet. The tight bodice stretched around firm, ripe breasts. Her chin was slightly raised; her mouth closed and set with a determined air that seems to say *I am and was and will be forever*.

A sharp clap of thunder startled me from my reverie. Outside the cave, rain beat a staccato rhythm upon mossy grass and gravel path. The lightning strikes were close. Each one lit up the sky like the sun at high noon.

With no place to sit inside the cavern, I knelt upon the packed earth floor in front of the Virgin. The ground was surprisingly soft. Being alone was new to me, and a little frightening. Up until a few days before my children, friends, family, and co-workers surrounded me at almost every hour of every day.

Prayer seemed necessary there in the deep silence. I pulled a rosary from my purse. The small, purple, glass beads—a going-away gift from my friend and neighbor, Martha—felt warm in my hand.

> *Hail Mary, full of grace, the Lord is with thee....Holy Mary, Mother of God, pray for us sinners...*

I was moving my family so far from everything we had ever known, but I was dying in Oklahoma, slowly dying, day-by-day. After giving up Bo, I felt in many ways I had stopped growing emotionally and spiritually. I was more mature and independent, certainly. I worked hard for my family—Fern and Dustin had a roof over their heads and food in their mouths—but I was still dependent on my parents. I was a fishing bobber on the water, without dreams or aspirations. Never much more than a woman-child, I needed to believe there was more for me in this world.

> *Yes, Mary, be with me, and be with my children, too. Can you see them? Are they OK? Sweet Mary, am I doing the right thing? Please, guide me, dearest Lady; protect me on this journey.*

A soft breeze entered the cavern doorway. I shivered beneath my damp sweater. The room filled with the scent of rain and wet pine. I glanced down at my left wrist for the time, but remembered that Bennett discouraged watches at the monastery, and I had left it in my room. Here we were on God's time, not our own. I heard my stomach grumble. I hadn't eaten since I left Santa Fe that morning. My body kept its own timetable, and I was hungry.

I placed the rosary beads back in my purse and leaned over to kiss the Virgin's feet. After extinguishing the candles, I exchanged the darkness of the Virgin's sanctuary for the darkness of the clearing. I followed the footpath to the refectory with another silent thank you to Bennett for the flashlight.

I was the only guest at the monastery that night. We—Bennett, the Abbess and I—ate a hearty meal of creamy potato soup and coarse multigrain bread in silence. The blueberry cobbler (with ice cream!) served for dessert was exponentially scrumptious, and I pinched myself to keep from making my usual yummy noises. After dinner, Bennett and the Abbess led the way to a small chapel for compline.

For the first time that day, I heard the beauty in my voice as I joined the others to sing and pray.

> *Keep watch, dear Lord, with those who work or watch or weep this night. Give your angels charge over those who sleep. Tend the sick, give rest to the weary, bless the dying, soothe the suffering, pity the afflicted, shield the joyous, all for your love's sake. Amen.*

I had always sought God's help and protection when I was in trouble or hurt or sick. But this prayer reminded me that happiness, too, is frail and vulnerable, and equally deserving of my care. To have joy was a great gift and I must guard it with my life.

My sleeping quarters for the evening were called a cell, but the room felt like one only in its limited size. In all other respects, I was no prisoner, but a welcome guest. The room was narrow and barely contained the single bed. A small window adorned one wall, and through it a generous full moon peeked through tall pines. There was no lamp or overhead light, but a tapered candle on the tiny nightstand next to the bed had been lit awaiting my arrival. I blew it out, undressed in the dark, and scooted under the sheets. They were rough against my skin and smelled like sunshine.

The day had been so full of thought and prayer and wonder, I was afraid that I might lie awake for hours, but my eyelids felt heavy, almost as if I had been sedated. I heaved an imperceptible sigh of relief.

But almost as soon as my eyes closed, the sound of singing filled the small room. Was I dreaming? There must have been hundreds, no, thousands of voices singing in a language I did not understand. Each voice was singing a unique note, and the harmony was thick and brutal. The beauty of the song was almost unbearable. I was eavesdropping on the choir of heaven. A veil was ripped, a threshold crossed. Angels gave me a private concert that night.

I still believe I experienced something extraordinary and inexplicable that night in the monastery. But now I no longer believe in God. So, if I could know these mountaintop experiences, these encounters with the mystical, these spiritual heights, how could I stop believing? How did I get from there to here?

It was a tortuous journey. My spiritual road map took me from being a Bible-thumping, Jesus died to atone for my sins Christian fundamentalist to a What Would Jesus Do? love mercy, do justice, walk humbly evangelical, and then finally to some mixed-up mishmash of Star Wars theology—God is love, love is a force, may the force be with you. Through it all, church was my home. Week after week I placed my widow's mite in the passing plate, shared the chalice, and ladled out hot soup to strangers and friends, not because I espoused a particular religious dogma, but because I loved and needed community. I realized that it was the community, and not the teachings, that called me to the best part of myself.

Eventually my spirit and my mind collided. No longer did the steady stream of pabulum spouted weekly from the pulpit feed me. I couldn't hear or recite the Apostles' Creed without making an internal translation of "I believe in God, maker of heaven and earth" into "I believe in love, the creative force in the universe."

I couldn't taste the bread or drink the wine without telling myself that all of life is sacramental and that everything I encounter is an exquisite reminder of the grace inherent in our very existence.

As much as I love Celtic hymns, I couldn't sing "Be Thou my battle-shield, sword for my fight," without thinking of St. Paul's armor and cringing. I couldn't sing "Your eyes are watchful, your ears are list'ning, your lips are speaking, friend at my side" without compulsively looking over my shoulder for the God stalker.

And after years of a conscientious and complicated quest to love myself, on Good Friday I could no longer kneel at the foot of a wooden and cross and sing the words, "Who was the guilty? Who brought this upon thee? 'Twas I, Lord Jesus, I it was denied thee; I crucified thee." No, I did not crucify thee!! And I had sweated too much blood and too many tears in therapy to wallow in that guilt for even a single day.

For more than fifty years, I believed that God was an external, supernatural being who was simultaneously creating, redeeming and sanctifying me. But I finally had to admit to myself that God, at least in the way I had always known God, was dead.

As with other deaths, the first year was the hardest. My first Easter without God, my first Christmas without God. I missed the Feast Day of St. Francis when my faith community gathered in the courtyard to sing a wonderful hymn about salmon, and blessed dogs and cats and guinea pigs with bowlfuls of holy water. I missed the Feast Day of American Independence when we served up apple pie with cheese slices and sang all four verses of "America the Beautiful," including verse two, the one most of our presidents have overlooked, which is all about mending our flaws and needing more self-control.

I missed holding hands and praying with total strangers—knowing that they were my brothers and sisters, that we shared a bond that transcended any racial, sexual, ethnic, or class identity. I missed singing music in a harmonious group that transported me to a place where I felt I was my deepest, truest self.

I still think the Jesus story is the best fairy tale ever written, and at times I am sad that I can't believe it anymore. I love the way the story is crafted—just enough reality to draw us in, just enough mystery to keep us hooked—humor, pathos—it's all there. Like a horror movie, just when you think it's over, there's that moment when the heroine turns her back on the dying monster to only find it's back wielding one more chainsaw. But this time what is resurrected is what is best in us, what we can barely believe is possible. Light shines forth in the darkness. The wrong is always made right, and we have the sure promise of eternity.

Roger's aunt died in the winter of 2008, and her funeral was my first since coming out as an atheist. I stopped claiming a belief in the holy three and believing that there is anything like an eternal soul encased in this mortal body. I acknowledged nothing more than the fact that I am a creature—just slightly higher on the evolutionary ladder than a pig.

The funeral had me thinking about death, and I understood the crux of the Christian appeal—we humans long for immortality. We think too highly of ourselves to ever believe that we don't live on in an afterlife created especially for us. Those that believe in reincarnation want to hold on to the idea that after all the mistakes in this life we are given an opportunity for a second chance. I wish there were a hell, but only because of all the evil people I would like to put there. At times I have been desperate to believe that we will all meet again in the great by-and-by, that the circle will be unbroken. At times, the knowledge that I will never see my mother again is unbearable.

The childlike faith I had in God was gone, and I ached with its loss.

In November 2009, I attended a benefit concert Aurora Chorus gave for a young Iraqi boy who had been injured in the 2004 shelling of Fallujah and was brought to the United States for treatment. Its members were Portland-area women, and its mission was to sing for peace. Throughout the concert I was utterly, unabashedly blown away. Women who sing for peace. Where do I sign up?

I got on the chorus waiting list and received an invitation to join on January 3rd. Within a couple of weeks, we began preparing for our May performance. That year's theme was "Well-behaved Women Rarely Make History." Some of the music was hard to sing—it changed keys, had up to eight different parts, and tripped me up with crazy syncopated rhythms. A single rehearsal was more of a workout than two hours on an elliptical machine.

Before the third rehearsal, Bunny, the membership chair, and very much our den mother, called for a new member orientation. At the meeting, we hardy band of nineteen newbies received a dog and pony show about the Aurora's structure—the Board of Directors, section leaders, music librarian, the harmonizers. We learned what we might expect at our retreat and the rules about absences. Bunny was still talking when choir rehearsal started up in the sanctuary next door (we rented space in a downtown Jewish synagogue). The chorus members there were warming up on the one song we were supposed to have memorized that evening, "Peace, Salaam, Shalom," which is sung in a round. From the room where we were sitting, I could finally hear how the parts wove in and out; floating, falling, melding disparate voices into the vocal equivalent of a Borchelu rug. At the end, I wanted to stand and applaud, but Bunny was still talking.

Finally, we were told to line up by height and walk into the room single file. We processed in through the center aisle of the sanctuary between the alto ones and soprano twos, and we formed two rows on the short dais where our gifted conductor usually stood. Then the chorus began to sing "Welcome to the Circle."

I was enveloped by the rich, thick harmony of their voices. One hundred and twenty women sang to me, caressed me, loved me, accepted me. A community of strong, powerful women called me to the best parts of myself.

I was the Cheshire cat. My smile nearly split my face in two. I looked across a sea of faces. Strangers caught my eye, held my gaze, and kept singing.

All across the room women held hands. Some encircled their arms around a neighbor's waist or shoulders. Some wept. I was so happy I was about to blubber like an American Idol contestant just awarded a golden ticket to Hollywood.

The song lasted a little more than three minutes. When it was over there was thunderous applause for us, the new members. The sound washed over me like waves crashing on Cannon Beach, and its rip tide pulled me into an ocean of good will. We left the dais and made our way back to our seats. As I walked down the aisle a fellow second soprano, and now a new sister-friend, whispered "Welcome Home."

This mountaintop experience was greater than the one I had in New Mexico. Once again, I heard angels singing. That night I fell in love with the powerful goddess that I could see and hear in these women. Friendship, family, and community now fill the "God-shaped hole" in my heart. I try to be more present, more aware of each moment. And as I daily acknowledge and claim the hope, faith and love that is in me, I'm comfortable knowing that this is all there is.

The Pathos of Things

In the spring of 2010, I accompanied Roger on a business trip to San Francisco. While he spent the day attending workshops and presentations, I wandered through parts of the city I had never visited and lost myself for most of one day in the San Francisco Museum of Modern Art. The painting *Personal Values* by René Magritte sent me spiraling into memories of my time at Sellers. The painting affects others in myriad ways. In fact, Alexander Iolas, who promoted and defended the Surrealists in the United States and elsewhere, and who was Magritte's New York dealer, wrote to Magritte complaining about the painting. He wanted an explanation:

> *I am so depressed that I cannot yet get used to it. It may be a masterpiece, but every time I look at it I feel ill.... It leaves me helpless, it puzzles me, it makes me feel confused and I don't know if I like it.*

I didn't know if I liked the painting, either, but each of the objects seemed to trigger feelings I had fought long and hard to repress, and when I returned to my hotel room later that day, the following poem came to me.

Less is More, More or Less

Today, I give you a Magritte poem. What feeling do these invoke?
a tortoise shell comb, a turned-down bed,
a matchstick and shaving brush on top of a Persian rug,
in the corner a closed window with red drapes,
an armoire, a glass chalice the color of the Mediterranean Sea.

Which is it? Longing or loss?
You tell me.

Not enough information, you say?
so, suppose I tell you
the tortoise shell comb is blue plastic purchased at the
Woolworth's on St. Charles Avenue,
the turned-down bed is a single bed, with blue chenille
bedspread hiding perfectly tight hospital corners,
the matchstick litters a concrete porch where teenage girls
smoke menthol cigarettes,
the shaving brush is my father's, stolen from his toiletry
set as a reminder of home.

There's a face in the closed window—it's a second story
window—it is my face and
the face in the window stares at the back of a girl on the
sidewalk below and
that girl is me, also.
The face in the window whispers to the back of the girl on
the sidewalk,
don't look back, don't ever look back.

The armoire has another identity, too—
a clothes closet filled with peasant blouses, dresses with
empire waists, pants with elastic waistbands and stretchy
front panels,
clothes discarded by young woman for others who will
come to find bodies stretched beyond recognition.
the girl on the sidewalk takes only what she is wearing,
what she wore.

The glass chalice has no color; it is
filled with amniotic fluid and water from the murky
Mississippi.

Now, which is it?
loss or longing?
I don't remember any more.

In viewing the Magritte painting, I was struck by what the Japanese call "mono no aware (物の哀れ)." The literal English translation is "the pathos of things," and it connotes an awareness of the transitory nature of those things which hold deep meaning for us.

The love of cherry blossoms is an example of mono no aware in contemporary Japan. The blossoms are beautiful, but they are valued more for their transience than their beauty as they fall to the ground within one week of budding. Portland prizes its cherry trees too, and they line the west bank of the Willamette River as it flows through the center of the city. Annually I walk beside a reminder that life, like beauty, is fleeting, and imbued in my appreciation of the pink blossoms is a wistfulness at their inevitable passing.

A comb, a matchstick, a turned-down bed—we live in a world where even the meanest and most mundane objects can hold beauty and value. We understand that the pathos of things is the bittersweet reality that everything turns to dust and decay. This in turn brings about an even deeper sadness as we become conscious of our own ephemeral existence. My answer to the question, "which is it—longing or loss?" will always be "loss."

I can never regain all of the minutes, hours, days and years that I was kept from mothering my son.

$400 and 24 Hours

All of my adult life I have carried the greatest guilt about signing the relinquishment papers. I hated myself for doing it. "No one forced you, no one held a gun to your head," screamed a tiny piercing voice in my head. "You should have said no. You could have stood up to them."

But I was young, and I was scared. They said that I—a young, fornicating sinner—was unfit to be a mother, and I fully believed them. It was weak and unconscionable to have gotten pregnant in the first place. I was a bad seed, completely incapable of caring for someone as innocent and vulnerable as my infant son. I was told over and over again that if I truly loved my son, I only had one option. The only thing I could do was let him be part of an all-American family with a hard-working dad and a stay-at-home mom—parents who could care for him in the best possible way.

I only knew that more than anything, I loved my precious son. So, I signed the papers and walked away, knowing I would never see him again.

When Bo was born in 1971, abortion was illegal, adoptions were closed, records were forever sealed. Parents, church authorities, social workers and well-meaning adult friends and relatives told me that his existence should be a secret I would carry to my grave. My extensive stretch marks were a river of scars that extended from five inches above my belly button to my pubic bone, so the fact that I had given birth was an impossible secret to keep in any intimate encounters. But aside from lovers and a few friends, I lived with this story buried deep in the recesses of my heart. I was imprisoned by my inability to name and own and acknowledge my profound loss. I was a mother without a child. Depression and anxiety were constant companions. When my daughter was born seven years later, followed my second son in 1980, I thought I would be set free, but I remained chained to a pain I couldn't articulate.

At Sellers the Powers-that-Be wanted us to believe that we were selfless in choosing to place our babies for adoption, and that they were fulfilling the Word of the Lord in their holy mission. They told us again and again that we should be thankful we had the opportunity to give our children to good families and a happily-ever-after life. That's right. Be thankful. But how could they expect me to be thankful for the loss? Was I supposed to be thankful for the guilt? Thankful for a lifetime of shame and silence and empty arms?

Not only were we expected to be thankful, we were supposed to be joyous about it, too. After my son was adopted, Mrs. LaPrairie, Sellers administrator, sent a letter that said, "Hope you're finally happy and at peace knowing that Bo is in a good home, and that you can move on with your life."

Happy? I was far from happy, plagued day in and day out with the uncertainty of never knowing what he looked like, what he liked to eat, who was taking care of his scrapes and bruises. I wanted to know who his heroes were. Did he have hobbies? Did he do well in school? Would he find true love? More than anything, I wanted to know if he was happy.

I repressed those feelings. I stuffed them into a bag of unwanted kittens along with the stones of my religious upbringing, my family myths, my southern culture, and I threw them all in the river to drown. But they didn't drown. All I felt was the heaviness of self-loathing and disgust.

My early twenties were plagued with risky behaviors—alcohol, drugs, and promiscuity. I attempted suicide and I was hospitalized twice for depression. I became increasingly agoraphobic, some days unable to leave my house, and on others, unable to leave my bed. By my mid-thirties, my mental health had improved thanks to Roger's love and acceptance, therapy, and anti-depressants. But my true healing didn't begin until I was able to speak the unspeakable and share my story.

After Roger and I moved to Portland in 2001, I took a writing class at The Attic Writer's Workshop. Facilitated Ariel Gore, novelist and founder of Hip Mama magazine, "The Language of Your Life" gave me the prompts I needed to start trolling through long-buried memories. The process was slow and tedious.

In the first class I was timid and unsure. When I was young, writing had been a large part of who I was. It was as important to my life as singing. I had dreams of being the next Truman Capote or Tennessee Williams or Carson McCullers. I was going to graduate college, move to New York, and write for *New Yorker Magazine*. But I lost my voice. Aside from the few letters I sent to friends from Sellers, the obligatory high school and college papers, and the almost desperate attempts at poetry, I didn't write again.

In my first memoir class I wrote about a trip to Antarctica I had taken earlier that year. I wrote about the Christmas visit to Oklahoma after my mom died when Roger asked me to marry him. I wrote essays about my Christian faith; I wrote stories about our drinking buddies in Hollywood and our life together there. But it wasn't until spring of 2002 that I opened up about Sellers, and I shared this story of "The Box."

> A box of stationery accompanied me on my trip to Sellers Maternity Home. I arrived in March. Six months later the supplies were exhausted with homesick letters to my parents, heartsick letters to the baby's father, Randall, and "this totally sucks" letters to my best friend, Dayna. As other young girls arrived, delivered their babies, and left Sellers, chatty letters made their way to new friends in small towns in Kentucky, Mississippi and Georgia. By September, when my 17-year old body was filled to bursting with new life, I had an empty box, the perfect size for all my keepsakes.
>
> The box contains nothing of consequence—simple mementos of a long ago, but not forgotten love—some photographs, a few letters, two typewritten poems, some cards from a flower shop delivered on now long dead and decayed roses and chrysanthemums. But for a few weeks in the spring of 2002, I lived in a state of total panic because I couldn't find it.
>
> At first, not having it was understandable. Roger and I moved from New York to Portland the previous summer, and we still had unpacked cartons in almost every room of our house.
>
> "Don't worry, Lani, it will turn up," Roger reassured me.
>
> That's right. We could cook, we had clothes to wear, we could listen to our favorite CDs. Not having the box was just part and parcel of the natural disruption of a move.

It wasn't as if I needed to look at the box on a daily basis. Yet after the November rains came and went, after flowers began their April bloom, the need to hold it in my hands erupted in my soul like Mt. Saint Helens and covered my every waking minute with a feverish ash.

I started looking for it in the unpacked cartons dumped in my office. These contained old tax returns and phone bills and saved Christmas cards. I searched through cartons labeled "Personal," and found my daughter's Minnie Mouse ears, my son's bomber jacket. I found a worn, pink baby blanket, quilted by my grandmother and embroidered with my name. This was where the box was supposed to be. Here, with the rest of my children's report cards and Whale of the Week awards and Cub Scout badges.

But when the box wasn't with my personal belongings, a raw panic set in. I looked through cartons in my husband's office, in the guest room and the basement. There were supplies for creating wood block prints. Roger's high school yearbook. Bank statements from 1989.

Roger's voice tried to soothe. "It's OK; we'll find it," but I was frantic.

"I've lost it. It's not here, it's not here."

Roger placed a comforting hand on my shoulder. "No, Lani, it's here; we'll find it," but I didn't believe him. I knew without a doubt that a carton containing the box, so small and inimitable and irreplaceable, had fallen off the moving truck or been left behind in New York.

For the first twenty years following the box's creation, I moved 36 times. The box traveled with me to four states stretching from the central plains and out to both coasts. During that time, I had at least 18 roommates. I moved in and out of my parent's home four times. I lived with my first husband's parents, my third husband's parents and my best friend's grandmother. The box and I lived with six different men who, at some point, I believed might be "the one."

In apartments and duplexes and rented houses, the box stayed under my bed. In student housing, the box rested among textbooks on the corner of a study table. In a commune complete with goats and chickens and scores of children, the box sat on the top shelf of an old armoire in the corner of my bedroom. The box moved with me to small rural towns, suburbs, and capital cities.

In all these moves, I had few possessions and little money. What I owned could fit in the trunk of my '68 Chevy or in the back of a rental van. With each move I packed my belongings carefully, making sure the box was never far from hand.

Then I met Roger, and my life became uncharacteristically stable. We bought our first home in 1992, and the box made its way from under our bed to a shelf on a bookcase to a box in the attic. We owned enough furniture to cramp a nine-room house. A huge moving truck came to our home in New Rochelle, New York. Strangers packed and numbered hundreds of cartons inadequately labeled "Garage," or "Kitchen," or "Master Bedroom" to indicate their intended final destination. A stranger drove these cartons, along with our furniture and appliances, to our new home.

The box had been with me, a part of me, through all of the changes and chances of life. Thirty years had passed since the first time I opened it to write a letter home. During that time I gave birth to and raised two additional children. I was witness to the birth of my grandson. I stood at the graves of my Memaw, my Grandma and my mother. I survived a flood, a fire, a tornado, an earthquake and its aftershocks. And through it all, this box—my sweet, tender box of stillborn memories—stayed near.

On this latest move, I wasn't concerned about the box. Maybe I was too worried with how my fine wood furniture was being handled, or how my delicate wine glasses were packed. Maybe I was only looking forward, and not looking back. Maybe I convinced myself that it didn't matter. But when the box had gone missing among the sometimes necessary but mostly needless trappings of everyday life, I had to find it.

Roger pulled out more and more unopened cartons. "Look through everything."

I found graduate school papers, old magazines, and a sack full of keepsakes from our first trip to Europe. My parent's wedding photos and the obituary card from Uncle John's funeral service. My heart sank from guilt. Did I stop caring? Did I forget to remember?

I slowly made my way through the house. Upstairs—guest room, both offices, library. First floor—living room, dining room, kitchen, bedroom. Finally, down in the basement, in a medium-sized cardboard carton marked "Personal—Fern," underneath my daughter's Cabbage Patch Kid, Katrina, I found my box.

Like the woman in the Gospel with the lost coin, like the shepherd with his lost sheep, I greeted the box's discovery with joy. Tears of relief streamed down my face. I knelt on the concrete basement floor, cradling the box like a baby.

The seemingly insignificant cardboard container was a shrine, an altar at which I worshipped. It held all I had left—all that I could touch, press close to my breast or kiss with my mouth—the only physical reminders I had of the son I gave up for adoption in September, 1971, when I was a 17-year old high school senior.

The box was quite the worse for wear. Its dated 70s top, resplendent in neon orange, pink and yellow flowers amidst a field of neon green, blue, and beige leaves, was torn. The formerly neon-blue bottom had faded to a soft teal. It had obviously been wet, and the paper was curled and frayed, exposing the cardboard underneath.

Wincing from stiff joints, I picked myself up from the cold, concrete floor; climbed two flights of stairs to my office and opened the box once again.

The contents of the box included the small rectangular card that was posted on the bulletin board at Seller's right after my son was born, along with the short pamphlet, "Instructions for Mothers," which was handed out routinely by New Orleans Southern Baptist Hospital Maternity Department.

Inside the box there were three hospital identity bracelets, two for me and one for Bo. I saved an empty bottle of medication that was prescribed to dry up my milk. Diethylstibesterol 5 mg. Take one tablet daily.

The box contained two letters from Mrs. LaPrairie—one telling me that Bo had been adopted and the other wishing me a Merry Christmas. I saved a card that said "Thinking of You" removed from flowers delivered by the Frank J. Reyes & Company, sent by my Uncle Carl & Aunt Ann.

The most precious items in the box were the two photos of my son. Both photos had faded with time, though the images rang clear in my memory. In the first photo, Bo turned his face away from the flash and his features are somewhat blurred. Bo wore the white booties I bought for him, the only gift I gave him of consequence—a gift he could not keep and were returned to me to place in my little box. In the second photo, his head is turned toward me, and although my face is in profile, it's easy to see that I'm smiling and crying at the same time.

I stared at the photos, trying to imagine the man my son must have become. In my imaginings, only the best and most beautiful things happened to Bo. He is never sick, he doesn't do drugs, he is never physically or psychically injured by the people he loves and trusts. And most of all, I hoped beyond hope that he would find a place in his heart to forgive and accept me, especially if there were ever a time when he wished he had never been born.

After writing "The Box", the stranglehold on my voice was broken. As the memories came to me, I began to write more and more about my time at Sellers. Writing allowed me to own my story, and this in turn gave me the courage to share it with new Portland friends and my faith community at St. Michael's Episcopal Church. Acknowledging all the unanswered questions I had about Bo's life gave rise to an increasing desire to search for him, despite admonitions from adults in my past. It would be a horribly selfish act, an invasion of privacy, an unwanted and unnecessary disruption for the adopting family, they said. For myself, I feared rejection, anger, even hatred from the son that I loved so much. What if his life didn't turn out happily-ever-after? How would I ever be able to forgive myself if he couldn't find it in his heart to understand, accept and forgive me?

At some point after going back and forth on the pros and cons, I decided, "fuck it." Whatever the outcome, I would live with the consequences. My mom died of heart failure at 56, my uncle at 57, their father at 48, and I already had high blood pressure, arthritis—the list goes on and on. Bo at least had the right to know about his genetic predisposition for depression and heart problems.

Online I found lots of Search Angels—folks who make it their mission to assist members of families separated by adoption to find one another. On one search site, I even found a post by a young man in New Orleans looking for his mother, and he had Bo's exact birthdate—September 3, 1971. Unfortunately, it was a few years old and the trail led to a dead end. Then on a Yahoo group for Sellers birth mothers and adoptees, I discovered a private investigator who only worked on these cases. LeAnn had been adopted from Sellers and wanted to find her own mother, so she had figured out how to find the information hidden away in closed records through other means.

Miraculously, only four hundred dollars and twenty-four hours later, she had found a name and a phone number.

With my permission, LeAnn called my son first and gave him my number. I wanted to give him time to process the fact that I was looking for him and allow him the opportunity to respond to me when he was ready. But he had been ready for years, and by 9pm we were together on the phone.

For the first five minutes we cried. The post I had discovered online was from him; he had started looking for me when he turned eighteen. His name had been changed to Keith by his adoptive family, and he lived in Louisiana not far from New Orleans. We talked for almost an hour and made plans to meet. Roger and I flew out in early October. His future-wife may have watched too many episodes of Jerry Springer, the trashy daytime talk show, as her first response upon meeting me at the airport was "This could have been so much worse. At least you have your teeth."

We spent that first weekend catching up on each other's lives. I brought my box with me and we delved through all its contents. I gave him one of the Polaroids that Miss Popwell had taken of him the day before I left Sellers along with the white baby booties. He showed me photos from his childhood. He did not have the happily-ever-life I had envisioned for him. At Sellers we were told that our babies would be placed in families where all the children were adopted so they wouldn't feel set apart from any biological children. Keith had two older sisters, both born to his adopted parents. We were told that our children would always know that they were adopted, so it was a natural and understandable part of their lives. Keith wasn't told he was adopted until he was twelve, and it came as a huge shock. Mrs. LaPrairie told me that my baby's adopted father was a business professional with plenty of time for his family, but he was a workaholic lawyer. His adopted mother left the family when he was two. The rest of Keith's life story is his to tell, but I was so angry about the many lies I had been told that I was unable to write about my experiences again for almost ten years.

We've been a part of each other's lives now for seventeen years. I attended his law school graduation and his wedding. My now teenage grandson flies out to Portland every summer to spend a few weeks with his Noni Lani and Grandpa Roger.

In the decades between World War II and Roe v. Wade, during the "Baby Scoop Era," an astounding 1.5 million girls and young women were sent to maternity homes and coerced into relinquishing their babies. Like me, these girls and young women were considered too young to be mothers.

Being unwed meant we were immoral fornicators, and therefore, unfit to parent. Most of us suffered the permanent loss of our babies, and we fell into a lifetime of worry, constantly wondering about our children's fate.

I received enough closure from reconnecting with my son and being allowed to parent to him in a long-distance sort of way that I thought maybe my story didn't need sharing with the wider world.

Then the 2016 election happened.

Women's reproductive rights are once again fueling a divisive national debate. Sex education focuses on abstinence only. Birth control is increasingly restricted. In state after state, laws have been passed making abortion illegal or at least unavailable, and a conservative Supreme Court threatens to overturn Roe v. Wade completely. Women are again being denied agency over their own bodies. The objectification and denigration of women is becoming normative once again, and the latest trauma-filled stories never have happy endings.

I finish this book with a plea that we don't turn back the clock.

This summer, my son came out to Oregon along with my grandson. Our initial greeting is always a little awkward, since in many ways we are still strangers. One day we drove to a new Chinese dumpling restaurant in Tigard, and I started telling him how I'm afflicted with a wandering bug. I never meant to live in Portland more than five years, but now we've been here for over eighteen. I'm a small business owner, so even heading out of town for the weekend is difficult these days. One of my guilty little pleasures is looking at real estate sites from all over the world. The location is usually associated with the latest foreign detective show that I've been binge watching (another guilty pleasure). Sometimes it's the Shetland Islands; sometimes it's Norway. Villages in Italy that beg for folks to buy a crumbling property for 1 euro. Keith started laughing and confessed that he does a similar thing. He signed up for an email alert about farms and ranches for sale. It's his way of escaping for just a moment the responsibilities of his life. As the years pass, we continually find other small ways in which we are similar.

I am reminded of my wish at the grave of Madame Marie Laveau about a distant future in which I would meet a young man who calls me "mama."

I don't know if I should thank the Voodoo Queen or the god I no longer believe in for our reunion. My husband, Roger, and my writing mentor, Ariel, certainly played a part. Mostly, though, it was my own determination to bring some closure to a long and painful chapter of my life.

My baby boy is nearing fifty. He is not the baby I remember or the young man I had dreamt about. But as I hugged him goodbye at the airport, he whispered in my ear, "I love you, Mama."

Acknowledgements

Many thanks to all the writing mentors who supported and encouraged me in this decades-long endeavor—especially Ariel, Krystee, Chloe, Fuff, Cheryl, Linda, Carol, Maria.

Many thanks to David Biespiel for creating The Attic Institute: A Haven for Writers, without which I would never have started this journey.

Many thanks to my editor, Megan Kruse, who was instrumental in getting me to clean up my act.

Many thanks to the girls and women I met at Sellers. For a short while we were part of the same story, and your friendship during those dark times kept me sane.

Many thanks to my sisters Kathy and Janet for your unyielding love for me even when it isn't easy.

Most of all, thanks to my husband, Roger, who has saved my life in more ways than one.

About the Author

Bo and Lani Jo, 2002

Lani Jo Leigh was born in Hawaii and lived in England as a small child, but came of age in Oklahoma, not far from land settled by her great-grandfather in the Land Run of 1889.

As a refugee from a high-pressure corporate career, she moved from New York to Oregon in 2001 to reinvent herself. She spent several years at the NW Film Center School of Film with a focus on documentary filmmaking. Subsequently, she wrote and directed three feature-length documentaries.

In 2012, Lani Jo and her husband, Roger, purchased the Clinton Street Theater, an independent art house, which serves as a vital community space for a wide variety of activists and artists. Having been silenced for most of her own life, hosting a space where alternative voices are celebrated provides unending satisfaction.

www.ingramcontent.com/pod-product-compliance
Lightning Source LLC
Chambersburg PA
CBHW020354080526
44584CB00014B/1015